THE HELOTS' TALE

BOOK II - REDEMPTION

DAVID CAIRNS OF FINAVON

Finavon Press

THE HELOTS' TALE

Helot: (in ancient Greece, esp. Sparta) a member of the class of unfree men above slaves owned by the state.

Collins English Dictionary

NOTE ON SOURCES

Historical records can not only be difficult to track down but can also throw up contradictions and false trails; the person you think is Joe Bloggs may be another Joe Bloggs and sometimes there is no available evidence to put you on the right track. It is quite possible that some of the historical events portrayed in the following pages could suffer from this problem, if so I offer my apologies and encourage the reader to reach out to me so I can perhaps correct and issue an updated version in the future. That said, this story is based on true events and the main characters and many of the supporting cast were real people.

Unless otherwise noted, all artistic illustrations in this book are the author's pen and ink sketches from photographs, paintings and drawings of places, events and people or copies of newspaper advertisements of the day.

A NOTE ON MONEY & MEASURES

The currency in use in the British Empire in the nineteenth century was Sterling: pounds, shillings and pence. Twelve pence equalled one shilling and twenty shillings (or 240 pence) equalled one pound.

Pounds were expressed by the £ symbol, shillings by 's' and pennies by 'd' (derived from the Latin, denarius). One pound, one shilling and one penny was written as £1 1s 1d.

In everyday speech one shilling and sixpence would, for example, be referred to as one and six and written as 1s 6d or 1/6, five shillings and ninepence, referred to as five and nine and written as 5s 9d or 5/9.

A guinea used to be a coin in circulation up until 1813 worth one pound and one shilling. Luxury goods were often priced in guineas even though the coin itself was no longer in circulation.

A sovereign was a twenty-shilling coin, a half-sovereign, ten shillings. A crown was five shillings, half a crown was two shillings and sixpence, the florin was a two-shilling coin, other coins were sixpence, a groat (fourpence), a three-penny bit (pronounced *thrupny*), two pence (pronounced tuppence), a penny, a halfpenny (pronounced *haypny*) a farthing (a quarter of a penny) and a half farthing (an eighth of a penny).

While relative values are very difficult to measure against contemporary times, to be considered lower middle class as an example, you would have needed an income of at least £100 to £150 a year – or about 40 shillings to 60 shillings a week.

The British Imperial system came into use in 1824, common measures:

½ pound (written lb) = 225 grammes

1lb = 450 grammes

1 inch = 0.025 metre

1 foot (12 inches) = 0.1 metre

1 yard (3 feet) = 0.3 metre

1 mile (1,760 yards) = 1.6 kilometres

1 pint = 0.568 litre

1 gallon (8 pints) = 4.5 litres

PROLOGUE

HE YEAR IS 1834. William IV reigns over the United Kingdoms of Great Britain and Ireland. Clearance of 'undesirable elements' is in full swing, including transportation of the Tolpuddle Martyrs who had the temerity to fight the system by forming a trade union.

Van Diemen's Land (modern day Tasmania) has been turned into an island prison housing tens of thousands of convicts alongside free settlers clamouring to use and exploit this cheap labour. Shaped by this and other momentous events of the time, the new colonies of Australia are beginning to develop a distinct Australian identity.

Two youngsters, unknown to each other, Robert Bright, a farm labourer in his twenties from Cambridge and Mary Ann Goulding, a fiesty teenager from the slums of London, have both been transported to Van Diemen's Land on separate ships for minor offences. They are to serve their 7-year sentences under a comprehensive penal system being strictly implemented by the martinet, Lieutenant-Governor George Arthur (who is also busy accumulating a personal fortune and unashamedly displaying dictatorial nepotism at the same time).

1

Robert has been assigned to Edmund Bryant to work his sentence for housebreaking on the *Trafalgar* farm near Launceston. Mary Ann has just arrived in Hobart after an exhausting journey half way across the world in a marginally seaworthy tub. She is in prison at the Cascades Female House of Correction awaiting her fate alongside her two friends, both sentenced with her in London for stealing a Dutch clock.

THE STORY CONTINUES ...

ASSIGNMENT

Hobart
Spring 1834

"To you that hear my mournful tale / I cannot half my
   grief reveal.
No sorrow yet has been portrayed / Like that of the
   poor Convict Maid.
Far from my friends and home so dear / My punish-
   ment is most severe.
My woe is great and I'm afraid / That I shall die a
   Convict Maid.
I toil each day in grief and pain / And sleepless
   through the night remain.
My constant toils are unrepaid / And wretched is the
   Convict Maid"

Verses from traditional 19th Century ballad:
The Convict Maid

* * *

IT BEGAN THE FOLLOWING MORNING. Conveyances of every description began arriving at the Factory bringing ladies (and those who considered themselves to be 'ladies') looking for a servant; the wealthy, the middle class and the aspiring artisan's wife making their way in Tasmanian society. They knew that a 'lady' had to have servants, or at least one servant to be able to merit that social rank, and convict servants were cheap so there was always a strong demand. All that was required was for the applicant to give assurances regarding their respectability and their ability to clothe, feed and house their servants as well as ensure their moral rectitude.

Stepping down from the assorted vehicles and entering the prison they produced their orders for servants on assignment and the women and girls were called in one by one for examination, 'Can you sew? Can you cook? Have you cared for children? Can you get up fine linen? Can you read or write? Have you worked on a farm? – the questions came thick and fast as convicts were drawn by lot to be interviewed and assigned to their new mistresses.

After interviewing different candidates a choice would be made and before the end of the week perhaps two thirds of those who had arrived on the *Edward* were assigned[1] to different mistresses and masters; driven off in carts and carriages to town and country houses to take up duties as nurses, housemaids, scullery maids, cooks, seamstresses and more besides. Those with scarce skills in particular demand such as pastry cooks were selected for assignment to government officials or others well placed in Van Diemen's Land society.

Not a few of the women had made friends on or before the voyage and there were some bitter farewells as they were broken apart to begin their new life. Mary Ann and Liz bade farewell to Emma, who had been assigned to work as a housemaid for a Presbyterian Minister's wife in the interior. As they parted, Mary Ann wondered if they would ever meet again but her eyes were dry, the time for tears had long passed.

She and Liz remained at the Factory for the time being waiting for the next batch to be assigned and thoughts of what this would bring were uppermost in her mind for she saw this as her escape from her miserable surroundings.

* * *

MEANTIME, over the next few weeks, each morning they would be woken by a bell at five thirty for muster at six o'clock. They would then work until eight o'clock when they would break for half an hour to breakfast on a quarter pound of bread and a pint of gruel. At half past eight they would be led through prayers before returning to work until noon when a dinner, which consisted of a half-pound of bread and a pint of meat-flavoured soup (often made from boiled ox or sheep's head to keep the cost down) and peas or barley, would be served. They would then return to their work until sunset and an evening meal at 7 o'clock (which was always a quarter pound of bread and another pint of soup). Following this meal they would be led in prayers at 7 o'clock by Hutchinson before being returned to and locked up in their dormitory.

Each morning the dormitories (there were four of them in the two Yards, one for each class and another for cooks and other staff) would stir with hundreds of women and girls awaking from their sleep to face the new day.

Mary Ann had heard about the lives of those in the Crime class and was happy to have escaped the drudgery and hard labour of the washtub or picking oakum[2] or other such tasks. Instead, she found herself assigned to a group of women working on sewing clothes for the inmates and, despite herself, she actually found some peace in her work as the women around her busied themselves in silence fashioning clothing.

She was shown how to cut the fabric from a pattern and how to sew the parts she had cut out together. Although she railed at being forced to do something against her will, she kept it to herself and, in actuality, she took pride in her small, neat stitches and even received a commendation from her supervisor for her work when she produced her first finished jacket.

It was, however, monotonously regular and boring apart from times at night after lock up when some of the women would sing in the dormitory or exchange what passed for gossip. The only change in pace came each week when the Doctor would arrive and ask if all was well, dismissing what he considered to be frivolous women's complaints.

But one day the prison collectively stood to attention.

Mary Ann heard the clamour at the gate as the Porter called out, "The Governor's coming down the road!" The matron exploded from a door and started ordering everyone to tidy up this or that, to button uniforms, to get back to work - as if God himself was about to appear. Hutchinson himself followed her out and scurried up to the gate to welcome their visitor, "Open the gate, open the gate!" he ordered the Porter as he checked his suit while he polished a shoe on the back of his trouser leg.

Cantering up to the gates on a magnificent black stallion, Governor Arthur was accompanied by his aide de camp, his son Charles, who was wearing a scarlet military uniform. An orderly followed in the rear on a less imposing charger.

Arthur looked resplendent in a semi-military costume with discreet scarlet piping along the seams of his black trousers, a black frock coat buttoned completely up to the neck despite the warm weather, a wide white stock supporting a square chin, a white feather cockade fastened on the side of a black beaver hat and a polished black belt around his waist from which hung a sword resting in a glittering steel scabbard.

Their approach was only announced by the thud of hooves on packed earth and the rattling of their accoutrements, but it was clear that Arthur expected all to be ready for his arrival, including an open gate.

He dismounted smartly, throwing the reins to his orderly and then, with his son in tow, marched in determined fashion through the gate. He glanced at Hutchinson and his wife as he walked past them, nodding his head in curt acknowledgment and continued on without uttering a word. Leading the way (with Hutchinson scuttling along behind) he then proceeded to inspect all he saw in minute detail. He opened doors without knocking, poked his nose into absolutely everything; the yards, the drains, the dormitories, the peeling plaster on a wall, the spinning lofts, the laundry, the cooking areas, the hospital, the nursery.

Mary Ann looked up as he opened the door of their work-room. He took two paces inside and, wordless, gazed at all in the room before turning, his scabbard striking the metal hasp of the door with a clatter as he walked out. She looked at an older woman working alongside her, "Bloody 'ell, what was that all abaht?" she asked in a low voice. The room had suddenly ceased to be a silent chamber with several women making similar comments about the apparition, but the chatter was soon stilled with a command from the supervisor, "Shut it! Quiet. Get on wi' yer work".

Arthur returned to the office. He commented on what he had seen that required improvement or attention, to which Hutchinson responded with assurances that action would be taken, then he wrote a few notes in the visitor's book before striding out of the door and through the gate, which the Porter had opened for him, with his son hastening behind in a flurry of scarlet like a large gawky tropical bird. In a few swift, efficient movements he mounted his horse and he was off, back to Hobart with the same indifferent, cavalier progress as he had arrived.

As many had observed before, Colonel Arthur did not

believe in wasting words or compliments.

* * *

A FEW DAYS after the Governor's visit, Mary Ann and Liz, along with perhaps twenty-five other girls, were interviewed by prospective mistresses. Mary Ann was called in to a room where an older woman was standing beside the matron. "Come in Goulding" the matron instructed, "Sit down here and answer Mrs. Kearns's questions.

Mrs. Kearns was perhaps in her fifties. Her grey hair was submerged under an expansive black hat with a flurry of small red feathers on the crown. She had a wrinkled face, as if the sun had dried out any moisture and the years had marked their passing with furrows, like the rings of a tree telling its age. She wore a respectable dark grey dress with the occasional piece of red lace and a red feather to signal that she wasn't actually in mourning and she clasped a bag in her lap as if worried that someone in this den of iniquity would steal it if she were to place it out of her sight.

"And where is it that you come from?" she asked Mary Ann, her unexpectedly soft voice betraying her own Irish roots.

"From England" Mary Ann replied, eying her inquisitor suspiciously.

"I know that, my girl" Mrs. Kearns replied with exasperation, "But where in England?"

"London" Mary Ann replied, wondering what this had to do with anything.

"Ah, London. That's a hard place, so it is" and Mrs. Kearns reflected on the fact that London was indeed a hard place before asking her next question, "What did ye do in London?"

"I was a nurse girl. I looked after sick people at an 'ospital" she replied and then, thinking that an additional skill might not go amiss," And I also 'elped me Mum and Dad wiv their weaving".

"Weaving? Can ye sew then?"

"Yeah. I've been sewing jackets and fings 'ere"

"Are ye any good at it?"

"I'm good at anyfing I turns me 'and to" Mary Ann responded, sitting up a little more straight as she emphasised the point.

"But not so good at stealing clocks?" Mrs. Kearns interjected with a sideways glance.

Mary Ann didn't respond to that awkward comment but just folded her hands in her lap and bit her lip nervously.

"I'm looking for a good girl to work around our house. Cleaning, making the beds, washing, mending, looking after the children, cooking and the like".

"I'm not a cook" Mary Ann quickly added, "But I can fine do everyfing else ".

"Can you then?" Mrs. Kearns said absently and then turned to the matron, "I think she'll do".

Matron looked at Mary Ann and then back to Mrs. Kearns, "Very well. As you know you have given undertakings to properly house, feed and clothe your servants and to ensure regular church going and attendance at muster as required. You are also bound to keep confidential the nature of your servant's conviction unless she agrees to make it known more widely".

Mrs. Kearns nodded, "I am sure I understand that all well enough Mrs. Hutchinson. It won't be a problem". Matron then turned to Mary Ann, "You will be released on assignment to Mr. and Mrs. Kearns's household, Goulding. Should you misbehave you could be returned to this House of Correction. It is in your best interest that you do work diligently and serve out your sentence; with good behaviour you could earn a ticket of leave in four years".

She then looked at both Mrs. Kearns and Mary Ann, "Any

inappropriate behaviour by either party can and should be reported to the local police office. I trust I have made myself clear".

Mary Ann stayed quiet and Mrs. Kearns responded, "I will have my man servant bring my carriage here tomorrow morning at nine o'clock if that is convenient and he will convey Goulding to our home".

"Where is 'ome?" Mary Ann blurted out.

"Launceston town" Mrs. Kearns replied and thanking matron, she departed in a rustle of black cotton and lace.

"Where is Launceston" Mary Ann asked.

"It's to the north of here, several hours by carriage" Mrs. Hutchinson replied, "And now you need to prepare yourself for the journey".

* * *

BACK IN THE DORMITORY, Mary Ann learned from Liz that she, too had been assigned, to a 'Scotchman', Mr. Ferguson and she would also be travelling north to a farm outside Launceston. They both wondered if they would see each other again, whether they would be within distance of each other and how they could make contact, but other than asking at the local police office (which neither of them wanted to do if they could help it) they were at a loss.

"We'll fink o' somefing" said Mary Ann as she and Liz hugged each other, their minds spinning with unspoken worry mixed with relief that they would be leaving their prison.

FOOTNOTE:

While Mary Ann and Liz were experiencing the consequence of parliamentary legislation, the Houses of Parliament, the instrument of their incarceration a world away in London, was consumed by fire (on 16th October, 1834). It was caused by burning wooden tally sticks in the furnaces of the Houses of Parliament (which were only designed to burn coal) destroyed the House of Lords and the House of Commons. Other buildings, such as the Law Courts, were badly damaged. Despite the ferocity and size of the blaze there were no deaths.

Thomas Carlyle, the Scottish philosopher, was one of the many who witnessed the conflagration that night. He later noted that, 'The crowd was quiet, rather pleased than otherwise; whew'd and whistled when the breeze came as if to encourage it: "there's a flare-up (what we call shine) for the House o' Lords."—"A judgment for the Poor-Law Bill!"—"There go their hacts" (acts)! Such exclamations seemed to be the prevailing ones. A man sorry I did not anywhere see".

VIGILANTES

*L*auceston
1835

BUSHRANGERS.

INQUEST ON THE BODIES.

The Inquest was held yesterday morning, before P. A. Mulgrave, Esq., Coroner.

The Jury met at 10 o'clock, at the Court-house, and, after viewing the bodies, returned: when the first witness called was Thomas Rogers, who being sworn, stated, that Brown and Jeffkins came to a hut at Port Sorell, where he was employed as a lime-burner, the 1st Feb., in a very bad state as to clothing; they had no shoes, but had pieces of leather and blanket tied about their feet; Brown had a grey jacket drawn on instead of trowsers, and Jeffkins had a blanket sewn up round him; they each had a ragged shirt and no other clothing; they appeared weak, scarcely able to stand; they were both armed with double barrelled guns; they tied him and another man; an old man who was in the hut they did not tie; they ordered him to get them something to eat; they said they had nothing to eat for five days, but a parrot and a cockatoo, and were three days without water; they remained all night and kept us tied. One kept watch whilst the other slept; they eat a great deal during the night; their stomachs would not retain the food they were so weak, and they frequently went out to vomit; next morning they got up before day and ordered the old man to bake a damper; told us they were going to a bark chopper's hut, three quarters of a mile from our hut; they marched us up to where the "barkers" lived; Brown went up, Jeffkins following; Brown asked a man at the hut where his comrades were; we then saw three constables coming over a hill at a short distance; Brown ran towards them; he immediately levelled his piece and fired; I saw a man fall; he then fired the other barrel; directly after I saw a gun fired by one of the party and Brown fell; Jeffkins ran up and said, "Get up you cowardly b--r, and come on"; Brown said he could not; Jeffkins rested his gun against a tree and fired; he cried to the party, 'Come on there is enough of you to eat me"; he presented his gun and fired, a second time; I saw him soon after fall, after hearing a gun fired from the other party; I heard something said by the party when Jeffkins was behind the tree, but do not know what it was; after the firing, when I went up to the party, I found the constable who was shot, and whose name was Smith, still living, but he died soon afterwards; Jeffkins died after the constable; they were both shot through the head; Brown was wounded in his body and had his left arm crushed by the shot; I called out to the constables when Jeffkins fell that there was no more bushrangers; I should know the constables who were of the party if I saw them. (The men, James Small, James Huckley (who were with Smith when he was shot), John Harris, Frederick Carman, Henry Chalk, William Birmingham, Richard Berbrage and Thomas Walker, were then brought and recognised by the witness). I saw nine constables in the party; six came up after the skirmish commenced; Brown and Jeffkins took clothes from us when they were in the hut on Sunday; they did not say anything, but took them from the box in the hut.

> *The Jury, without retiring, returned the verdict. "Murder against*
> *Brown and Jeffkins. Justifiable Homicide in the case of their death."*
> Launceston Advertiser, 26th February 1835

* * *

THE NEW YEAR saw continued raids from bushrangers and others in the Norfolk Plains and Launceston districts. Despite some success, including bringing the notorious bushrangers, Brown and Jeffkins to account, the settlers were very uneasy and after a year of sheep and cattle stealing and other depredations, a public meeting was called for the thirteenth of October, at the Tasmanian Inn in Launceston, to force Governor Arthur's hand. Bryant had personally suffered and was finding it hard going since McTavish had left to return to Scotland. His new overseer was taking time to 'break in' and with routines disrupted, he had lost more of his stock with night raids.

The Tasmanian Inn was unusually noisy and very busy for a Tuesday. It was uncomfortably warm and cigar smoke hung like a sweet fog over the assembly while the clink of glasses being filled with beer and whisky interrupted the indistinct clamour of conversation.

Men of all shapes and sizes, some dressed in tailored suits but most in riding clothes and wearing dusty boots, packed into the room. Some were already seated, waiting for the meeting to begin, others were standing, talking with animation and at the back of the room James Cox of Clarendon waited, a self-assured man of about forty-five years of age. He was the local magistrate, a banker, businessman and landowner and was one of the wealthiest men in Van Diemen's Land. He was a keen sportsman and, sensing that the room was readying itself for the starting gun, he strode up to the head table set out for the "dignitaries". In addition to Cox, there were several others seated there including Edmund Bryant.

"Gentlemen, welcome to this public meeting called by and for the inhabitants of the districts of Morven and Breadalbane. It will not be news to you that there is a general consternation about the repeated robberies being committed in our district. Despite our best endeavours to establish a civilised community, where good, God-fearing men can live, work and prosper, we find that we are still at the mercy of felons and bushrangers because of the lack of government action and the ever-increasing convict population. Despite promise after promise from Governor Arthur, we do not have a competent police force to protect us and, indeed, the protection which has been afforded to other parts of the Colony and denied us is driving felons from these more favoured districts to prey on our own. It is not good enough". Several of the attentive audience banged tables with their glasses and some clapped while others shouted out their support.

He held up his hands for quiet, paused for breath and went on, "This meeting has been called to debate our situation and, with the agreement of the meeting, I intend to propose remedies and actions. I am going to open up the meeting for comment and, once we have established the mood and will of the meeting, we should propose resolutions that can be placed in front of the appropriate authorities. I open up this meeting for comments and suggestions". He resumed his seat.

As if a cork had been let out of the bottle, several men jumped up waving their hands or papers, eager to say their piece, "It's a disgrace!" cried a heavily bearded man sitting in the front row, aggressively pointing his cigar for emphasis, primed for action, "While we have to make do as best we can, Arthur is enriching himself. He's nothing but a corrupt autocrat doling out riches to his family and confederates while stuffing his own pockets with profits from the sale of illegally procured lands. And all this while leaving us to the mercy of his off-casts and convicts".

Cox waved the man down, "I can empathise with these senti-
ments, but this is not the time nor is it the place to make wild
claims or accusations that cannot be substantiated. We are here
specifically to address the issue of inadequate policing in order
to live in our homes without fear and to manage our enterprises
without predations".

There was a general hubbub and a few cries of frustration
but the meeting settled down and continued in a relatively
orderly manner thanks to the projected authority of the
Chairman.

Before too long discussion turned to raising funds from the
local community to protect themselves if the police were unable
to do it and, after an hour of debate and discussion, Cox
summarised everything and asked the meeting to agree a series
of resolutions:

Proposed by Mr. Gleadow:

"That this meeting view with alarm the repeated robberies
committed in this district and, notwithstanding the frequent
promises of the government to extend to these Districts the
same protection which has been afforded to other parts of the
Colony having similar claims, the breach of which promises has
caused this neighbourhood to become the resort of abandoned
characters who have been driven by an efficient Police from
more favoured districts, justifies this meeting in expressing its
Want of Confidence in the promises made by government".

He looked up and asked, "do I have someone to second this
motion?"

A man from the audience raised his hand, "Seconded by Mr.
Henry Reed".

"All those in favour?" - a forest of hands shot up, "And those
against?" No-one.

"Motion carried unanimously" declared Cox.

He continued, "The second motion is proposed by Mr. John
Sinclair:

That this meeting deeply regrets that they are compelled by the unjustifiable neglect of the Government to enter into a Public Subscription to ensure that protection for their property against the frequent and almost daily depredations that occur, which, in justice, they are entitled to receive from, and has been promised by the Government".

Once more he surveyed the room.

"Do I have a seconder?" Another member in the audience raised his hand. "Mr. Donald McLeod seconds the motion. All those in favour?"

Again, the motion was carried unanimously.

Another motion was carried unanimously regarding the formation of an 'Association for the Suppression of Felonies' and that the land and stockholders of the Northern Division of the island be invited to become members and that a fund be raised to support this.

A committee was then formed which included Cox, Bryant, Gleadow and Captain King and seven other gentlemen and it was agreed that an annual subscription should be levied on the members to fund the Association.

Cox then adjourned the meeting and the head table exchanged handshakes, congratulating each other on a job well done while others left the room and still others congregated in groups of three or four to continue the discussion.

Bryant soon disengaged himself, giving as an excuse his need to get home before the evening meal, and, together with two neighbours, set out on the road south.

* * *

BACK HOME, Bryant described the day to his wife and his brother, Francis who was stopping over for the night. He expressed satisfaction that things would improve as a result of their deliberations and, with the mood softening, while pouring a glass of port after their meal, Bryant idly threw out, ""They're talking about forming a cricket club in Longford[1]".

"Oh yes?" said Francis with polite interest, for he was no cricketer. Bryant added, "I was a fair batsman at school and a good slip fielder; I was even told by the headmaster once that my batting reminded him of Fuller Pilch[2]. My poke was as good as his, I swear. Maybe I should try out?"

Francis shrugged his shoulders and said, "Why not, if you have the time".

Bryant warmed to his theme, "It's been a while, of course. I'll need some practise, but I still have my bat and pads and there will be a cricket ball somewhere".

"And who is going to bowl?" asked his brother, "It won't be me, I haven't a clue where cricket is concerned, other than eating sandwiches on the village green at the tea break". And he laughed at his joke. Bryant considered this for a moment and then said, "I could get some of the servants to bowl and field. We could make a good enough pitch behind the barn".

His wife had been listening quietly in the corner as the two men talked, but this latest comment made her drop her crochet work, look up and exclaim with an unusual steeliness, "Definitely not, Edmund".

"Why ever not, my dear" Bryant responded with some alarm.

"If it ever got out, and the getting out would be certain, I am sure, I would never be able to hold my head up in society. Cavorting with convicts indeed. It's out of the question". Francis looked from Anne to his brother and nodded his head, "Anne is right, Edmund. You have to maintain your station. Lowering yourself to their level will not only cause scandal but make it impossible to maintain their respect. You could find them disobeying orders and abusing your good nature. It wouldn't work."

Bryant was about to protest, when his brother added, "And remember, if you show undue indulgence to your assigned convicts, Arthur may well turn around and strip you of them all. He's done it before. He wants the screws turned, Edmund, don't throw away all you've achieved for a plank of willow and a red ball."

Bryant realised that he was outnumbered and, more to the point, they were probably right, "Well, I can still try out, even if I don't practise" he pouted.

"Of course you can" soothed Anne and she returned to her crochet with a hint of a smile crossing her face.

"So, what is this Association for the Suppression of Felonies actually going to do?" asked Francis, hoping to change the conversation and restore harmony....

RESTART

&

*L*aunceston
  1835

Come the 6th June that year, John Batman entered into a treaty with the local Wurundjeri to – as he believed – acquire land around the Yarra river and at Corio Bay to the south-west (modern day Geelong), representing the first recognition of indigenous ownership of the land by white settlers. On 8th June he then wrote in his journal: "So the boat went up the large river... and... I am glad to state about six miles up found the River all good water and very deep. This will be the place for a village." This last sentence was to become famous as the "founding charter" of Melbourne. The New South Wales Governor, Richard Bourke however took a poor view of this and declared the treaty null and void, unauthorized and in direct conflict with the British government's assertion that there is no pre-existing indigenous sovereignty anywhere in Australia.

* Conflicts between settlers and Aborigines had been steadily increasing during the preceding few years as settlers moved further inland to take up land grants. Governor Arthur had struggled to resolve this conflict and had sponsored an English missionary, George Augustus Robinson, to round up the approximately 200 surviving*

Aboriginals, giving assurances that they would be protected, provided for and eventually have their lands returned to them.

Robinson befriended Truganini[1], a daughter of Mangana, Chief of the Bruny Island people, to whom he promised food, housing and security on Flinders Island until the situation on the mainland calmed down. With Truganini's support, he was able to reach an agreement with the Big River and Oyster Bay peoples, and by the end of 1835, Robinson had been feted in Hobart for his accomplishment and nearly all the Aboriginals had been relocated to the new settlement[2].

* * *

MARY ANN STRAIGHTENED up and put both reddened, calloused hands on her back as she worked the aches out of her body after half an hour or so scrubbing the kitchen floor. Mrs. Kearns would pick fault for even the tiniest of spots that she missed so she had been meticulous in scrubbing every inch of the floor.

She had put some rags under her knees, but they provided little comfort and she grasped a nearby table as she pulled herself upright, letting out an involuntary sigh.

It was August and winter had arrived in Launceston with a vengeance. An unusually cold winter, it had also been accompanied by rainy days that seeped into the spirit and made people short-tempered, although the farmers were happy enough with the prospect of good crops in the Spring and Summer to come.

As she opened the door, a storm-threatened sky greeted her and she looked up at the angry clouds before casting the slops from her bucket onto the rough ground outside and, with an involuntary shiver, turned back to put the pail and mop away in the laundry area.

She had been working on the kitchen floor while the cook was out shopping for the weekend meals. The cook, Sarah Birmingham, was an assigned convict like her from England. She was taller than Mary Ann, a thin woman with a pale, pockmarked face, brown hair that was usually hidden under a mop cap and unfathomable grey eyes. She had been a plain cook before being transported for 14 years in 1831, four years earlier, but she bullied Mary Ann because of her junior position in the household and because she was a good ten years older.

A rustling of clothing and a creaking of wooden boards announced the arrival of the mistress, "Are ye not finished yet?" she asked impatiently.

"I've just done the floor and put the mop and brush and pail away" Mary Ann replied with a hint of exasperation.

"Well, you took your time. Lay the fireplaces now afore Mr. Kearns comes home and when that's done collect the clothes to be washed from the bedroom and get on with the laundry".

"Yes, Mrs. Kearns"

"Well, get on with it, girl".

Mary Ann went outside again, this time to collect logs that Robert Diver, the groom-cum-handyman, had chopped the previous day and stacked in the wood shed. She had previously cleaned the ashes from the fires at six o'clock that morning before breakfast was served. Now she would replenish the logs beside the fireplaces and prepare the grates with paper and logs ready for the evening.

She was now living with Mr. and Mrs. Kearns in a house on the southern outskirts of Launceston town. It was not overly imposing compared to some of the finer houses in the town and country but it did have three bedrooms, a drawing room, a dining room, a study and a housekeeper's 'office' used by Mrs. Kearns to run the house. It also had quarters at the rear with a kitchen, laundry, wood store and servant's quarters where she shared a bare room with Cook. There was additionally a small stable block where a carriage and one or two horses were normally kept and where Diver slept. It was unlike anything Mary Ann had experienced before and she was initially overawed.

She was also eating better than she had ever done as the servant's food was usually remnants of the family's meal. Consequently, the whole experience in the first few months was, on the whole, at least tolerable. But she did chafe at the knowledge that she was not free and she missed the times when she would walk the London streets with Liz and Emma or wander in and out of the busy markets wherever her will took her. And she missed her family. Missed them sorely.

The master of the house was a successful merchant who operated from a warehouse in town importing and selling a variety of goods, mostly to government departments. Their children were grown and had long flown the nest but occasionally one of the daughters would call with or without her husband which would require Mary Ann to play the diligent servant.

Upon taking up her assignment, she had been told that her duties would be to keep the house clean, to retrieve, empty and clean chamber pots daily, to help with the washing and ironing, (something that Cook also had to do), to clean and lay the fireplaces in winter, to wash and dry the dishes, cutlery, pots and pans and assist the cook and mistress as and when required. She was provided with basic work clothing, two drab brown dresses, white, full-length aprons and a mop cap that Mrs. Kearns insisted she wear when she was in the main part of the house. The apron was a burden. It struggled to stay clean and she would often have to replace it during the day if she was to avoid harsh words about her 'slovenly' appearance.

Mrs. Kearns was a woman with ideas about her station in society. Besides enjoying the benefit of having two assigned women to handle the work, she also believed that having a cook and servant girl was necessary to announce her status.

When people came to call, as they did from time to time, she would insist on Mary Ann staying nearby to fetch and carry and, of course, always with her starched white apron and mop cap on display. But however hard Mary Ann tried, it never seemed good enough, and Mrs. Kearns could have an acerbic tongue. She bit back her impulse to reply with equal venom because she knew that this could land her back in the Factory – there was a big, new House of Correction in Launceston now – and she did not want to risk that.

On Sundays, Mr. and Mrs. Kearns, with Cook and Mary Ann sitting on top of the carriage, would be driven to the Anglican St. John's church in Launceston for the 11 o'clock service conducted by Reverend Browne. The church sat in quite open grounds looking over the growing town of Launceston. A new clock and bell had just been installed in the church, the bell brought over from London, and there was great pride in the fact that it had been cast in the same foundry as the Big Ben bell. Trees lined the front of the church grounds and a grassed open area lay beside the cemetery, waiting on the passing of souls to fill it, Mary Ann thought.

Mr. and Mrs. Kearns would be driven to church by John Driver. Mary Ann and Cook would leave earlier and walk the three quarters of a mile. On arriving, they would occupy seats at the rear with Robert Diver while the Kearns took up their position nearer the front with the 'gentry'. The church had been built some ten years earlier and was the centre of social activity on a Sunday; a place to see and be seen.

Although Mary Ann usually found the service to be boring, she enjoyed singing the hymns that she knew and the chance to break the monotonous drudgery of long hours of hard work at the house.

She also enjoyed the opportunity to talk with Robert Diver without either of them worrying about being chastised by the Kearns for taking time away from their duties. Diver was in his mid-twenties; he came from an English village in Cambridgeshire where he had worked with horses. He had been transported for life for horse stealing (although none of this information had been disclosed to Mary Ann, just as she kept much of her past to herself). He was a good natured, easy-going person who had an obvious warm relationship with the horses and he kept himself to himself during the week and stayed out of trouble if he could.

The Kearns would drive back after socializing with other notables outside the church and Mary Ann and Cook walked back together usually in a tense silence. Once 'home' they would have some of the afternoon free to themselves. This Sunday, Mary Ann went to the stables where John Diver was busying himself with the carriage and horse.

"Would ye like to join me in a walk after dinner[3]?" Robert asked Mary Ann as she helped him unhitch the horse and put him back in the stable. Mary Ann quickly responded, "Yes, I'd like that" and smiled coyly at Robert. They both knew that servants were not allowed to 'become familiar' with each other but a walk into Launceston would do no harm and the day was clear albeit it brisk.

Later, after dinner, Mary Ann changed into a simple dress that she had been wearing when she was delivered to the Edward less than a year ago, although it seemed like a lifetime had passed since then, and sought out Robert at the stables. He had his Sunday best on with a red polka dot neckerchief tied around his throat and a rather threadbare grey jacket over an equally timeworn black waistcoat and black trousers that had probably never seen a crease, at least not one in a continuous line down the front and back.

The young couple left by a side gate and walked steadily side by side along an unpaved road that would take them to Charles Street following the route they had used a few hours earlier back from church.

COUNTDOWN

⤡

$\mathcal{T}$rafalgar
1835

Ninety-nine out of a hundred are very desirous of going....

They say that their Characters are lost in this Country, that there would be no Possibility of their getting any Work if they go Home....

Applications are numerous to go by the first Ship; that is the general Cry .... I do not mean to say that is the Case with all of them, but they are looking forward to going to a fine Country.

Evidence taken on board Convict Ships and in Chatham Dockyard, presented to the Lords Select Committee appointed to inquire into the State of Gaols and Houses of Correction.

26th May, 1835

* * *

AT THE END of the year, Bryant was particularly exercised that two of his prize horses, an iron grey, three-year old filly and another strong chestnut yearling, had either strayed from one of the Trafalgar paddocks or been taken. He wondered if the men were not as alert or not as concerned to protect his property with the arrival of the new overseer, Allsop - or worse, because these men were thieves by nature and inclination, this was an inevitable outcome. However, there was also no arguing that bushranger and other nefarious activity had increased across the district.

The departure of McTavish, returning to his home in Scotland, and the arrival of Mr. Jeremiah Allsop in April (Bryant had found him via an advertisement placed in the Launceston Advertiser in January for an Overseer) had brought about a subtle change in the atmosphere at Trafalgar. McTavish had been fair, if gruff, was comfortable with his responsibilities and authority and had developed an effective way of handling the men. Allsop, however, perhaps understandably, was very much more concerned with proving himself to Bryant and he had obviously determined that the best way to do this was to work the men as hard as he could. This naturally had produced some grumbling and Bryant sensed an underlying tension amongst the farmhands that had not been there before.

To try to tease out information about his horses and perhaps about goings-on at Trafalgar, he decided to place an advertisement and offer a reward. He sat at his desk, dipped his quill in the ink bottle and began writing.

* * *

ON SUNDAYS, after church, Robert had taken to going on long walks by himself. Breathing in the fresh air, watching and listening to the birds, occasionally running across a kangaroo or a rabbit, maybe a Tasmanian devil or some other strange animal running wild. In the summer, even when it rained, he would still walk - relishing the cleansing tears of the Tasmanian heavens.

With Bryant's posting of a reward, Robert had used one these perambulations to explore Magpie hill, which is where Bryant's missing horses had last been seen, to check if there were any tracks or other indications as to where they might have gone and possibly with whom.

At the back of his mind he had a vague thought that, if he could track them down, maybe Bryant would be so gratified that he would organise a pardon for him. But as he was studying the ground and looking over the hills and valleys, the thought also occurred to him that, if he did find the horses, would he want to snitch[1] on a fellow convict or, worse, what was to stop Allsop telling Bryant that he had been involved in their disappearance to curry favour? With doubts in his mind rapidly piling up, he concluded that he was wasting his time and gave up the chase to return back to Trafalgar.

A week later, he was nearing the end of a tiring day in one of the wheat fields where he had been clearing out weeds, readying for the harvest. Stopping for a moment to wipe his brow after the salty taste of sweat ran into his mouth, he gazed heavenwards figuring that it was about time to stop as the sun would soon slip below the horizon. He was interrupted by a shout, "There's bloody cows in the field!"

A black and white speckled cow and a strawberry coloured steer had strayed onto the wheat field through an open gate and they threatened to destroy some of the crop. The man who had shouted ran back towards the farm to raise the alarm while Robert and others began to chase the two bovine intruders to stop them trampling the wheat. There weren't enough of them and every time they moved the cattle one way, they turned away, creating more damage. This was a hopeless, frustrating task.

Then Allsop arrived. He had brought with him more men

and after another twenty minutes they were eventually able to corral the two animals. Breathing hard, the men rested their hands on their knees or sank down onto their haunches while Allsop inspected their catch. It was impossible to decipher the branding on the cow, and the steer had no branding at all. They were certainly not Trafalgar beasts. "We'll need to impound them until we can find the owner" Allsop stated with a puffed up air of authority.

"That's stating the bleedin' obvious" Colegrave muttered to Robert. Robert smiled back.

"Who said that?" demanded Allsop, whose hearing was apparently acute.

No-one answered, and after a pregnant pause Allsop stared at Robert, "Was it you?"

"No sir" replied Robert, taken aback.

"Was it you?" he barked at another man nearby. He also replied that it was not.

Allsop's face was turning a reddish colour and Robert imagined steam about to come out of his ears with rising apoplexy.

"All of you", he roared, "Raise your hands".

Everyone tentatively raised their hands, wondering what was happening.

"Now, everyone who *didn't* make that insolent comment put your hands down" said Allsop, shifting his gaze rapidly from one man to another.

Everyone put their hands down and one or two (not in Allsop's line of sight) smirked at the silliness of it all.

"Damn you. I'll teach you respect before I'm done, mark my words" and then, realising he was making a fool of himself, he ordered Robert and Colegrave, who were close to him, to take the cattle, which were now snared with a halter, to a fallow paddock on the other side of the farm and then get back to work on the field.

"I've got my eye on you, Bright. Take care my man. I'll have no slacking".

* * *

LATER THAT EVENING Robert was lying on his bed, the bile of anger rising. His roommates had left him to his own devices for he was in a foul mood. He was having to work hard to bite back an instinct to storm out and challenge Allsop's sneering accusations that he was a 'slacker' when he knew that he pulled his full weight. Where was the justice? Breathing deeply and closing his eyes to focus on other things, his anger however subsided soon enough and he finally relaxed when the cooling comfort of a breeze began to blow in through the windows of the leaky hut.

His thoughts turned to freedom. He began counting on his fingers the number of weeks and months until the twenty-third of July, 1836 which, he hoped, would be the date that he'd become a Ticketer[2], assuming that there was no trouble between now and then. Two weeks in January, four in February, that makes six. Five in March, that's eleven and four in April; fifteen. Another four in May; nineteen, five in June makes twenty-four and three weeks in July. Twenty-seven weeks to go, give or take a few days including that extra day in February because this was a leap year.

Of course, that would not be the end of his sentence because he still had a further three years to serve after that but it would give him an element of freedom that he was beginning to ache to experience again. There had been times, like today, when it had been necessary to grit his teeth, put his hands in his pockets and "turn the other cheek" as the Minister had put it once in some distant lifetime back in England.

There had been times when he could have struck out at the injustice of unearned harsh words, when he could have responded to taunts from would-be bullies, when his frustration sputtered and boiled at the restraints placed on him. He reflected that he had not had a drop of alcohol in more than three years and, unlike many who had run off to escape the heavy hand of Arthur's police, he had forced himself to buckle to the unyielding yoke and routine and constant oversight of the Van Diemen's land penal system. All to get through this four-year period unscathed, to be free.

He would often think about his mother, father and brother, Benjamin back in Cambridge. As he lay on his couch, he wondered how they were all getting by in the squalid Cambridge lodgings that he had learned to call home. He thought about working for Honest Bill, calling for customers at Christmas time on a cold winter's morning. And he thought of Sarah and meeting her by the mill; her smiling face, pretty hair, girlish laughter and the warm glow he felt just being with her, holding her hand, stealing a kiss.

And he wondered whether he would ever be able to return home and, indeed, what waited for him if he did. With night falling, he dropped off to a troubled sleep.

A notice appeared soon after in the local papers:

Poundkeeper.
Public Pound, Prosperous,
South Esk, Jan, 13, 1836.

IMPOUNDED at the Public. Pound, Prosperous, South Esk, in the District of Launceston, by E. Bryant, Esq., of Trafalgar, 13th January, 1836.

One black and white speckled Cow, illegible brand on the off hip.

One strawberry coloured Steer, white on the breast and rump, no brand.

Damages claimed, £2.

Poundage fees 6d.; food and water 3d, per head per day.

If the above animals be not claimed and redeemed within the time allowed by law, they will be sold by me, at the above pound, on Wednesday, the 17th day of February, 1836, according to the provisions of the Impounding Act.

AWOL

Launceston
February 1836

"IF YOU DON'T PUT your back into it my girl, you'll be back to the Factory, by God you will". Sarah Birmingham, the cook, vented her anger on Mary Ann, who was at the wash tub. She had been scrubbing a particularly persistent grass stain in one of the master's shirts without much success and as a result it was taking longer for them both to get through the morning's wash than her fellow servant thought necessary. Particularly as there was dinner to prepare and she needed to get on with the cooking.

"I can't work magic, Sarah" Mary Ann retorted, "If you can do any better, show me".

"I'll not put up with that insolence you little strumpet" Sarah Birmingham replied furiously as she banged a wooden spoon on the tub to emphasise her displeasure.

Mary Ann bit her tongue for there was little this woman could do other than put a flea in Mrs. Kearns's ear (which Mary

Ann fully expected her to do when she had the opportunity). The real reason for this bitterness, which had been building for weeks, was, she suspected, the fact that Mary Ann and Robert Diver had developed a friendship which excluded this woman and, by extension, she fretted at Mary Ann's youth and her own fading prospects of finding a husband.

This idea passed quickly across Mary Ann's thoughts and she replied under her breath to this thought, "Well, there's nuffin' I can do 'bout that, you ugly old cow" and she did what she had been doing for weeks past; she just kept her head down and soldiered on, hoping for the best.

* * *

THE NEXT WEEK Mary Ann was in the kitchen, taking a chamber pot outside to be emptied and cleaned while Sarah was working at the table, rolling some pastry. As Mary Ann reached the door she heard a crash behind her and turned with alarm. The cook had spilled a good pound of flour onto the floor, a bowl lay broken in pieces and a white, diaphanous cloud hovered in the air. "Look what you've made me do, you clumsy girl" Sarah cried out with fury, "You need to watch where you're going. If it's not one fing it's anuvver". Mary Ann was about to protest her innocence when Mrs. Kearns appeared at the doorway.

"What's going on here?" she demanded.

"That clumsy girl got in me way and made me drop the flour" Sarah explained with a pleading tone. Mary Ann retorted, self-righteously, "I didn't do nuffing. I was just goin' out the door".

Mrs. Kearns looked daggers at Mary Ann, "You're nothing but trouble, you stupid, clumsy girl. Now clean this mess up or I'll be having words with Mr. Kearns. You need to sharpen your act my girl. Aye, sharpen your act". And with that she turned and left the kitchen.

As Mary Ann turned her head away from the departing Mrs. Kearns to Sarah, she saw that she was no longer angry, she was just standing there triumphant, hand on her waist and smiling.

"You evil cow" Mary Ann spat out, loudly enough for Sarah to hear but not so loud as to reach beyond the kitchen.

"Strumpet" was the immediate response and then, "Well, get on with clearing up this mess that you made".

Mary Ann was sorely tempted to physically attack her nemesis but held back. She knew that this would be the last straw and she wasn't prepared to give this damn woman the satisfaction. So, instead, she quietly collected a brush and pan and began sweeping the floor. Sarah left her to it, walking out of the kitchen jauntily. She left Mary Ann seething at the injustice, made all the worse for her impotence.

* * *

THAT EVENING she went out to the stable block to find Robert. She needed someone to talk to, needed some way to vent her own frustration.

It was twilight, the sun had set but there was still plenty of light and it was a calm evening as February gave way to March.

"Robert, are you there?" she called as she reached the stables.

"Mary Ann?" came the reply.

"Yeah. Are you doin' anyfing?"

"No. Hold on, I'll come down".

Robert appeared from the shadows, pulling on a waistcoat, "What's goin' on?"

"I just 'ad to talk to someone. I don't know if'n I can keep it all togevver much longer with those two bitches in there".

Robert put his hand on her shoulder, squeezed and said, "Yes you can. There's worse can 'appen to you, you know that".

"I know, but there's only so much anyone can take. It's just so unfair. No matter what I do, it's never good enough and I could fair shut that evil bitch's norf and souf[1] at times to stop the lies comin' out of it".

"You'll just 'ave to pocket[2] it, Mary Ann. Thought you'd figured that out by now".

Mary Ann exhaled a bitter laugh, "Yeah – you're right, no point in getting' me tail down, I s'pose.

"That's more like it, girl".

Robert looked up at the sky, "It's a fair night. Ow's about you 'n me taking a couple of hours off. Master and his witch of a wife are out so they won't miss us.

We can go to a place I know near 'ere".

Mary Ann's initial response was to refuse, but then a bile rose up within her breast and she changed her mind, "Yeah. Why not".

Robert broke into a broad grin, took her arm and led her to the side gate, "Alright, let's go". And without further thought the young pair stole quietly away until they were a distance from the house. And then they ran together, laughing with abandon.

About half a mile away, walking north along Wellington Street, Robert took Mary Ann's arm again and turned her right at a crossroads, "Let's see what we can find on old Dickey White's Street".

"Strange name for a street" Mary Ann observed.

"Yeah, I s'pose it is. It's really Brisbane Street but Dickey White's Street is what it's called".

Mary Ann looked puzzled and Robert smiled and explained, "Apparently Dicky White came 'ere from Norfolk Island and 'e pegged out the site of the *Launceston* 'otel – a big, fancy pub in town. The street we're on now leads up to the *Launceston* so it got the name Dicky White's Street".

"So, where are we goin?" Mary Ann asked.

"I thought we'd look up a friend o' mine at the *Robin 'ood and Little John* pub – it's just up the road".

"What's wrong wiv this one?" Mary Ann asked pointing to a

sign hanging outside a pub showing a man's head and shoulders poking through the world and on the other side his heels and backside hanging out the other side of the world.

"That's the *'elp me through the World* pub – it's alright, but I knows Jimmy Osborn at the *Robin 'ood* and we'll get in wivout trouble and we can stay late[3]".

They walked on together talking busily and soon after Mary Ann saw another pub sign with a painting of the two famous outlaws in their forest green tunics and people coming and going in and out of its door. Beneath the sign were some words, but of course they meant nothing to Mary Ann, "What does that say, Robert?" she asked, pointing at the sign.

"It says, Robin 'ood is dead and gone, Come and drink wiv Little John". Robert chuckled and took Mary Ann's arm again to escort her into the rustic bar where several men were already drinking as well as two women sitting with two men at different tables.

Mary Ann had been so enthralled at the freedom and easy-going confidence of Robert Diver that she was quite giddy with excitement and all thoughts of her status had been left behind at the Kearns house. But as she crossed the threshold a big red flag went up in her mind. What was she doing here? What trouble was she getting into? But, before she knew it, they were sitting at a table and Robert had ordered beers for both of them. This was unaccustomed freedom laced with the dizzy spice of drinking alcohol and Mary Ann was almost light-headed.

"Well, bless my soul!" An older man, late twenties or perhaps thirty, tall, well-built with a shock of black hair tied in a pony tail at his neck had caught sight of Robert and he came over to their table. He continued, "Bob Diver! What a sight for sore eyes!" Robert looked up and broke into a grin, "John! I didn't know you were out!"

"So's I am. Been a few months working fer a geezer by the name o' Lloyd. Lives near 'ere. It's me night off." Robert, was now standing and he turned to Mary Ann, who had been examining this newcomer with interest, "Mary Ann Goulding, meet John Hurley. John, meet Mary Ann – we works togevver near 'ere too. But watch yerself, Mary Ann 'cos 'e's a bit of a wild 'un" said Robert and he winked and smiled at her. She blushed a little as John Hurley took hold of her hand and smiled at her, "How do, miss Mary Ann".

The three of them spent the next hour drinking their beers and Mary Ann was beguiled by the attention bestowed on her by this man who had just appeared from nowhere.

She began to relax, "So, Mr. 'urley, 'ow did you get to be 'ere at the end of the world?" Hurley sat back in his chair and took a draft of his beer, "I've been 'ere since March of '31 serving me time. Got seven years fer 'ousebreaking in London. What about you?"

"I got seven years too, fer liftin' a clock from a shop in Oxford Street".

"So we're both Londoners" Hurley stated with a clap of his hands. "I was a waterman on the Thames. Good one, too. Even rowed Doggett's[4] when I was a kid, but it got tougher wiv the steamers takin' trade and even swamping some o' the wherries. Must say, I'm glad to be off the river, but I'll be 'appier still when I 'ave me ticket".

With that he stood up, swung his beer in front of him and impulsively broke out in song, serenading Mary Ann while the others in the bar clapped along as he sang happily in a not unpleasant voice, keeping his eye on Mary Ann, just as all other eyes were on him:

> 'Ave you ever 'eard tell of a young London
>   waterman?
> Who, from Blackfriars did regular ply.
> And 'e fevered 'is oars wiv such skill and dexterity
> Pleasing each maid and delighting each eye.

And 'e sang so sweet, 'e sang so merry
The couples all jostled to 'ire 'is wherry
And 'e became known as the young lover's ferry
But 'e could not find a true love of 'is own.

Til there came a goose girl from Stratford St. Mary
And she wanted taking to Farringdon Fair
But she 'ad not the ha'p'ny to pay for 'er wherry
And stood on the steps in a pretty despair

But she sang so sweet she sang so merry
'E put 'er and all of 'er geese in 'is wherry
And 'er pretty face was a far fairer ferry
'E rode 'er across to Farringdon Fair
They were married next May time in Stratford
   St Mary
And now they 'ave watermen one, two, three, four
And they fevver their oars with such skill and
   dexterity
Rowing the people from shore to shore
The couples all jostle to 'ire their wherry
And everyone goes by the Blackfriars ferry
And they sing so sweet, they sing so merry
While 'e stays at 'ome with a love of his own[5]

Some of the men clapped him on the back and Mary Ann applauded enthusiastically when he had finished, "That was lovely, John. And what a fine voice you 'ave".

Hurley gave an elaborate bow and returned to his seat, "A pretty song for a pretty girl, Mary Ann". But just as things were getting interesting, Robert pushed back his chair, "We need to get back, Mary Ann. It's getting late."

This was the last thing Mary Ann wanted to hear and it brought her back down to earth with a bump. She looked a

Robert, then back to Hurley, then to Robert with a pout, "Oh! Just as I was beginnin' to enjoy meself".

But she knew he was right and rose from her chair, "I do 'ave to go, John".

"If you must, Mary Ann. I'll see you again?"

"I'd like that. Where? When?"

"I'm 'ere most Saturday nights. Per'aps next Saturday?"

Mary Ann smiled, nodded and walked to the door with Hurley and Robert either side of her.

Outside, Hurley and Mary Ann stood close by and Hurley put his hands on her shoulders, lowered his head and kissed her cheek.

Mary Ann didn't resist. Her heart beat in her ears and her stomach was fluttering. Things were just going so fast. Hurley stood back, "Next Saturday then". Mary Ann smiled her acquiescence and hurried after Robert back down Brisbane Street, looking over her shoulder once to see Hurley standing there looking after her until she turned the corner into Charles Street.

This would take her past St. John's Square and out of town back to their lodgings. The sun was long a-bed and the night lamps opposite the entrance door of each pub, hanging the regulation ten feet from the ground, lit their happy way home.

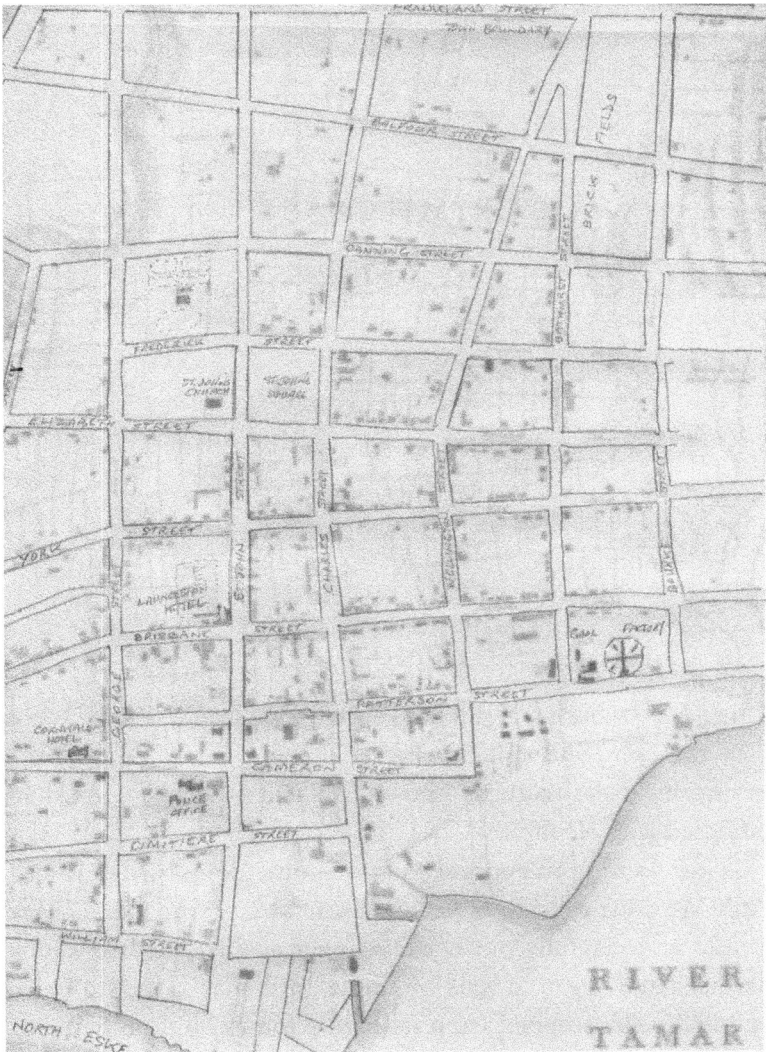

Launceston

CRIME CLASS

Launceston
March 1836

MARY ANN PLODDED along diligently beside John Diver. It was a pleasant night. She smiled to herself and giggled, walking a little erratically if the truth be known, for her head was somewhat muddled with alcohol.

They were soon approaching the house. John turned to her, "Shh! We don't want to wake anyone up". Mary Ann looked back at him and playfully put her forefinger against her lips, shook her head and began to walk on tiptoe until, that is, she stumbled and had to be stopped from falling by John's hold on her arm. "Mary Ann" he whispered urgently, "Pull yerself togevver. You need to get back to yer room wivout waking anyone up. Can you do that?" Mary Ann looked up to him again and nodded her head.

They were now at the side gate and John eased it open, grimacing as the un-oiled hinges squeaked in the silence of the night. He pulled Mary Ann behind him and took her to the kitchen door where he opened it and, kissing her on the head, gently pushed her over the threshold whispering, "Off to bed now. Quietly. Very quietly."

John made his way back to the stables and disappeared. Mary Ann stood still for a moment in the dark taking in the ticking of a clock, the scurrying of a small animal, maybe a mouse, but otherwise all was at peace. She stealthily crept towards the stairwell leading up to the room that she shared with Sarah Birmingham. She had no idea whether the Mr. and Mrs. Kearns had come back from their evening but she knew she needed to be as quiet as that mouse just in case. One step. Two steps. On the third step the wood groaned and she stopped, frozen, listening. Another step, one more, another groan from the next step and she held her breath, poised like a cat alarmed at the subtle scent of a lurking dog in the dark.

Nothing stirred. The silence hovered in the air like a physical shroud. She almost jumped out of her skin when the grandfather clock downstairs began to chime. It was 10o'clock and it rang its bells for an agonisingly long time, all the while Mary Ann held tight to the bannister and held her breath. After the 10th strike the house fell silent once more and she began ascending the stairs again. Eventually she reached the top and she let out a small breath before turning down the hallway towards her room.

On reaching the door, she looked back behind her. Nobody there. She slowly turned the doorknob and opened the door, praying that it would stay silent. Thank God, it kept her secret. She entered the room and turned around as she shut the door behind her. Gently, very, very gently. Then she turned again and crept to her bed.

"So where 'ave you been?"

Mary Ann almost jumped out of her skin. Sarah Birmingham's voice came from the dark like an avenging angel. Accusing. Threatening.

"Bloody 'ell, you made me 'eart jump into me mouth" Mary Ann whispered back.

"I'm still waitin' for an answer?" Birmingham replied in an unfriendly tone.

"I've been out walkin'. Wanted some fresh air, if'n you wanna know"

"It's not what I *wanna* know, it's what the Mistress will *wanna* know" Birmingham retorted, emphasising the 'wanna'.

"Why would she be any the wiser?" Mary Ann asked.

"Because I'll 'ave to let 'er know, of course" Birmingham responded petulantly.

"Why? I've done no 'arm to you or the Master"

"No 'arm? You'll bring this 'ouse into dis-re-pute wiv your pub crawlin'. And don't pretend that you ain't been drinkin', I can smell it on yer breath". She stumbled over the word 'disrepute' – she had obviously heard the phrase before but had not used it herself. Now was the time and she articulated it with a flourish".

"Please Sarah, don't be a snitcher. I'd cover fer you". Mary Ann pleaded.

But Sarah didn't respond; only turning her back to Mary Ann and smiling to herself as she settled back to sleep, well satisfied with the night's events and relishing the morrow.

Mary Ann, however, found it hard to sleep but eventually she drifted off in the wee small hours, hoping that the threat was just to make her uncomfortable and nothing would come of it.

* * *

COME MORNING, both of them were up as usual busying themselves with their routine chores. Despite a mild hangover, Mary Ann made a good fist of everything and was emptying the chamber pots when Sarah told her that Mrs. Kearns wanted to see her in the drawing room.

"Why?" Mary Ann asked, dreading a confrontation.

"Why d'ye fink?" Sarah spat back at her.

"You bleedin' cow" Mary Ann replied with fury, "Just you wait, your turn'll come".

She made her way to the drawing room, tidied herself as best she could and knocked on the door.

"Enter!" came a muffled stentorian voice.

She opened the door and made her way into the room to find both Mr. and Mrs. Kearns standing by the hearth.

"Who gave you permission to be absent last night?" came the charge from Mrs. Kearns in a shrill voice.

"I just went out for a breath of fresh air" Mary Ann responded indignantly.

"And came back drunk after midnight" added Mrs. Kearns.

" I did no such fing!" Mary Ann retorted angrily.

"And who were you with, you disreputable girl?"

"I wasn't wiv anyone. I told you, I just went out for some fresh air".

Mrs. Kearns turned to her husband, wringing her hands, "See Mr. Kearns. See what lies and misbehaviour I have to put up with?", obviously rehearsing accusations that she had flung his way before. Mary Ann wondered if they knew that she had been out with John, but she wasn't go to be the one to snitch on him.

"I do indeed Mrs. Kearns, I do indeed" he replied with stern deliberation, "It is not to be tolerated in a Christian household, not tolerated I say" and he glared at Mary Ann. "There is nothing for it but that we pay a visit to Justice Clarke and let the law take its course". He then turned away, picking up a book that had been lying on the mantelpiece. And as he opened a page he spoke over his shoulder dismissively, "I will arrange for Diver to take us to the Police Office this morning. You will pack your things, Goulding and be ready for me in an hour". And with that dismissal, Mary Ann gritted her teeth, exited the room, swore revenge on Sarah Birmingham and began pulling together the few meagre personal items she owned. There was nothing else to do.

In front of the magistrate she was charged with being absent without leave and sentenced to one month's Crime Class at the Launceston House of Correction. Before the evening of March 4th was out she had been 'escorted' by a constable a short distance along Paterson Street to the Female Factory to serve her time.

* * *

THE LAUNCESTON FEMALE FACTORY had been constructed on supposedly 'modern' principles.

It was a large two storey octagonal building known as a 'Panopticon'[1] – a design that had been promoted by reformers in England to allow for observation and separation of inmates.

Mary Ann was put through the same procedure that she had experienced at the Cascades a year and a half earlier, including an examination by the doctor. But this time she sported a large yellow 'C' on her dress signalling that she was in the Crime Class. Because she had a short sentence she had been issued with used clothes, but they were clean, if frayed. She was to be confined with other incorrigibles who were to be taught a lesson, sharing a cell with another 'Crime Class' convict.

Launceston Female Factory

She was walked from the office at the entrance back to the cells at the rear of the building by a turnkey and up a set of stairs.

As Mary Ann was locked into the cell she saw that it was already occupied. Her new companion was a quite pretty young girl of 18, about the same height and build as Mary Ann with brown hair, a fresh complexion and dark brown or hazel eyes set in an oval face. Both arms were tattooed and, like Mary Ann, she was wearing a dress with a large yellow 'C' on the back and another on her sleeve. As the turnkey locked the door, the girl sat up in her hammock to examine the new arrival. Her small mouth pursed and she offered up a cheery, "Make yerself at 'ome luv".

By now Mary Ann was more weary than angry and the Factory no longer held any terrors for her, she had seen all this before. Indeed, this place was better than the last – which was not saying much – and in four weeks she expected to be assigned again so things really hadn't changed much other than she was shot of the two witches. The face opposite her seemed vaguely familiar and even with the few words spoken she suspected that this girl was from the east end of London, like her.

The girl swung her legs to the floor and offered her name, "Sarah, Sarah Davis. You?"

Mary Ann looked at her, "Mary Ann, Goulding" she responded and after a pause, "Do I know you?" Sarah frowned and said, "Dunno. Where are you from and 'ow did you get 'ere?"

"I was workin' near 'ere and I walked".

"No, I mean where's your 'ome and what ship did you come out on?" Sarah insisted.

"Me Mum and Dad 'ad an 'ouse in Spitalfields, but I lived in lodgings near Oxford Street when I was stitched up; and I came out on the *Edward*" Mary Ann expanded.

"Bloody 'ell! I'm from Spitalfields too and I came out on the same tub, though don't 'member meetin' you - then or before".

"There was a lot of us on the ship I s'pose an' most o' the time everybody seemed to be spewing their guts with sea sickness". Mary Ann responded and both girls burst out laughing at the image; belly laughs that made them both shake. It was the first time for a long time either had laughed without restraint.

As they recovered, Mary Ann asked, "Where did you live back 'ome?" and leaned forward with interest to hear the answer.

"Me family 'ad lodging's off Red Lion Street, near the Ten Bells[2]".

Mary Ann's face lit up, "I know where you were! Me Dad would 'ave an 'alf at the Bells. Our place was off Befnal Green Road. Just fink, we probably walked past each uvver on Commercial Street and never knew it and now 'ere we are in this God-forsaken 'ole".

The two girls continued swapping stories for another hour. Happily reliving experiences, emotions, places and events which, with the passing of time, had taken on a warmer glow than the grim reality warranted. But the talk conjured up heart-warming images of family and time had misted the hunger and deprivation that both girls had survived. It was a wonderful release for them both and when, eventually, they lay their heads down to sleep, Mary Ann wept a tear and whispered a prayer for her mother and her family. And herself.

The following weeks were a mix of drudgery and hard work at the laundry tub or picking oakum, sweat pouring from her brow at the tub and fingers aching and sore from the tar.

It was broken by the laughter and mutual empty threats against officialdom in the evening where they both tried to outdo each other describing punishments that they would visit on their tormentors if they could as well as girlish fantasies about friends and associates on the 'outside' like John Hurley...

This routine was broken about three weeks later when Sarah was hauled off to solitary confinement on the 25th of March for swearing at one of the 'trustee' convicts set over them to super-vise their work.

To be fair, Mary Ann thought, Sarah used a swear word in

most sentences so this was probably inevitable, but it was much quieter of an evening as she served out her remaining few days of the four weeks sentence without Sarah's company and she thought more than once of her friend subsisting on bread and water in a dark, dank solitary cell. And about John Hurley.

PERMISSION

*L*aunceston
1836

IT WASN'T long before Mary Ann was assigned again at the beginning of April after she had completed her four weeks at the Factory. It seemed that there was an insatiable demand for servants; not surprising when the only cost was board, basic clothing and lodging. She was happy to hear that she was not going back to the Kearns' establishment. This time she was to be the only servant at a house in Brisbane Street – a short distance from the Factory – in the household of a Mr. and Mrs. James Green.

This was a smaller house. There was no cook and no handyman or groom. Indeed, no horses. Mary Ann was instructed by Mrs. Green in her duties – she was to keep the house clean, wash and iron, do some basic cooking for breakfast and dinner and look after the three children as needed. Saturday afternoons were hers until the evening meal and on Sundays she would be permitted time off to attend St. John's church. Obviously, she would also have time off to report monthly to the Police Office as required.

Mary Ann did her best to ingratiate herself. The children were in their early to mid-teens so there was little she was required to do with them and they often acted as if she were invisible, which suited her fine. James Green was an ex-Army free English settler with black mutton chop whiskers and a full head of speckled black hair.

He stood ramrod straight, always wore a suit with a waist-coat, regardless of the weather, and dominated his wife. She, in turn, dominated the children and resolved to dominate Mary Ann who determined to play the mouse; she wanted to meet John Hurley again, having been forced to miss their previous assignation, so bending the knee was a small price to pay.

The first Saturday she was able, she made her way to the *Robin Hood* pub hoping to find John there, but no luck. She remembered Robert Diver telling her that he was friendly with the publican, a Jimmy Osborn if she remembered rightly, so she sought him out, asked after both Robert and John and left a message with him, promising to be back the following Saturday.

The week ground its way through the days. March and April had been unseasonably wet and gloomy with more rainfall than would normally have been seen even in winter and May witnessed more of the same. It had a knock on effect on more than just the mood of the populace. Costermongers were marking down the prices of potatoes, for example, because settler farmers had been forced to dig them up and bring them to market before they rotted in the soaked soil.

It was into this turgid weather that Mary Ann ventured out the following Saturday, 14th May. She did her best to make herself presentable and left the house at 3 o'clock. Thankfully it was dry and, although it would likely be turning chilly in the evening, the temperature was tolerable. Darkling clouds scudded across the sky and a freshening breeze blew in from the harbour. The *Robin Hood and Little John* was only a short walk down Brisbane street so she hurried on her way hoping that the rain would hold off for a while.

At one time she would have hesitated to step across the threshold of a tavern, but she had toughened considerably over the last two years and didn't hesitate to enter. Inside several men and a few women were standing and sitting, drinking, talking in hushed voices. It *was* the afternoon she thought, so no time for anyone to have gotten into their cups yet. She looked around the room but couldn't see anyone she knew so she made her way to the bar and asked for Mr. Osborn.

The barman looked over his shoulder to an open door behind him and called out, "Jimmy there's a lass here looking after you. Better not let your missus know!" The publican soon appeared, a large man with bushy eyebrows, wiping his hands on his apron as he walked up to Mary Ann and he cast a caustic comment to the barman before reaching her, "Hello Miss. You'll be looking for your fellers I suppose?" Mary Ann confirmed that she was indeed and asked if he knew if either man would be coming today? But before Osborn could answer, a loud, "Mary Ann!" sailed across the room from the doorway and there stood John Hurley, larger than life.

She turned and beamed a big smile at him and he returned it, striding across to the bar. Upon reaching the bar he grasped her at the waist and swung her around. She frantically held onto her bonnet with one hand and squealed with delight as she hugged his neck with the other. "So you've been in the Factory?" he asked once he had put her down again.

"Four bloody weeks of washin' cloves an' pickin' rope from tar. I wanted to meet you again but that cow Sarah Birmingham 'ad it in fer me".

"Not to worry, Mary Ann. Bob told me 'ow you kept yer mouth shut and kept 'im outa trouble. I'm proud 'o yer. Good on yer girl". Mary Ann muttered, "Tweren't nuffing" and John called to the barman, "Two beers, Seamus" and dropped a couple of coins on the bar.

They went over to a nearby table. "Ave you seen Robert today?" she asked.

"No – e's workin' – ain't gonna be able to make it today. Ain't I enough?"

Mary Ann giggled girlishly and replied, "Of course you are. I was just wondering".

"When do you 'ave to get back, Mary Ann?"

"I'm gonna 'ave to leave in an hour or so, but until then I'm all yours!".

They spent the next hour talking animatedly like two conspirators. She told him about her experience in the Factory, about Sarah Davis, about her new situation, but mostly she revelled in being with him, relishing touching his hand and hearing his voice.

He told her about how he had been caught housebreaking and given seven years, that he was also working for a local family by the name of Lloyd and that since arriving on the *Red Rover* in 1831 he had had a hard time of it with spells on road gangs and sentences of hard labour. It seemed that this assignment with the Lloyds was, in his mind, an opportunity to break the cycle and he was trying hard to keep out of trouble.

An hour flew by and then another half hour before Mary Ann forced herself to break off their tryst, promising to do her best to meet him again same time next week, same place. As John left her on the pavement outside the pub he pulled her close so she was on tip toes and, with a strong hand cradling the back of her head he gave her a long, lingering kiss full on the mouth.

Each Saturday over the following three weeks Mary Ann and Robert Hurley met at the Robin Hood and then would go for a walk along the harbour front. They were never short of things to discuss, mostly turning towards what they would do once they had served their time. Early in June they were walking back towards Brisbane Street from the docks when two intoxicated ruffians staggered out of a pub and bumped into them.

John pushed Mary Ann behind him and grabbed the culprit by his arm, "Do that again matey and you'll be fuckin' sorry" he spat out with venomous intent. The drunk tried to get John's hand off his arm and, as he struggled, his friend then tried to intervene. Before Mary Ann knew what was happening John had thrown a punch at the second man that made him stagger backwards before falling onto his backside in an almost comical manner. The man he was holding then attempted a wild swing but John blocked it easily with his free arm and drove his knee into the drunk's groin causing him to double over with a cry of pain and vomit into the street as he too fell to the ground.

The commotion was beginning to draw attention and Mary Ann pulled John back, "Come on John, we don't want trouble. Let's get outa here". His immediate reaction was to pull away from her but then the red mist subsided and he turned back to Mary Ann. Together they walked quickly away, leaving the two drunks struggling to get up, cursing their attacker. No-one followed them, probably not interested in challenging this dangerous man, and they ducked into a side street, and hurried away from the ruckus.

"What was that all abaht, John?" Mary Ann asked as they slowed to an ambling walk.

"I dunno. Somefing just came over me when that drunk barged into you".

"Well, fanks for the protection, but I like you outa prison if'n you can manage it"

John smiled and stopped Mary Ann, turning her to face him, "Mary Ann, you're good fer me. And I fink you like me, you do don't you?"

"John, you know I like you. On this prison island we both need someone to 'ang onto when times get rough"

"Well, I've been finking" continued John, "If we was married we could be togevver instead of scratching out time whenever it please our masters. What d'ye think?"

Mary Ann wasn't sure she had heard him aright and she was just stood there with her mouth slightly open.

"Well? Will you marry me?" John asked again.

"I 'aven't thought about it, John. Can we get married? I mean, while we're serving our time?"

"We'd 'ave to ask permission but I know lots who 'ave gotten married long before their time's up so why not us?"

Thoughts washed around Mary Ann's head; she did like John; true and a man would provide her with some security in this land; being married would give her a leg up in the society they inhabited. But marriage? Is this what she wanted. Then she decided, yes. Why not. Time to start rebuilding her life.

"Yes, John, I'll marry you" she said after a space of a few seconds that seemed more like an hour to them both.

John wrapped his arms around her and she put one hand on his face as he bent down and gave a her a long, passionate kiss. People walking by looked at them and, depending on their social status either thought it inappropriate or gave no thought to it at all but John and Mary Ann cared not a fig either way.

Disentangling themselves, John promised to enquire about how to apply for permission to marry and the pair of them finished their walk, John seeing Mary Ann back to her lodgings (she didn't think of the Green's house as 'home' understandably) with smiles on their faces and hope in their hearts.

Winter was on its way and the darkening skies foretold roughening weather, but Mary Ann walked into the house with a spring in her step, caring nought for the quickening breeze and the hint of rain in the air. For her, the sun was shining brightly.

MICE AND MEN

Launceston
1836

The best laid schemes o' mice an' men gang aft a-
gley,
An' lea'e us nought but grief an' pain, for promised
joy.

Robert Burns: From 'To a Mouse', 1786

* * *

ROBERT HURLEY HAD BEEN BUSY. He knew that to get married he
would need permission, but how to get this and from whom?
He had no idea. However, when he reported to the Launceston
police office for his monthly muster, it occurred to him that the
constable would know and he was passed to one of the clerks in
the office.

The clerk explained that this was in the gift of the Lieutenant Governor while they were serving out their sentences and that a written application would need to be made. As Robert could not read or write, the clerk offered to prepare the paperwork for him but he was told that his proposed bride would also need to be present.

He was not meeting Mary Ann that Saturday because he was required to work that day, but the next day Mary Ann would be at church and he would find time then to let her know the good news. He felt strangely elated. He liked the girl, he liked her bravado and ready smile, he liked being with her. She was pretty enough and she had a certain manner that made him feel wanted and needed. Something told him that maybe this was a turning point, maybe this would put them both on a new path and perhaps, maybe a better future. Love? Who had time to love in this world? But this was good enough and a wife also brought other benefits to a man - in and out of bed.

On Sunday, 3rd July 1836 he woke with a sense of anticipation. The one thing better than receiving good news was giving it, he thought. Dressed in his shabby Sunday best, with a scarf wrapped around his neck, he made his way to St. John's for the service at 11 o'clock. It was a cool day but the sky was relatively clear and the sun rose into the heavens with a smile on its face. By the time he arrived, Mary Ann was already inside and stragglers were entering to take up the pews at the back of the aisle. John took a seat at the end of a pew, by the aisle and scanned the people to see if he could see her. And there she was, three rows further down, a small figure bent over a hymn book that she couldn't read, her bonnet perched on her brown hair, bunched into a pony tail.

The church was quite full, maybe 400 people in attendance, and they made a rumbling noise as they rose at the beckoning of the minister, shoes scraping, papers rustling and a couple of books falling to the floor with a thud. The Reverend Doctor Browne opened with a benediction and the congregation remained standing as the organ released its first sonorous note and the congregation joined in to sing the first hymn.

The service continued on its predictable course, sitting, kneeling, standing, listening, singing (or opening his mouth to give the impression of singing) and thinking – not of God's eternal message but wondering how she would react to the good news and mapping out the steps to accomplish his goal. They would marry here, he thought. The good Reverend would do the job.

The service over and the final blessing pronounced, Reverend Browne walked down the aisle with the congregation emptying the pews filing behind him. As Mary Ann passed him by, he smiled at her and she smiled back, her eyes lighting up. John joined the rear of the procession and made his way out past the Reverend who had been captured by a number of parishioners who were now talking to him earnestly. Mary Ann was standing to the side, arms wrapping a thin shawl around her to keep warm, waiting for him to appear.

"Mary Ann!" he cried out once he saw her a few yards away.

"John!" she replied with a happy smile.

"Come on, let's get away from 'ere. I've got some good news" he said as he put his arm around her shoulders and directed her away from the crowd, the horses, the carriages milling around them.

Once on their own Mary Ann said, "So what's this good news, then?"

"I spoke to the constable yesterday and 'e 'as a clerk wot can make out the papers for us to get married. You and me need to be there so I was wondering wevver we could go togevver next Saturday and get it movin'. What d'ye fink?"

Mary Ann reached up to him, put her hands around his neck, pulled him down and gave him a kiss full on the mouth, "That's wot I fink, John 'Urley. Next Saturday it is. Yeah!" she shouted as she clasped both hands together tightly, "Next Saturday, 'ere we come!"

So, on the 6th July, they made their way together to the Police office, sought out the clerk and gave him the information he needed, receiving his promise to submit the request to the Secretary. It took another nine full days for this to work its way through the bureaucracy but at last, on 15th July, 1836 the Secretary had received the application and submitted it to Lieutenant Governor Arthur for approval.

And they waited.

Both Mary Ann and John were kept hard at work and worked hard at keeping out of trouble.

And they waited.

July passed. August wound its wintery way through the month. September arrived and delivered warming winds that breathed a promise of summer.

Still they waited with growing concern and frustration.

It was mid-September when John was pulled aside by the constable at his muster. The constable took out a letter from a file on his desk, "It's from the Lieutenant Governor, dated 8th September" he started. He read it to himself and re-read it before looking up at John, "Your request to marry has been denied, Hurley".

John took a step back. This was the last thing he'd been expecting, "Denied? Can they do that?"

"You may be out on service, Hurley, but you're still serving time and the Governor can do what he likes – Port Arthur, Norfolk Island, road gang. Whatever he likes. Perhaps you can try again once you have your Ticket, but it's still his call even then until your time's up".

"It ain't fair. It just ain't fuckin' fair" he said softly as he took in the news. The constable handed him the letter but it was just scribbling to John and he despondently crumpled it up and dropped it to the floor. He shook his head and walked out the door wondering how to tell Mary Ann.

The pair were unable to meet on Saturday the 17th so it was not until after church the next day that John caught up with her.

"They've turned us down" he said grumpily as they stepped aside from the usual melee outside the church.

"Turned us down? Who 'as? For what?" Mary Ann asked, not quite sure what John was talking about as he had just blurted this out without any preamble.

"They've refused permission for us to marry" He said with exaggerated pauses between each word.

"Refused? What does that mean?" and again, "What does that mean, John?"

John began to get angry. Not really with Mary Ann, but she was the only person he could vent his anger against, "It means the fuckers won't let us get married and God knows if or when they ever will".

Mary Ann had difficulty processing this and didn't reply.

John stepped into the vacuum with a raised voice that had some nearby churchgoers turning their heads, "It's fuckin' over. The fuckin' Governor 'as the final word and 'is fuckin' word is No. Fuckin' buggerin' bastard!"

Mary Ann tried to calm him down but the red mist was rising and the frustration he had been harbouring burst out.

"We're finished Mary Ann. All our 'opes and plans. All fuckin' finished". And he kicked out at a clump of grass sending earth flying, fortunately not in the direction of any bystander.

"Come away John. Let's talk and decide what's to do" Mary Ann urged him, grasping his arm. She was beginning to worry that his anger would lead to violence and in the present company that wouldn't do either of them any good, not at all.

Her quiet insistence calmed him down and he reluctantly let himself be led away from the church precinct along St. John Street heading for Brisbane Street and the docks.

But it was a morose and surly conversation. While Mary Ann felt it to be a blow, she was not distressed. She figured time was on her side. But John had taken it as a personal slight and his anger clouded everything. In Brisbane Street he stopped and said, "I'm no good for anyfing right now Mary Ann. You should get back to yer lodgings, I'm not fit company. I'll see yer next Saturday". And with that he gave her a short, distracted kiss and went on his way, leaving Mary Ann outside the Green's house wondering just what was going to happen next.

The week crawled by. Washing, cleaning, ironing, cooking, emptying chamber pots, going to bed tired and falling to sleep with a troubled mind to wake up tired and do it all over again. It was soul destroying but at least she had food and a roof over her head she thought.

On Saturday she made her way to the Robin Hood as she had done for several weeks now to meet John. But although she waited a good hour, he didn't turn up. No-one there knew where he was either. They'd received no message.

On Sunday, he was not at church and the following Saturday she walked to the Robin Hood determined to find out just what was going on. As she walked up to the entrance she saw Robert Diver at the entrance talking to another man.

"Robert. Ow's tricks?" she called out.

Robert turned at her greeting and smiled at her, "Where've you been Mary Ann. 'Aven't seen you for weeks".

"I've been around, just not crossing your path I s'pose". Robert's friend had walked off so Mary Ann took the opportunity to ask Robert if he had seen John Hurley.

"Won't see 'im fer a while Mary Ann. Got into a fight wiv a couple o' lags at 'is work and was put away last Saturday. Been given two months in prison wiv 'ard labour then 'es being sent to Reibey's Ford road gang I 'ear".

Mary Ann was taken aback at the news but was not totally surprised. She had wondered when they parted if he would control his temper. Obviously not and, with his past record it was only going to lead to something like this. She thanked Robert, who offered to buy her a drink, but she turned it down and she went back the way she had come, dreams deflated and vowing to put this behind her and get on with life, wherever that took her.

A brilliant sun in a blue sky, the warmth of a fine day, birds busily going about their business and the emerging blossoms of trees and shrubs did little to lift her spirits as she walked slowly back to her lodgings.

The collapse of all hope of marrying John Hurley (and the greater freedom she expected that to bring) weighed heavily on Mary Ann's mind as 1836 wound its way to the year end. She kept to her task but began to fret at the strict control exercised over her by the Greens in an environment where she could taste and feel freedom all around her.

* * *

AFTER CHURCH one Sunday in October Mary Ann was making her way towards St. John's Street when she caught sight of a man and woman with a toddler in the man's arms on the other side of the road. She had to look twice before she was sure, but there she was. Emma Wells!

Mary Ann crossed the street and caught up with the pair, "Emma! Emma Wells!" she called out. The woman ahead stopped and quickly turned around, "Bless me soul! Mary Ann! Where did you come from?" Mary Ann ran the last few steps and the two girls hugged each other with unabashed delight.

Emma explained to the man standing by her, "This is Mary Ann Goulding. She came out wiv me" and, for Mary Ann's benefit, gesturing towards her companion, "This is me 'usband, Bill Watson. We got married last year and this is our son,

William" she added, putting a doting hand on the youngster's brow as he cuddled up to his father.

Bill introduced himself with an accent that unmistakably betrayed his Scottish origins and Mary Ann replied with a demure, "Pleased to meet you, I'm sure Mr. Watson".

"So, you're Mrs. Watson now?" Mary Ann laughed merrily.

"Yeah, 'ave been since August last year. We were in Campbell town souf of 'ere but Bill's found work in Launceston so we moved up 'ere last munf. Where are you stayin'? And what are you doin'?"

"I work for a family on Brisbane Street. Keeping 'ouse 'n fings". Been there since April. 'Ate it!" and she laughed again not without some bitterness.

"I know. It's not London, is it?" Emma replied and she quickly added, "But fings could be much worse. I never fought I'd be married wiv a wee boy by now!"

The two girls chattered happily for another two or three minutes before Bill interrupted, "We need to get 'ome, Emma. William needs seeing to".

An unpleasant odour emanating from the youngster's behind told its own story and it seemed that her husband was becoming a little irritated so Mary Ann let go of Emma's hand, which she had been holding tightly while they were talking, "Of course. But we need to get togevver soon".

"That would be wonderful" Emma replied.

They exchanged addresses – it seemed they were no more than a mile away from each other - promised to catch up the following Sunday, and parted with smiles and good wishes.

Mary Ann's smile quickly left her face and her temporary good humour soured with each step as she walked back. Although delighted to meet an old friend, it brought back thoughts of what might have been with John Hurley and she was back in a despondent mood by the time she walked into the house.

* * *

As THE NEW year arrived she began to bristle whenever she was criticised or instructed to do more. It wasn't helped by Mrs. Green's pregnancy which meant that she was being relied upon to do more and more to cover for her mistress's incapacity. It was made all the worse by Mary Ann finding out at the beginning of December that Emma and her husband had fallen out over something and Emma was now serving 15 days in the Factory, committed on her husband's charges! Improper conduct to her husband, whatever that meant. Life seemed to be so bloody unfair.

As SHE STEPPED into January she was not in a good place.

TANTALUS

Trafalgar
1836/1837

The Punishment of Tantalus: Zeus brought Tantalus to the Tartarus and put him into a lake with a fruit tree above him for eternity. Although he was close to the fruits and the water, whenever he tried to take a piece of fruit or drink a little water, the tree and the water would move away from him, so that he could not reach them.

Greek myth

* * *

1836 WOUND its way through a cool, wet Autumn into Winter. The twenty-third of July had come. And gone. And still Robert remained an assigned man without his Ticket. And there was nothing he could do about it other than protest to Allsop - which protest fell on stony ground - or the constable at his monthly muster; and the constable was also not inclined to take any action (and Robert did not have the money to make it worth his while). So Robert soldiered on and his frustration festered.

Winter lingered into Spring. A cool Spring. Robert was in the hut after the day's efforts talking to Colegrave as they huddled around a small fire, "It's bloody well burnin' me up 'aving to pocket Allsop's snide gibes" Robert said as he gnawed on a crust of bread, "But I knows I 'as to keep a clean sheet to get me ticket even though I should've 'ad it by now". Colegrave nodded his head knowingly, "Yeah, 'e's a brown nose[1] wi' Bryant and no McTavish to the men; but 'e's what we 'ave and I'm sure yer ticket'll come through. It 'as to". Robert nodded in agreement and added, "But I'd just love one chance to give that brown nose of 'is a nose ender[2]". And they both laughed, relieving the tension.

They were still laughing when Robert Taylor walked in with a smile on his face.

"What's ticklin' yer, Robert?" asked Colegrave.

"Bryant's just told me that I'm gonna be 'is man next month at Macquarrie Plains. "I'm to plough for Trafalgar in the Southern prize meetin' at the Woolpack Inn".

"Good on yer, mate" enthused Colegrave and Robert clapped him on the back too and commented with a wink, "I 'ope there's some siller to win".

Taylor said he didn't know but they all agreed that it would be a good day out at the very least. Both Colegrave and Robert praised Taylor's ploughing skills as they talked about the challenge and, soon after, with lights out they drifted off to sleep dreaming of days long past when they had enjoyed similar competitions as free men or boys.

The next two weeks went quickly and late November Taylor headed off the day before the competition with the best wishes of many of the men.

* * *

A COUPLE of days later Bryant and his brother Francis returned, with Taylor driving a wagon that rumbled into the Trafalgar yard with Bryant's prize bull, Trojan attached by a rope. They were in an excellent humour. Bryant's bull had won the 'Best Bull' prize and Francis had won Best mutton ram and ewe, Best heifer and Best roadster with one of his favourite horses. Taylor had not won the ploughing competition but had received an honourable mention and Bryant was fulsome in his praise. There had been nine others competing and the standard was high.

At the end of the day's work, Bryant called the men together with Allsop standing to the side and he announced, "As you will have heard, the Bryants and Trafalgar have been very successful at this week's Southern Association prize day. I think it only right that this evening everyone at Trafalgar should share in this achievement". There was a buzz of excitement and Bryant continued, " I've set up a cask of ale in the mess hall for everyone to celebrate our success. I expect you all to imbibe with moderation - there is work in the morning - and I expect everybody to be prompt. But tonight it is right to celebrate. Thank you all."

There was a roar of acclamation and much jollity as the men made their way to the mess hall. For many, including Robert, it was a luxury that was both a novelty and a rarity.

In the mess hall there was a pushing and shoving as the men strained to fill mugs with this unexpected indulgence. Allsop was standing at the table with the cask, overseeing its distribution, so the scene was more controlled than it might otherwise have been. Robert and Colegrave followed Taylor, who made his way to the front receiving the congratulations of the men as he did so, and once served, each took their prize outside and sat with their backs against the timber wall, knees bent, looking out over the distant pasture and forested hills.

'Ere's to you Robert" said Colegrave.

"And 'ere's to the champion Ploughman what gave us a taste o' victory" added Robert, lifting his mug in salute. They clinked the mugs together and Robert took a deep draft. It was the first time he had tasted a beer since that eventful day at the Anchor in Burwell more than four years ago. The light amber liquid filled his mouth, it's yeasty scent filled his nose, and the soothing, cool fluid melted as it drained into a welcoming, dusty throat.

TICKET

Trafalgar & Launceston
1837

TRAFALGAR: The New Year had arrived. And Robert Bright, like Mary Ann, was in a dudgeon with no further news on his ticket of leave. The situation was also now being exacerbated by the fact that Bryant's lease on Trafalgar only had a year to run and he had resolved to look for a larger property rather than renew the Trafalgar lease. Consequently, as each month passed, Bryant focused more and more on preparing for the sale of his stock and crops to accumulate the capital he needed to make the move and he drove the hands all the harder. With each month, Robert became more and more frustrated.

* * *

LAUNCESTON: The summer months also crept slowly by for Mary Ann who was being pressed hard by her master and mistress to keep on top of her household duties. She was seeing Emma every now and then, walking her son together after church mostly. Emma had resolved things with her husband, but things were not as she would have liked at home and she was consequently not an uplifting companion.

Come Easter, falling early that year on the 3rd April, Mary Ann made a sullen figure in church, begrudgingly going through the motions. Arriving back at the house she was instructed by Mr. Green to clean up the kitchen and wash the floor after two of the children had created a mess with an attempt at making a cake. Mary Ann couldn't help but retort, "Why can't they clear up their own mess?" which shocked her master who had become accustomed to her obedience, albeit with lessening enthusiasm as each month rolled by.

"I'll have none of that, my girl! You will do what you are told and like it, do you hear?"

"You can't make me like anyfing I don't wanna like" Mary Ann retorted, which maddened Green. He took a step towards Mary Ann, who was a good six inches smaller than him. But she stood her ground which only seemed to infuriate him further, perhaps because of the implied challenge. Unable to control himself, he struck Mary Ann across the face with the back of his hand, "Take that sneer off your face and get to work or you'll answer for it. I'll have no insolence from the likes of you in my own home".

The physical blow forced her take a step to the side but she controlled her anger, put her hand to her mouth to feel a trickle of blood running down her chin and looked daggers at her master, wordless. He looked back, also silent, and then he performed an about turn and marched out of the kitchen leaving her on her own to complete the assigned task.

* * *

EVANSDALE: Bryant was in Evansdale as Robert was stewing over the Ticket of Leave delay and while Mary Ann was battling with the Greens. He was at a meeting of the Association for the Suppression of Felonies. The agenda having been completed, Bryant was talking to James Cox, the Chairman, and John Gleadow while the other committee members took their leave:

"So, Bryant, I hear you are going to be moving on from Trafalgar" remarked Cox as they relaxed in their chairs around the board table.

"Yes, indeed. Barclay's lease expires early next year and I think it's time for me to acquire something larger" Bryant responded.

"Have you anything in mind?" asked Gleadow.

Bryant raised his eyebrows, anticipating a possible lead from Gleadow, who was a partner in a prominent Launceston firm of solicitors, Gleadow and Henty, and often dealt in property transactions, "Nothing specific at this moment, but I would like to stay in the same general area"

Gleadow came straight back, "We represent John Batman. Don't hold me to this, but I believe that he could be interested in putting Kingston on the market. That's not far from Trafalgar. Would that be of any interest?"

Cox interjected, "Batman? I understood that he'd settled in Port Phillip - or Melbourne[1] as I hear I should say now - and he's not in the best of health."

"That's true", said Gleadow, "I was talking to Mr. Blackhouse just the other week and he was telling me that he is much of an invalid these days, even needing a rush-work perambulator to help him walk. A sad thing for a man who has done so much, although he is not universally liked, I will grant you that, and some will shed no tears".

"Tell me about Kingston" said Bryant, whose interest was piqued, having a genuine interest in the possible acquisition of acres won by Batman for apprehending the Brady gang.

Gleadow raised both hands off the table as if about to present Bryant with a wondrous gift and began, "Well, Kingston covers more than 7,000 acres in the Ben Lomond foothills; it has livestock, buildings and a fair number of assigned men on the land. I couldn't be precise as to numbers at this point, but I can certainly find out. Not all of the land is prime, of course, but there is no reason why a good man, like yourself, Bryant could not do well there"

"When do you think it would come on the market?" asked Bryant.

"We don't have any instructions at the moment" Gleadow responded and then quickly added, "But I would be more than happy to speak to Batman on your behalf. I'm sailing to Port Phillip to meet with him in a month anyway".

"Do that, Gleadow" Bryant said enthusiastically, "I may well be interested in a transaction if you can get me the full information and an indication of the price, assuming Batman is interested in selling".

James Cox stood up from the table, "Well, Bryant, it sounds like you may have a new adventure ahead of you". He smiled and then, speaking to both Bryant and Gleadow, "Eliza and I are planning on holding a winter ball at Clarendon on the 15th of July. If you and your good ladies are free, we would be delighted to see you there. I've also invited John Glover[2], who I am sure you will find most interesting."

He added with a laugh, "Just as well Batman won't be able to come" and then continued, "We may be able to encourage him to show us some of his latest work". Without waiting for a response, which he correctly assumed would be an eager acceptance, he added *sotto voce*, "We shall have to ask for your forbearance in advance as we have some work underway on the house, but that should not unduly affect us for the evening. The fifteenth of July then. Eliza will see to your formal invitations".

Bryant could not wait to get back home to tell Anne the

good news, unsure of whether she would be more interested in the Kingston opportunity, as he was, or the ball, as she would probably be.

* * *

LAUNCESTON: Tensions in the Green household had been increasing with Mrs. Green's moody and erratic behaviour brought on, Mary Ann believed, by the late stages of a difficult pregnancy.

At the end of May, 1837 they came to a head. It was mid-afternoon and Mary Ann was finishing the laundry, preparing to hang it on the line at the back of the house. It was hard work and the sweat ran down her face with the effort. Mrs. Green appeared at the door, "I thought I told you to tidy the children's rooms?" Mary Ann had already performed that particular task and responded, "I 'ave, Miss".

"If that's tidying, we have a different view of the word"

"I did it after everyone was up this morning. If the children 'ave been back in their rooms since then, it's not my fault if'n there's a problem".

"Well, go up there and finish the job properly this time"

"I'll do it when I've 'ung the washing, Miss"

"You'll do it now!" her mistress responding angrily.

Mary Ann looked at Mrs. Green as if she were talking to a stupid woman, "I said I'll do it after I've 'ung the washing. I need to catch the sun if it's gonna dry before nightfall"

Mrs. Green exploded at the challenge to her authority, "We'll see about that when Mr. Green comes home. You are not going to disobey my orders you lazy child".

Mary Ann put her hands on her hips, "Alright, I'll go 'n tidy the rooms. You can finish the washing" and with that she brushed past the 'stupid woman' with her speechless mouth hanging open and stomped up the stairs, struggling to keep her temper under control.

That evening Mrs. Green pulled her husband into the drawing room as soon as he came through the front door and, with tears of frustration, berated him for allowing a servant so much latitude and complaining that Mary Ann had refused to obey her orders and had even told her to do the washing herself. The cheek of it.

James Green drew himself self-importantly up to his full height and told his wife to calm down. He would resolve this matter immediately. Disobedience of orders and insolence would not be tolerated.

He was tempted to birch the wayward girl, but knew that this could backfire if she were to report him to the authorities so instead he hauled Mary Ann roughly in front of him, shouted down her protestations - which only seemed to fuel his fury and, with spittle bursting from his mouth in his anger, told her to pack her belongings.

Mary Ann sullenly wrapped her pitifully few personal items into a ball and, with this small package under one arm, Green took a firm hold of the other arm and marched her ferociously down Brisbane Street to the police office near the Female Factory where he laid out his charges to the constable in an angry stream of self-righteousness; charges which had evolved into 'refusing to work'. Without ceremony, in a whirlwind of events, Mary Ann found herself back in a prison cell waiting on 'justice' to be processed.

* * *

THE FOLLOWING MORNING, first thing on the 29th May 1837, Green and the constable took Mary Ann to see the magistrate, where charges were formally laid. Mary Ann put her side of the story but the magistrate was having none of it and pronounced a sentence of two months in the Crime Class at the Female House of Correction, Launceston.

Come the afternoon, she was busy at the wash tub with other women in the Crime Class yard of the Factory. She didn't regret what had happened, indeed was still relishing the look on the face of that 'stupid woman' when she had told her to finish the laundry herself and two months was neither here nor there. This, she could handle. She was becoming toughened by the system.

* * *

TWICE A DAY, the women would be called to prayers in the chapel which was housed above the Superintendent's and his family's lodgings in the centre of the Factory. A stream of mostly subdued women and girls would climb the stairs and shuffle into the pews to be led in prayers for twenty minutes by the Superintendent before being sent back to work again. It was an opportunity to exchange gossip and information and find out what was happening or could happen, including sourcing contraband alcohol and tobacco or food or coffee which, considering the daily Crime Class diet consisted of a just 1/2lb of poor quality meat and 1lb of bread, was valued.

Mary Ann also noticed that the Factory was more crowded than when she was last there. Although built to house 100 inmates it must, she thought, have half as many again. She was in a dormitory room designed for one or two and there were four women there now.

One of them was an interesting character, an Irish girl by the name of Margaret, or Meg Drury. She was a little taller and a couple of years older than Mary Ann with the pale complexion and full black hair associated with the Irish and she was serving a six months sentence. Amazingly, it was her husband who had put her there. Apparently, or so she said, he was a member of the crew on the ship that had brought her here, and they had been married, so she was assigned to him. However, after a row, he had reported her to the magistrate and here she was.

Talking with her at night, Mary Ann found out that she had been shipwrecked[3] on the way to Sydney and had been one of a handful of survivors who made it to an island to the north of Van Diemen's Land after the wreck. From there she had been picked up and sent to Launceston.

She described the shipwreck one night. Described how the ship had struck a reef during the night which broke open the prison below deck, "What an uproar to be sure! Panic gripped us all and what a scene! Women, girls and children struggled to get out of that watery coffin, clambered up on deck. But, as I stand before you, I tell you no lie, once on deck, a lot of the women made for the stores where the rum was kept instead of trying to save themselves! They broke the cask open and just drunk their fears away. Got so drunk they just drowned when the ship went down".

This statement was greeted by appropriate oohs and aahs and 'well I nevers' before Meg carried on, "The crew got boats away but so many tried to get in them, all but one sank. I was helped onto a raft of timbers and we drifted all night and a good part of the morning until we reached King Island".

"What 'appened next?" Mary Ann asked with an expression of incredulity. "Well, the men built a rough shelter with the wood from the wreck and some of the food and drink also washed up so we managed to keep body and soul together until, about two weeks later, we were discovered by a sealer who kept us alive with wallaby meat that he'd hunted. Strange man. Lived with three native wives and seven little 'uns"

Meaningful glances were exchanged before Meg carried on, "About two months after the wreck a ship picked up most of the survivors but I was hunting for food with two of the crew, including my husband-to-be and we got left behind".

"So 'ow did you end up 'ere?" one of the other girls asked.

"They sent another ship to find us and the washed up stores and dropped us off at Launceston". She added, "And while we were stranded I got to know my John and he ended up marrying me! Silly sod. He's the reason I'm in here now".

* * *

TRAFALGAR: As May passed and the cool, wet days of June fell away one by one, Robert was told by Allsop that he should expect his ticket of leave to be processed soon, which was certainly a welcome piece of news, although it was still not in his hands and it was much later than he had hoped. The frustration of being so near yet so far was a daily burden. Not just for himself, but also his companions who bore the brunt of his bad humour.

Autumn's gold and umber shades coloured the days as they slipped by, then the colours faded as winter began knocking timidly on Trafalgar's door. With an eye to maximising his capital, Bryant sweated the farm hard which resulted in long, tiring days for the assigned men preparing the fields, mending fences, ploughing and sewing crops, harvesting, threshing and keeping the flocks of sheep (about six thousand all told) and herds of cattle (a hundred head of heifers with calves and steers, bulls and bullocks) safe from bushrangers and in good shape ready for a grand auction planned for early the following year.

Three weeks later, on the 21st June 1837, while Mary Ann was serving time in the Launceston Factory, a Government advertisement in the Launceston newspapers confirmed that Robert Bright, *Georgiana II*, had been granted a Ticket of Leave.

Robert had reported to the Constable on the 25th June in his normal monthly muster, but the notice had not arrived at the police station by then, so he was still unaware of its availability.

On the following Friday, Allsop came up to him with a

folded copy of the Hobart Town Courier dated the 30th June and showed it to Robert, "You have your Ticket, Bright". Robert knew how to make his mark on a piece of paper, but that was the extent of his literacy skills, so with Allsop pointing at what he was being told was his name (which he had learned to recognise) and looking up at Allsop's grinning face, he initially feared that this was a sick joke. But Allsop was deadly serious, "What are you going to do now, Bright?" he asked. Although Robert had been waiting for this moment for almost a year, he hadn't actually thought that far ahead and stared back at Allsop, mouth open, wordless.

Allsop laughed again, "Well man, you'll need to think on it. If you want to stay on at Trafalgar, Bryant's told me he'll be happy to pay you the going rate. You can stay in your hut, too".

Robert looked again at the paper and now responded, "Well, Mr. Allsop, I dunno. Gi' me a couple o' days to let it sink in".

"And you need to pick up your ticket from the Constable" added Allsop.

"Yeah, I do. I will" Robert replied.

With the coming of Saturday and Allsop's permission to go into town, Robert presented himself at the police station and requested his ticket. The Constable had it waiting and handed it over without ceremony. It consisted of four pages; the official ticket with the signature, a second page with the description of Robert on his arrival in Hobart on the *Georgiana* and the third and fourth were blank for subsequent comments, if any.

"Mind, you are still required to attend muster, Bright" intoned the Constable as he handed the document over, "This allows you to seek employment on your own account, to acquire property and to marry with permission. You shall not carry firearms and you shall not leave the District. And you shall carry this paper with you on all occasions. You will be bound to good behaviour and to regularly attend to religious affairs. If you don't behave yourself, this ticket will be withdrawn. Understood?" Robert took the ticket and muttered his assent. He folded it and tucked it carefully into his pocket. Then he patted it twice and turned around, pacing slowly out of the station, his boots echoing on the wooden floor. "Have a care, Bright" the constable called out as he left the office.

In some ways, Robert thought, this was as precious a trinket as he had ever owned. He even felt a little light-headed. The overcast skies and uncomfortable wind that was now whipping the dust across the street and the threatening rain just didn't bother him. Not one little bit. He might not yet be free, but he was free to work for someone of *his* choosing or for himself and a Certificate of Freedom, final, absolute freedom, would be his in two years if he kept his nose clean.

He thought about calling into a pub to celebrate but the constable's parting words echoed inside his head and he decided against it. Time enough for that, he decided.

The creaking of a shop sign swinging in the wind faded into the distance as he walked back to Trafalgar with a spring in his step and a smile on his face.

PATTERNS

❧

*L*aunceston
1837

AT THE BEGINNING OF AUGUST, Mary Ann found herself
assigned to another family. This time it was a Mr. Amos Langmaid, a boot and shoe maker with a shop and premises on
George Street. At least that was how the papers worded the
assignment. In reality it was his wife who had turned up at the
Factory to make the arrangements.

A new Governor, Sir John Franklin[1], had been posted from
England to take up his duties in Hobart in January and Queen
Victoria had ascended the throne two months earlier in June on
the death of her uncle, William IV. Mrs. Langmaid was the
epitome of the coming Victorian age, although she would not
have known it. She seemed to only own full, sober dresses, her
hair was worn in a severe bun and her nose was regularly
buried in the bible from whence she drew her inspiration and a
strict moral code.

She had sharp features, thin lips, a pale complexion, all

framed by mousy hair. She secretly fretted at her husband's 'tradesman' status and hoped for more, forever pushing him to 'better himself' by associating with the movers and shakers of Launceston society. Her husband was proud of his craft, customer-focused, but not as driven as his wife to become a social animal unless it furthered his business interests. He went along with his wife's machinations – anything for a quiet life.

Mrs. Langmaid was the mistress of the house, was clearly eager to make her mark in Launceston society and made it obvious that she intended to brook no insolence or disobedience from her newly acquired servant, "This is a Christian house with Christian values" she lectured Mary Ann on her first day and emphasised that she was expected to 'pull her full weight'.

It was more of the same for Mary Ann. Mrs. Langmaid was strict and gave her little time to herself. She worked from dawn to sunset, Monday to Saturday, collapsing wearily into her bed at night. On Sundays she would go to church and Sunday afternoon she would have to herself, although Mrs. Langmaid insisted that Mary Ann obtain her permission to leave the house and her destination had to be approved too. What free time she had was usually spent meeting up with Emma to spend an hour reminiscing, complaining, making plans and playing with her son.

Emma, however, was too quiet for Mary Ann. She had her own life, had no intention of risking more prison time and she would not put her certificate of freedom in jeopardy – as much for her son's sake as her own. Mary Ann, on the other hand, was straining at the leash. She had no family constraints and was finding the oppressive regime of Mrs. Langmaid hard to bear.

* * *

ON SATURDAY, November 25th, the Langmaids were out at a social event. Mary Ann had been given permission to visit Emma while they were out but her mind was set on more.

Once the Langmaids had left, she spent 20 minutes in her room brushing her hair, putting on what passed as her best clothes and making herself feel presentable. It had been a warm, sunny day and there was little or no chance of rain so no need to worry on that account. Down the stairs and out the door, she headed into town looking for the Robin Hood pub once more. Whether there would be anyone there that she knew or not, she just felt a need to be amongst people, free from oversight, regardless of the rules.

Outside, the streets were busy. People walking to and fro, individuals with a deliberate demeanour, couples more carefree, smiling and laughing, all social strata; gentlemen, ladies and those occupying less heady heights of society. Carriages and horses rumbled by and, up ahead, the swinging signs of public houses and hotels enticed all and sundry to participate in the evening's entertainment.

From the Robin Hood, there came the sound of music, laughter and, every now and then, people would exit or more often enter, letting the sounds of singing, conversation and music spill out onto the lamp-lit street. In the far corner of the bar a fiddler was playing a lively tune, perched on a stool. The bar was reasonably full, most people from the lower strata of society, mainly men but women too. Although gambling was illegal, there were men playing dice at one of the tables with roars of approval when the numbers fell kindly. A few men stood next to the fiddler, singing along and drinking freely.

Mary Ann looked around the bar, hoping to find somebody that she knew but before her eyes could capture anyone, she was approached by one of the men in the bar carrying two glasses of beer. He proffered one to Mary Ann, "I've not seen you here before. Can I buy you a drink?" Mary Ann eyed her benefactor. He was a few inches taller than her, probably about the same age and he had an engaging smile that beamed from a weather-beaten face.

"I don't mind if I do" Mary Ann replied, returning the smile. Her new friend returned the smile and led the way to an empty table where they both sat down.

"My name's Jonah, what's yours?"

"Mary Ann" she replied, "And weren't you supposed to be swallowed by a whale?"

He laughed and replied, "I guess my parents had a strange sense of humour or didn't read the Bible much. Truth to tell, I didn't know them very well – both died when I was a boy".

"I'm sorry" she replied, "That must've been 'ard".

"That's life. Or not, whichever way you want to look at it. But you just have to get on with things don't you?"

"You can say that again." She took a sip of her beer and, looking up into his eyes, asked, "What's 'appening 'ere tonight?

"Well, they've got some music and a couple of me mates are meeting me here soon so I suppose we'll have a drink or two, sing a song or two, maybe even have a dance or two" Mary Ann chuckled as he gestured towards her as if to invite her onto a dance floor.

Before she could reply, he stood up and waved at a couple of men who had just entered the bar, "Over here" he called out and, as they approached the table, he introduced Mary Ann to them both. "Mary Ann, say hello to Bill Andrews and Jack Starr and watch yourself with them, they can't be trusted to behave themselves". Mary Ann remained seated and smiled at Jonah's teasing remark. The taller of the two, the one called Jack, asked if they needed a refill and then went to the bar to buy drinks. He returned a few minutes later and placed a glass of beer in front of Bill, the foam slopping over the side as he did so. He raised his own glass with the toast, "Your good health" before taking a deep draught, wiping the clinging foam off his face with his hand as he returned the half-full glass to the table.

It wasn't long before more drinks arrived and more again so that Mary Ann soon found herself feeling a little tipsy and somewhat uninhibited. She found herself up on the floor with Jonah in an energetic dance as the fiddler worked his magic and after this, breathless, returned to the table where a refreshed glass of beer was waiting. The evening continued in much the same vein until 10 o'clock had come and gone. By now Mary Ann was very much the worse for wear.

Two of the girls at another table had disappeared with their male companions through a side door, although Mary Ann had not noticed this, and the atmosphere in the bar generally became more noisy, more unrestrained as time passed. An argument broke out and two men squared up to each other, but before blows could be exchanged the landlord had intervened and ejected them both leaving the crowd to resume its carousing.

An hour passed before the landlord cried out, "Last orders" as he rang a bell behind the bar, "Last orders, last orders". Jonah and his friends argued over who was to buy the final round before Jack 'won' the argument and headed off to fill their glasses one final time. Another half-hour passed by as the party drained their glasses. Then to the insistent clanging of the bell and a call of, "Time, gentlemen please" Jonah helped Mary Ann to her feet and they headed for the exit.

She stumbled and would have fallen if Jonah had not caught her. "My, Mary Ann, you're almost floor'd[2] . My lodgings are just round the corner, come on". Mary Ann was in no condition to protest. Her head was swimming and she was having difficulty putting one foot in front of another. As they left the pub the night air helped clear her head a little and she feebly protested, "No, I need t'get back t'me own lodgings".

"You're in no state for that" Jonah said. Indeed he was

himself not in prime condition but was better able to handle the night's drinking. He put Mary Ann's left arm around his neck, holding her hand with his left hand and put his right arm around her waist, part carrying, part walking her down Brisbane street.

About 100 yards on they came to his lodging house and he opened the door. All dark, still, hushed. He whispered to Mary Ann, "Keep quiet, don't want to wake anyone up" and then almost carried her up the stairs to his bedroom, opening the door and depositing her onto the single bed in the room. Mary Ann groaned but didn't move. It felt like she was viewing the world from a merry-go-round. Everything was spinning in an awful, sickening, dizzying manner and she just wanted it to stop. She dared not move an inch for fear of sending another jolt of pain into her befuddled brain. She let out a soft moan. Thankfully, eventually, everything closed down to a black unconsciousness and the merciful escape of a deep sleep.

* * *

SHE WOKE with a splitting headache and opened her eyes slowly only to quickly close them again before trying once more. For a moment she didn't know where she was. And then she remembered. She let out another groan, this time because she realised that she would be in trouble for staying out all night. Jonah was still asleep, uncomfortably curled up on the floor and Mary Ann was reluctant to wake him but knew it had to be done.

"Jonah", she called. No response. "Jonah", this time louder. Still no response except for a snort and a twitch. She slowly raised herself into an upright position, her head hammering and her body telling her to go back to bed but she forced herself to sit up and, her foot on Jonah's shoulder, prodded him until he responded.

He opened his eyes and, looking up at Mary Ann looking

down on him, he attempted a weak smile. He was also obviously not feeling in tip–top shape either. "I 'ave to go, Jonah. There might be a chance that I can sneak back in before they know I've been gone". He struggled up, raising his hand to his head as he did so and said, "Yes, of course" then, "Where are you going?" Mary Ann explained that she didn't have far to go and that the sooner she left the better it was likely to be. She got up onto her feet – a little unsteadily – and splashed her face with some water from a jug by the bed. Then she made her way to the door. Jonah called out, "See you again?"

"I'll try. At the Robin 'ood one Saturday?" Then, as she opened the door, "Thanks for last night, it was fun; I think". And with that she hurried down the stairs and out the door.

Unfortunately, even though she was back soon after dawn, the doors had been locked and she was unable to get in. Not knowing what else to do, she just waited until the household stirred.

'Mrs. Langmaid was the first up and Mary Ann knocked on the door when she saw her. Mrs. Langmaid came to the door, opened it and, instead of pouring invective at her, as Mary Ann was expecting, simply said, "Go to your room. Prepare for church and ask for the forgiveness of the Lord. You are past my strength".

She went to church that morning under a dark cloud and on the following Monday, November 27th, she was taken by Mr. Langmaid first thing to see the magistrate once more where she was committed to the Factory Crime Class again, this time for three months. She was becoming hardened to the system and was not in the least overawed by the magistrate, the constable or the court. Indeed, once it had become apparent on the Sunday morning that she was likely to be sent back to the Factory, she simply shrugged her shoulders and resolved to take it in her stride. It seemed that this was the pattern of life and she would just get on with it.

FATE

Launceston
1838

Petitioners emphatically deny [Assignment] to be in the mass of cases a condition of hardship, but affirm it to be, on the contrary, one of great physical comfort.

From Petition to the Queen by Free Settlers (including Edmund Bryant and John Atkinson, J.P.) opposing discontinuance of Transportation and Assignment March 5th, 1839

* * *

THE HEAT of a burning sun still radiated from the yard and buildings as the first day of January, 1838 drew to a close. With nightfall, the temperature had dropped but it was still close and the bare surroundings, the heavy, musty air, all did nothing to improve the spirits of the three women lying in their hammocks in a dormitory cell.

Mary Ann was confined with two fellow prisoners in the Crime Class and after another strenuous day at work in the laundry her hands were red and raw and her belly was grumbling. Their daily rations were deliberately minimal – ½ lb of stringy meat on the bone and 1lb of bread that tasted like sawdust. No vegetables, no coffee or sugar or any other so-called 'indulgences' to take their minds off the blandness of the diet. Well, she thought, it's better than bread and water in solitary, which both of her companions had experienced before and had been talking about as they readied themselves for bed.

The two women were Rachel Holmes, a black-haired 24 year-old from Preston in the north of England, who wore scars on her cheek and forehead from past beatings and Ann Murray, from London, a striking, freckle-faced 28 year-old with long black hair and bright blue eyes.

Ann had been sentenced to six months for 'Absconding' and had also, at the same time, had her 7-year term extended again, this time by 12 months, for repeated infractions. She had a month left to serve at the Factory. Rachel had been sentenced to six weeks for being in town, drunk, without a pass and was due to finish this particular sentence in a week. Mary Ann would outstay them both until the end of February.

"What will you do when you get out?" Mary Ann asked of Rachel.

"Find a pub and have a drink to toast you both" she replied.

Mary Ann chuckled. The three of them had hardened through their ordeals and took pleasure in talking up their disdain for authority, taking pride in their free spirits although never pushing things so far as to create unnecessary hardship for them while serving out this particular sentence.

"What about you, Ann?" she asked.

"I'll be sent to some bastard to wash 'is socks and empty 'is piss pots if 'istory is to tell us anyfing" and she paused and said wistfully, "But what I need to do is find a man to settle down wiv and get on wiv me life proper. I'd like a family one day".

That particular comment made them all think. There was silence until Ann added, "I'm not gonna let 'em beat me down. Good fings 'appen for those what want it" and after another pause, "G'night". Mary Ann and Rachel murmured their good-nights and thinking on Ann's words closed their eyes to sink into a tired sleep.

* * *

ON HER RELEASE at the end of February, Mary Ann left in defiant mood, a mood matched by the weather which was, as one newspaper described it, 'very boisterous'. On Monday, 26th February it had blown a hurricane, several boats had been swamped and some lives lost. On the Wednesday night, rain began to fall from the heavens in a torrent and continued incessantly all day and through Thursday night. It was into this maelstrom that Mary Ann was released on the 1st March. She left the Factory with a thin, angular man, clean shaven, with sparse, mousy hair plastered back onto his head. His name was Russell and this was the next person to whom she had been assigned. She clambered into his waiting carriage, thankful to escape the elements and the groom cracked the reins as the hooves of the horse struck the pavement and the carriage rumbled off into the rain-soaked day. They only had a short distance to travel and Mary Ann was soon inside his house being shown her room and receiving his expectations.

On Friday morning, the 2nd March, although the rain had thankfully stopped, the skies were still threatening but the temperature had moderated and it almost touched 70°F during the day.

The temperature wasn't the only thing to warm up. Almost immediately, her new master began to make suggestive comments to her that made her feel extremely uncomfortable. After beating off a physical advance. which left her attacker with a fat lip, she decided enough was enough and simply walked out of the house as soon as she was able. She had no idea where to go but after walking aimlessly for twenty minutes decided to ask Emma to put her up for the night until she could figure out what to do next.

Emma was solicitous but worried about the consequences of taking Mary Ann in, even for one night. But Emma's husband was away and Mary Ann persuaded her to shelter her after promising to go to the Constable in the morning and explain herself. Instead of a pleasant evening reminiscing with a friend, it was an awkward few hours and after a simple evening meal of meat stew and cabbage with bread Emma put her son to bed and she and Mary Ann made their way to Emma's bed where they both settled down for a night's sleep.

First thing in the morning Mary Ann did as she promised. She walked to the Police office and tried to explain why she was there only to be bundled off to the cells while the constable sent a colleague to fetch Mr. Russell. He arrived soon after, protested his innocence – which the constable accepted without question - and, at the same time indignantly accused Mary Ann of being absent all night without leave.

On the 3rd March, Mary Ann was sentenced by the magistrate to ten days in solitary confinement on bread and water. She recalled the description of solitary by Ann Murray just a few weeks earlier, never expecting to experience it herself so soon. But she wasn't going to give anyone the satisfaction of showing that it troubled her so she received the sentence stoically, giving no response as she was led away and marched inside the octagonal prison. The sense of injustice, however, gnawed at her.

She was taken to the Factory's cells at the rear of the complex, down a passageway with twelve heavy wooden doors, each with iron bolts. The turnkey opened the door of one of these cells, handed her the daily allowance of a pound of bread and a small piggin[1] of water and pushed her inside without comment.

The cell was effectively a bare stone coffin, about six feet deep by four feet wide into which no light penetrated. Cold, damp, dark as the grave and silent. There was nothing to do but huddle into a corner and think. Her ears strained to hear anything.

* * *

As the days passed, she focused on each sound, perceived or real, fixating upon anything to occupy the mind. Her thoughts wandered to days long gone, family and friends, the hustle and bustle of Covent Garden, the Punch and Judy show she had seen when she was little.

She would be let out once each day and allowed to walk the stone corridor for one half hour, the indirect light initially blinding, her body aching as she stretched her limbs. There would be no talking and then she would be returned to her dungeon and the next twenty three and a half hours would crawl interminably by.

She lost track of day and night and would sleep fitfully, wake with a start, drift again and usually, when the turnkey arrived, she would be startled into wakefulness by the sound of the bolt being withdrawn, the rush of air, the explosion of light.

She was almost perpetually hungry but this was nothing new and so gave it little thought at all, pacing her sampling of bread and water as best she could across the hours. But most of all she was angry, defiant, determined not to be broken, determined to show them all that while they could take her liberty they were not masters of her spirit, "A pox on all of 'em!" she shouted into the tomb as she steeled herself.

* * *

ON HER RELEASE on 12th March, Mary Ann left her cell with her head held high and a personal sense of triumph. She found that she was being assigned to a Mr. Joseph Pettingell and took up lodgings with him and his family in the centre of town. Mrs. Pettingell, with the support of two of her three daughters, gave lessons to 'young ladies' in music, drawing, oriental painting and dancing while her husband tried to make ends meet with contracted work; instruction in writing and drawing, book-keeping, engrossing[2] and copying letters, making and colouring charts of buildings and estates and restoring and varnishing paintings.

Prior to setting up home in Launceston they had run a boarding school in Evandale but they had been unable to make ends meet and Joseph had filed for bankruptcy the previous September and consolidated everything into their current lodgings at 2 Cameron's Buildings, St. John Street in Launceston.

Mary Ann found a chaotic situation. Mr. Pettingell was a disorganized individual, scratching to make ends meet and as a result counted every penny and demanded toil every daylight hour of every day from Mary Ann. His wife was nevertheless devoted to him, and their three daughters – a child and two teenagers – were just insufferable, unhappy about how life was treating their father and looking for someone to take it out on.

As is often the case, forced to humble themselves to secure business and being treated as second class by their clients, they sought to vent their sublimated anger on Mary Ann. Especially given their recent fall from grace and worried that his tattered reputation might suffer further, the master was determined to control his servant with an iron fist and he insisted that Mary Ann was home at night seven days a week, attended church regularly and acted properly in all respects.

* * *

SHE WAS WORKING in the kitchen one morning when a young man appeared at the door with cap in hand. He was several inches taller than her, perhaps 5'5", with reddish hair, a complexion burnished by the sun and wind and blue/grey eyes. Although he was wiry rather than well-built, he had broad shoulders and appeared to be well-muscled from physical work. Mary Ann was quite taken with him. He politely asked to see Mr. Pettingell, explaining that he had been referred by a Mr. Sprunt of Evandale for whom he had been working recently. Mary Ann told him to wait at the back door and sought out her master.

"There's a man says 'e's been told to come 'ere by Mr. Sprunt of Evandale".

Pettingell stopped his writing and looked up with a puzzled frown on his face, Sprunt had been a neighbour and client of his when he was a schoolmaster in Evandale, "What would Mr. Sprunt require from me, I wonder? Show him in Oh, and what is his name?"

"I dunno, I'll ask 'im". And with that she returned to the kitchen.

"What's your name?" she asked as she returned to the kitchen.

"Robert Bright" he replied, still holding his cap in his hand.

"Well, come on in, e'll see you in 'is workroom" and she added with a smile, "And good luck" as she showed Robert through the kitchen to an adjoining room.

"Robert Bright" she announced and stepped aside to let Robert pass into the room.

"Very well. You can go, now".

Mary Ann left the two men together and closed the door behind her as she left.

"Well, Mr. Bright. What does Mr. Sprunt want of me?"

"Nothing sir. It's just that I worked for him and when I told him I was looking for work in Launceston he suggested I call on you. I have a letter" and Robert proffered a sealed letter to Pettingell. He took the letter, opened it, read the few lines and then put it on his desk.

"It seems that Mr. Sprunt has a good opinion of you, but I have nothing that I can put your way at this time. Where are you staying?"

"I've lodgings at 20 Canning Street, sir. I'm doing some odd jobs for a carter".

"If I come across anything, I will let you know".

Robert tried one more time, "I can turn my hand to most anything, sir".

"I'll keep that in mind. Good day, Bright" then he opened the door and called for Mary Ann, who appeared quickly (she had been waiting behind the kitchen door, anticipating the call).

"See Mr. Bright out".

Robert followed Mary Ann back to the rear door.

"I 'ope you got what you were lookin' for" she said as she stood by the exit.

"No. Not really. But I'll keep looking" he replied.

"Nice to meet you, Robert Bright" she said with a smile, looking at him with upturned eyes as he stepped past her.

He stopped, a few inches away from her, and said, "Nice to meet you too, Mary Ann. I hope we meet again".

"It's a small town" she answered.

"I suppose it is. Cheerio for now then".

She smiled and shut the door as he walked with a steady step into the yard, pulling on his cap, and off the premises.

* * *

MARY ANN FOUND the going very hard at the Pettingells and struggled to settle into a routine. After a couple of weeks she had had more than she could take and refused to pick up after the two girls who had been deliberately making work for her. They ran crying to their father and he came storming in to the laundry to 'put this servant in her place'.

"What is the meaning of this insolence?" he shouted, raising his right arm as if to strike out, but keeping far enough away to avoid any physical harm.

"You need to keep those two girls in line. I'm not 'ere to be played wiv by two outa control children" Mary Ann responded defiantly.

"We shall see about that!" he responded between gritted teeth, somewhat taken aback by Mary Ann's belligerent tone, "You shall come with me this minute to the Constable's office and we'll see what's what, by Jove we shall". And with no further notice, on March 3rd they marched off on a journey that was becoming familiar to Mary Ann.

Pettingell charged her with idleness and repeated insolence. While she would dispute the idleness charge, deep inside she acknowledged the charge of insolence, but the bastard had it coming she thought to herself.

This time the sentence was increased to 14 days in solitary on bread and water and Mary Ann found herself back in her dungeon marking off the days to her release on the 8th April.

As the door of the cell closed with a thud and the bolt was shot home, she resumed her position in the corner of the cold, dark, damp cell and tried to focus on pleasant things. Like that Robert Bright?

* * *

ROBERT HAD RETURNED to his lodgings after calling on Pettingell unsure of what to do next. He had left Evandale because work was difficult to come by since Bryant had quit Trafalgar. He had been offered work by Bryant at his new farm but Robert felt that it was time to exercise the relative freedom that came with his Ticket. Continuing in essentially the same role, albeit at a larger farm, wouldn't do that.

He found physical work with local merchants in the Evandale, Longford and Perth area and worked hard and diligently. But while he managed to accumulate a few shillings, he had not settled into anything regular. In March, he was hired by Robert Marlow of King's Meadows, to help load and convey some furniture to Launceston that he had purchased from the insolvency of the Tasmanian Inn at Cocked Hat Hill (although the owner, Mr. Carolan, insisted on people calling it 'Prospect Hill' because he thought the existing name 'grossly' vulgar and cocked hats were, after all, unfashionable in these modern times). Robert had been to the inn once before when Bryant had attended a meeting of the Association for the Suppression of Felonies, but that was the furthest north he had travelled.

Although the Inn was only 6 miles from Launceston, his drive into the principal town of northern Van Diemen's Land was his first and he was quite taken by the bustling town and the number of people and businesses operating, so much so that he resolved to return once he had settled matters in Evandale to try his luck, expecting to find more opportunity there.

However, delayed in returning, he failed to report for the monthly muster and found himself hauled in front of the magistrate on the 7th April and, despite his excuses, he was dealt with severely; handed one month's hard labour to drive home the lesson that, while he held his ticket, he was not a free man yet.

It was to be a salutary lesson.

* * *

AT THE FEMALE FACTORY, the interminable days had crawled by and Mary Ann had withdrawn into herself, losing track of time and becoming disoriented. But she clung to an inner strength that expressed itself in a bravado whenever the cell door was opened and, although impotent, she shouted curses on all who had brought her to this place when she was shut in.

At last, the 8th April arrived and she walked out into the sunlight and fresh air once again, her spirit unbroken with a mocking smile on her face.

FREEDOM'S CALL

Launceston
1838

THE SAME DAY that Mary Ann was released, Robert was sentenced to work on a road gang at Reiby's Ford[1] and found himself in the company of about 75 men breaking rocks under the relentless rays of the sun and the armed supervision of an overseer and soldiers.

Although he didn't realise it at the time, it could have been worse because many road gangs chained the convicts. On this particular piece of the road, that wasn't the case. Nevertheless it was unrelenting, hard work and disobedience or insolence or just not working hard enough could earn a brutal punishment as Robert witnessed when one of the gang was publicly flogged. The poor man tried to face his torture bravely, holding back his cries of anguish for the first few stripes. His raw back was repeatedly torn open, the blood splattering the ground with each vicious crack of the whip, leaving angry wounds like chopped meat.

Until, mercifully, the fiftieth lash fell and the unfortunate victim was untied, collapsing onto the floor before being hauled away by two fellow convicts.

At night the convicts were confined in squalid conditions and during the day they were provided with the minimum of rations to keep body and soul together. This was the harsh side of Governor Arthur's penal code and Robert wanted nothing more to do with it if he could help it. At the end of the month, he thankfully left Reiby's Ford and resolved never to come back.

* * *

ON HIS RELEASE, Robert found work collecting wood for Robert Marlow, whose King's Meadows property was near the Tasmanian Inn. Loading and driving a cart and delivering fuel to merchants in town didn't pay much, but it was a start. His co-worker was a fellow Ticketer, Joe Hunter, a bluff Yorkshireman with a checkered history. He was 29 years of age, the same size and build as Robert, with a slightly pitted face and reddish-brown hair pulled back into a pony tail. He had arrived in 1831 on the *Gilmore* and was a brickmaker by trade but, unlike Robert, he had found it difficult to stay out of trouble and had experienced spells on the treadwheel, on chain gangs and, most recently, in April, had been sentenced to six hours in the stocks for missing muster and being drunk. But he had an irrepressible, optimistic personality and Robert found him lively company.

Their work for Marlow was paying them enough to keep a roof over their heads and provide food and drink. Especially drink where Joe was concerned.

Through the winter months they were both kept reasonably busy and then in September, having completed the day's work, they visited the Hibernia Inn[2] at the corner of Bathurst and Brisbane Streets – four blocks down from where they were staying. The pub was owned by a freed ex-convict, Josiah Pilcher, and the two men had heard about it from fellow workers as being worth a visit. The evening was a merry one. They had been paid, the pennies in their pockets were jingling and tobacco, drink and good company were in prospect.

They left in high spirits late that evening, walking back to their lodgings, arm in arm, stumbling and singing at the top of their voices.

That is, until a constable confronted them and arrested them both for disturbing the peace.

They spent that night and Sunday in a cell sobering up and, in front of the magistrate the following Monday, 10th September, they were both fined 5/- for being drunk, admonished and released. It could have been worse but their behaviour had not been violent and they had been contrite, which softened the magistrate's outlook.

Sober and poorer, Robert vowed not to let that happen again. He wanted his Certificate of Freedom and he was not going to buck the system, no matter how much fun it had been carousing with that lushy cove[3], Joe Hunter.

* * *

IT HAD NOT BEEN uneventful for Mary Ann over these past few months either. She survived the solitary confinement through force of will. Indeed, it hardened her and fueled a resentment and fierce independence. She was a different person to the girl who had stolen a Dutch clock for a 'lark' in London town. She had thought much about her family while alone in the cell and her anger at the disproportionate treatment and raw injustice of her situation welled up to carry her through their attempts to browbeat her into submission. She left the Factory more defiant than ever and determined to 'stick up for herself'.

She had been assigned to another master, a Mr. George –

again in Launceston – and had as much success with this position as before. She did her best to play along but after twelve weeks the drudgery and boredom became too much and she took the opportunity to break free for an evening on the town.

Inevitably, on the 12th July she found herself back in the Crime Class at the Factory for six weeks for being absent without leave. She was returned to the George family in the middle of August after serving her time but all trust had broken down and the atmosphere was poisonous.

On Saturday, 1st September she walked out of the house and made her way into town. It had been a fine day and with the going down of the sun there was a languid warmth and a sense of freedom in the air. Ignoring the possible consequences, she made her way to Brisbane Street and quickly fell in with three young men outside one of the many pubs in town. She had by now graduated to gin from beer – it was cheap and easier to drink than the bloating drafts of beer, but it also addled the senses more assuredly.

As the night wore on she lost any inhibitions and with the chimes of midnight striking she found herself with one of the boys on some straw in a warehouse near the docks. Both of them were stupid drunk and they made a poor attempt at fumbling with each other's clothing as long-constrained passions drove both to search and explore. But it all came to an ignominious conclusion when the boy rolled over and vomited copiously, retching again and again while Mary Ann tried to comfort him, not too effectively as she, herself, was much the worse for wear. After perhaps an hour of this, they both fell back exhausted. He collapsed into a senseless stupor and Mary Ann gave up resisting attempts to stop the room revolving and fell into a deep, drunken sleep as well.

·   ·   ·

SHE WAS WOKEN by the sound of a horse and cart outside the building and she did her best to wake her paramour. His snoring continued regardless and concerned that she might be caught, she eventually gave up her hopeless task and left him to it, sneaking out of the warehouse and heading back to the retribution she knew would be coming.

On the Monday morning she was in the police cells and on the following Wednesday 4th September she appeared before the same magistrate that Robert Bright would encounter in six-days' time.

"You again?" the be-whiskered gentleman sitting at the bench exclaimed, for it was the same justice that had sentenced her only a few weeks before.

"What do you have to say for yourself?" he looked down at the charge sheet and continued before Mary Ann could respond. "Absent without leave all night. It gets worse".

"I lost track of time sir. I didn't mean no 'arm'"

"No harm! No harm? You consistently disregard rules. You get up to God knows what on your nocturnal jaunts and you tell this court that you 'lost track of time' and mean no harm. Well, let us see if you can lose track of time over the next fortnight. Fourteen days solitary confinement on bread and water". He banged his gavel on the table, "Take her down".

Mary Ann was taken away and within the hour was treading the now familiar steps to the solitary cells in the Factory and, with a sigh, settled back into the corner of another damp, dark cell with 1lb of bread and some water to see her through the next 23 ½ hours.

AS THE SAYING GOES: this too shall pass, and it did, and on the 18th September, not bowed at all, although disoriented and blinking furiously in the light, Mary Ann was released into the service of Mr. Birch. The first few weeks of washing, ironing, sewing, cleaning etc. proceeded on their normal track. She went the extra mile to avoid being accused of insolence, disrespect or disobedience but a caged bird still needs to spread its wings and at the end of October she decided to break out of her cage.

It was a Friday, three days before Gunpowder Treason Day[4], bonfires had been built on rough ground in readiness and she felt that a spirit of revolution was in the air. She didn't know where she would end up or for how long she would be gone, but she decided that she had to get out of this stultifying situation.

Her first stop was Emma's lodgings where she begged Emma to put her up again for a night, which extended to two nights. But both Emma and Mary Ann knew this couldn't last. She was putting Emma and her husband in jeopardy if it was discovered that they were harbouring a convict on the loose so, with a heavy heart, she left her friend and wandered the streets for a couple of hours before making her way back to the Birch household to turn herself in.

On arriving, the master blurted out, "Where have you been?" to which Mary Ann gave a sullen, "Ere and there, nowhere special".

"Well, what have you been doing?" he persisted.

"Just finking".

And so the interrogation continued, producing no information of any value because Mary Ann certainly wasn't going to create trouble for Emma. At length the master marched her back to the Constable, told him that this assignment was not working out, explained the situation but chose not to press any charges as he just couldn't be bothered with the disruption to his busy life. The constable took her into custody.

Within a few days, with the demand for servants still much greater than the supply, she had been assigned again, to a Mr. Bishop. Mary Ann was surprised that no punishment had been meted out and resolved to try to make things work this time when, on the 10th November, her new master advised her that the authorities had, in fact, not taken a lenient view but had instead extended her 7-year sentence by 12 months as a punishment for absconding. It came as a blow but, in truth, it was hardly an unexpected turn of events and she shrugged it off, biting her tongue rather than making a blustering comment and risking further punishment.

About two weeks later, November 27th, Mary Ann's patience ran out yet again and she decided to make another bid for freedom. Her master and mistress being out for the night, she threw caution to the wind and went out on the town once more.

Being mid-week, it was quieter than on a Friday or Saturday (which was normally pay day), but she decided to make her way to the Robin Hood, hoping to meet up with someone she knew (and someone with the money and interest to buy her a drink or two as she had absolutely nothing of her own). She hoped to spend a couple of hours in good company and get back before she was missed.

As luck would have it, when she entered the room she saw Robert Diver with another man standing in a corner, drinking their beers and quietly observing the people in the room. Robert saw her before she saw him and he broke into a smile and called out, "Mary Ann!" She looked and also smiled, almost with relief at having found someone she both knew and trusted.

She made her way over to the pair and was introduced to his friend, Charlie. Robert bought Mary Ann a gin and Robert and Mary Ann updated each other on what had been happening in their lives. It had been a pleasant hour or so when an argument broke out on the other side of the room. Before anyone knew what was happening one of the men had thrown a punch that knocked the other man to the floor. Another man jumped on him from behind and the three of them were trading blows and insults as they all attempted to regain their footing. Then a fourth man crashed a chair over the back of one of the men getting up off the floor and a small riot was in full swing.

This continued for a couple of minutes when two constables appeared at the door and within minutes calm had been restored. However, everyone in the bar was interviewed, including Mary Ann, and when she was unable to produce a pass or authority to be in the bar, she was arrested, taken back to the police office and charged with being in a disorderly house.

Back in front of the same magistrate on the 28th November, Mary Ann received short shrift and was sentenced to two months in the Crime Class at the Factory.

She found that now, those working at the wash tub received the same rations as those in the Assignment class because of the physical effort required and, because the women put to work were not strictly supervised they operated at a relatively leisurely pace, so it was not the punishment that it might have been. At times they could hear convicts in other parts of the prison singing – apparently there was little work available to occupy them and they would spend most of the day simply milling around, gossiping, singing, even dancing to pass the time.

* * *

CHRISTMAS and the new year passed and being by now familiar with the workings of the prison she had discovered that there was a way to make life a little more bearable thanks to the endemic corruption fostered by the low wages paid to prison staff. It seemed that the nurse and sub-matron, unhappy with their meagre pay, had instituted a system whereby inmates could buy goods such as coffee, tea, sugar and tobacco for cash or even sexual favours.

The nurse would provide pen and ink and paper at 6d a sheet so letters could be sent out with women leaving, often concealed in their stays and immune from search by the gatekeeper. Goods were 'ordered' via the sub-matron and the nurse; she then arranged for items to be brought in to the prison concealed by visitors or by prison staffers. It had even been known for spirits to be brought in over the wall. And, with the gatekeeper away at muster at 7pm, the gate would be opened by his wife to let in the contraband that was not brought in by other means.

It was a profitable business and it contributed to a less than strict regime within the eight walls of the Factory, especially evident in the Crime Class section. It also led to a regime where some of the longer-term inmates began to exercise control over others by incentives or intimidation. Some of the inmates had also paired up in lesbian relationships and some would fiercely defend their partners – it had even been known for released prisoners to commit a crime immediately to return to the Factory and rejoin their partner.

The Superintendent and his wife, the matron, were either unaware of what was going on or were simply unable to control everything and, as the factory became more and more over-crowded it became more and more difficult to re-establish control.

Mary Ann did her best to avoid getting involved in all the comings and goings. Life was difficult enough without compli-cating it further.

LIAISONS

⁂

*L*aunceston
1839

On January 27th, 1839 Mary Ann walked out of the Factory gates again with a defiant air in the company of a handyman who worked for a Mr. Mosely, her new master. As she followed the man up the street, she wondered what this assignment would bring. Truth to tell, she didn't expect much different and she didn't care.

Three weeks later, on the 22nd February, she was back in front of the magistrate charged with disorderly conduct. She rationalized to herself that the stupid housemaid already working for Mosely had it coming to her. She was a churlish older woman who took delight in making disparaging comments about Mary Ann. Every day, slurs were delivered with a curled lip in a pockmarked face, sneering at Mary Ann's work or appearance – always delivered out of the hearing of the Master or Mistress of the house of course. In the end Mary Ann had taken a bucket of dirty cold water and, to the crone's astonishment, had emptied it over the bitch. So here she was again, facing a charge of disorderly conduct.

SENTENCE: 10 days in the cells on bread and water, but at least not in solitary this time. She took it stoically, even thanking the magistrate with a curtsy as she was led away.

ON THE 6TH March she was released from the cells, hungry but cocky. They had tried to break her over the last year and failed. She was in control, not them.

Her new master was Mr. Atkinson, a Justice of the Peace, and she wondered, as she walked back to his premises, whether his position within the legal system might not make life more difficult for her. However, things went rather well, she thought, as March passed, then April and May, all without incident.

Atkinson was a busy man, a pillar of Launceston society and actively working on countering ideas coming from the Mother Country that he feared might lead to the abolition of transportation and the assignment system[1]. This would, of course substantially damage the economic base of many free settlers – himself included – as it would substantially increase the cost of what had until now been virtually free labour.

He was immersed in his own affairs and was unconcerned with the running of the house, which he left to his wife. Mrs. Atkinson was an unremarkable woman, spare and several inches taller than Mary Ann. She was officious but fair enough, not showing favour to any servant at least and, in keeping with his public assertion that assigned convicts lived a comfortable life, Mary Ann enjoyed a warm, dry room, adequate food, Sundays off after church, working hours from 5 a.m. to nightfall and a comparatively easy pace. She was responsible for the upstairs rooms, changing beds, emptying chamber pots, setting fires, sweeping and cleaning as well as being responsible for keeping clothes and linen clean at the washtub. Compared to previous households, this was a much easier situation. She was, however, not allowed to be out after nightfall without a good reason and so far, despite wracking her brain, she hadn't been able to think of one...

One late afternoon in May, a pleasant day with the sun shining from a blue sky and a fresh breeze airing the house, Mr. Atkinson arrived home with several other gentlemen. They were in earnest discussion about the merits of the American penitentiary system versus the system in Van Diemen's Land as they entered the drawing room. It sounded like gobbledegook to Mary Ann and she paid no attention. She kept in the background until Mrs. Atkinson called her over and told her to see to the two grooms waiting outside with the gentlemen's carriages. "They will be there for an hour or two. Get them something to eat and drink while they're waiting" she ordered. "Yes Mrs. Atkinson" Mary Ann replied and hurried to the kitchen to ask cook for something she could take outside.

Equipped with two pork pies and a jug of beer with two tankards, Mary Ann did as she had been bid. "'Ere you are gents. Somefing for yers while you're waiting"

The nearest groom had been brushing a fine bay horse and put the brush aside as he turned to reply, "Why thankee Miss, much appreciated I'm sure". He took the pie and poured himself a beer. By now the other man had made his way over to help himself.

"Why, Mary Ann! Bless me!".

The second man was Robert Bright. It turned out he had been hired to drive two of the men to the house – apparently this was part of a larger group involved in managing some sort of plea to Parliament in England. Robert didn't know much about it but explained to Mary Ann that he'd been working for them on and off for a couple of months now and this journey to Launceston was becoming a regular thing.

"I wondered if I'd see you again" he commented as he chomped his way through his pie. "And 'ow long 'ave you been 'ere?"

"Since March" Mary Ann responded, "And where are you lodging while you're in town?" she added.

"Oh, we're staying in town. We'll be there for a couple o' nights I 'spect. D'you wanna get togevver later? When you're finished 'ere I mean. I should be free after seven tonight".

The question both delighted and worried her. Delight at the thought of seeing someone who quite appealed to her, worry that she doubted she could get permission to be out. But she was not prepared to let this Robert know that she wasn't in control and, without knowing how she would do it, she agreed.

"Shall we meet at 'is 'otel? It's the Cornwall Inn² on Cameron Street".

Mary Ann agreed and, collecting the empty jug and tankards, returned to the kitchen, her mind working overtime to find a way to keep the appointment.

Mary Ann sought permission to visit Emma that evening – she figured that this would be seen as harmless enough - but Mrs. Atkinson refused, concerned that her guests might stay longer and that she might have to organise an impromptu dinner. Better safe than sorry, so all staff kept on stand-by.

However, the meeting broke up well before nightfall and after the noisy exit and the hollow sound of carriages and horses grumbling and clattering away, the house settled down. The servants finished their duties and Mary Ann made her way to her room. Once there, she stuffed a pillow under the bed to hopefully give anyone making a passing inspection the impression that she was in bed, then changed into her 'walking out' dress and, opening the window as quietly as she could, she climbed out and stealthily made her way off the premises and into the street.

Cameron Street was only half a mile away and, walking briskly, she made good time. Butterflies fluttered in her stomach, perhaps because of her escape and the penalty if found out or maybe because of the assignation.

A little flustered, she finally reached the Cornwall hotel and saw Robert waiting, on his own, leaning against a post under the balcony, beside the entrance. She waved as she saw him and had to stop herself breaking into a run, 'Slowly does it, girl' she whispered to herself. Robert saw her at the same time as she waved and he straightened himself up and smiled a welcome, "I was wondering if you was gonna make it" he said as she reached him.

"Well, 'ere I am, as I said I would be" she replied, slipping her arm into Robert's, "What are we gonna do?"

"I don't know the town much, you're the local, d'you 'ave anyfing you'd like to do in partic'lar?" Robert replied.

Mary Ann was tempted to suggest the Robin Hood, but only because it was really the only place she knew and then she suggested a walk down George Street to the harbour to enjoy what was left of the fading light as the sun began to kiss the horizon, leaving an orange trail behind.

They walked at a leisurely pace and talked. Robert told her about how he came to be in Van Diemen's Land and that he was expecting his Certificate of Freedom next month – the seventh anniversary of his sentence, a world away in England – and Mary Ann did the same, although skipping the detail of her regular run-ins with the authorities.

"So when you gets yer Cerstificate, what are you gonna do?" she asked.

Robert explained that he thought about trying to get back to Cambridge to his family but that he also wondered how he could manage it and, anyway, maybe he could make a better life here, "There's work if you look for it, there's some what's done well for themselves like that Josiah Pilcher – he owns the Tasmanian Inn just up the road for goodness sake". Mary Ann considered that. She, too, wondered about going home after her time was done and had dwelled on it a lot in solitary, but, like Robert, she also wondered if there was a better life to be had in Van Diemen's Land once she was free.

"What time do you have to be back?" he asked.

Mary Ann thought on her answer. She wanted to say that she was her own timekeeper, but Robert deserved better than that, she thought. She surprised herself when she answered, "In an hour or so".

They stopped to watch the sun disappear beneath the horizon across the Tamar river and Robert suggested that, as they had limited time, they make their way back, buy a pie and an ale at one of the many pubs in town and return her to the Atkinson's home before she got into trouble.

They did just that. It had been a quiet interlude but both Robert and Mary Ann knew something special had happened and as Robert left her at the corner of the street (Mary Ann explained she should return on her own) they looked intently in each other's eyes as Robert nervously leant towards her and, holding her gently, they kissed. Mary Ann put her arms around him and together they shared a long, slow, tentative kiss that promised much and left much unsaid.

"Can I see you again?" he asked.

"Try and stop me" Mary Ann replied with a giggle.

"I'll call when I'm in town with Bryant again. It'll probably be in the next week or two with all these meetings he has to attend".

Mary Ann nodded her understanding.

"G'night, Mary Ann. Until the next time"

"Yes, Robert. The next time"

They broke apart and Mary Ann turned and walked the last

fifteen yards back to the house while Robert stood his ground, watching, with a strange light-headed feeling. Just before she reached the gate, she turned and gave Robert a half-disguised wave before softly opening the gate and stealing around the back of the house to regain her bedroom before anyone could see that she had been away.

* * *

A MONTH later Mary Ann was leaving church on the Sunday morning when, to her surprise, she saw Robert standing by a carriage, stroking the horse and calming it as people wandered by. She walked up to him, a little unsure as to how he would react as they had not been in touch since their last meeting, "Hello Robert". He started with surprise then broke into a sheepish smile and replied, "Thank goodness. Hello Mary Ann"

" What are you doing 'ere and why thank goodness?" she asked.

"I'm taking my people back from church. I hoped you might be here. Look, Mary Ann, I can't stay long, they'll be here any minute, but I wondered if we could meet up Thursday evening again if you can make it?"

Mary Ann, didn't hesitate and said impulsively, "Course I can. Where d'ye wanna meet?"

"The 'Cornwall' again, like last time?"

"I'll be there"

He reached out and touched her hand tentatively, "That'll be good. See you Thursday. Take care of yourself".

"Thursday" she replied and squeezed his hand in response before stepping away and leaving him to busy himself with the horse as Mr. Marlow and his wife walked up to the carriage.

* * *

So, that Thursday evening, Mary Ann repeated her escape act and headed into town to meet Robert. She walked with a smile on her face, making people she passed on the street wonder what this young girl was so happy about. There he was, as before, waiting outside the Cornwall hotel and he didn't wait for Mary Ann this time but instead walked briskly towards her as soon as she appeared. He put his hands on both of her shoulders and said, "I missed you".

Mary Ann didn't know what to say but there was no need, he leaned down and kissed her instead, squeezing her arms as he did so..

"Here, I got this for you". Robert produced a simple bead necklace and offered it to her.

"Robert, you shouldn't 'ave" she protested.

"But I wanted to" he replied, pressing it upon her, "Let me put in on" and he fastened it around her neck as she stood there, feeling quite special.

"There. It suits you".

Mary Ann spontaneously reached up and kissed him quickly, "Thank you, it's lovely".

Night was falling so they decided to have a pie and something to drink at a pub where they could find a table. Mary Ann suggested they go to the London Tavern a little further along the street. She had walked past it many times before to attend muster at the police office, which was next door to the tavern. The sign swinging in the breeze with a picture of London and St. Paul's cathedral had struck a chord so, a few minutes later (for the tavern was just one block away at the corner of St. John's Street) Mary Ann crossed the threshold. Being past four o'clock the police office was closed so she felt safe.

Seated at a table with a pie and a jug of ale between them, Mary Ann asked, "What 'ave you been doing?". She actually wanted to say *Why has it been a month since I saw you?* but didn't want to appear too needy or controlling. Robert explained that he'd been kept at work in Evandale and King's Meadow and hadn't been back to town until this week. He also explained he didn't know how to get a message to her.

They were only four blocks from St. John's church and it occurred to Mary Ann that the best way to meet was to use the church as a constant point, "I'm always at church Sunday morning; that's probably the best way" she suggested and Robert agreed. I'll remember, he said, "Always St. John's?"

"Yeah, always St. John's and boring ol' Reverend Browne" Mary Ann laughed and Robert joined in with her, the infectious chuckle making it impossible to remain straight-faced.

Around them the small bar was in a constant state of flux as people, mostly men, came in, hovered around the bar and went out. A few stayed at the bar and talked to each other and in the far corner of the bar four men were playing 'two-up[3]'. When Mary Ann commented that they should leave in case a constable came in and found them gambling, Robert dismissed her concern, "The 'cockatoo[4]' at the door'll keep them out of trouble I reckon" and they talked on, at times holding hands. The time flew by.

At eleven o'clock Mary Ann told Robert that she needed to get back and they both reluctantly finished their drinks and walked out into the night. A breeze off the river had picked up and it was cool – it was June after all – so Robert put his arm around Mary Ann and they walked slowly back to the Atkinson's home. A few yards down from the gate they stopped and said their goodnights. They hugged, kissed and reluctantly parted, promising to see each other soon. Mary Ann walked softly back to the house, glad to see that it was in darkness, opened the gate and made her way back to her room, thankfully without waking anyone. Robert made his way back to his lodgings, counting the days until he could spend time with her again.

THE PATRIOT KING

*L*aunceston
June 14th, 1839

THE NEXT MORNING broke with blue skies and a chill in the air. Mary Ann made her way downstairs as dawn was breaking to fill a log basket to prepare the fires for the day ahead. She was making her way back when Mrs. Atkinson silently appeared in the hallway dressed in black, like an evil avenging angel.

"And where were you last night, my girl?"

Mary Ann's face fell. She realised that they must have checked on her room while she was out and she didn't know whether to confess or cry or what.

Mrs. Atkinson didn't wait for a response, "Mr. Atkinson will be taking you back to the police office this morning. I will not tolerate disobedience of my orders and certainly not absconding from this house without permission. Go to your room until Mr. Atkinson calls for you and may God forgive you your wicked ways". She stood aside, Mary Ann placing her logs on the floor before making her way back up the stairs wondering what would happen now; guessing that it would be the Factory yet again. She shook her head with annoyance and began to collect her few belongings, resigned to her fate.

It was the same old routine with the magistrate. This time he recommended extending her sentence by another 12 months for absconding, subject to the approval of the Lieutenant Governor of course, and he ordered her return to the House of Correction while a new assignment was organised. At the Factory, while being examined in the office, she was ordered to take off the necklace which she had been wearing ever since Robert gave it to her but she refused, "It's mine, you ain't gonna steal it".

The clerk told her she would get it back when she left the Factory, but Mary Ann was having none of it and a tussle ensued when the constable tried to take it from her forcibly. Soon another constable arrived on hearing the commotion and despite Mary Ann's protestations the necklace was taken from her,

"You wait here and no more trouble" the constable ordered, a little out of breath, and then left the room. A few minutes later he returned and took her to the Superintendent's office. He gave three quick taps on the door.

A disembodied voice came from behind the door, "Enter".

As the door swung ajar she saw the Superintendent seated behind a desk writing something in a ledger. She was taken before him by the constable and was left to stand on her own as he stepped back two paces. She felt like a recalcitrant schoolgirl in front of the headmaster. The Superintendent finished writing, put the pen down and looked up at her.

"Your necklace will be returned when you leave this establishment but I will not tolerate disobedience". He shook his head, tired of the inability of inmates to comprehend simple regulations, "Ten days in solitary on bread and water for you Goulding; you will obey orders while you are here. Perhaps ten days will give you time to consider how to behave in future".

There was no point arguing further and Mary Ann was marched back through the Crime Class building and on into the solitary cells where she was locked up once again in another small, isolated, musty dungeon to contemplate her sins.

The darkness enveloped her and she fumed with the injustice of it all. Rather than quench her spirit however, this treatment fuelled her anger and simply strengthened her resolve. She would not be broken by this bloody system. She bloody well would not and she struck the wall with her fist so forcibly that it made her wince.

* * *

TEN DAYS LATER, she came out of solitary disoriented and hungry once again but with her spirit undiminished. A few days later, at the end of July, she was released. The Atkinsons wanted nothing more to do with her, but it seemed that Michael Kennedy, the Clerk of the Peace at Launceston court had need of a servant.

* * *

ROBERT, meanwhile was faring better. At the same time as Mary Ann was leaving the Factory, he was in Evandale attending his muster, as all Ticketers had to do. When he reported at the office, the Constable called him over. He was an older man, slightly overweight with mutton chop whiskers; a freed convict who had been in Van Diemen's Land for many years and who had bent to the system. "Well Bright, that's it."

"That's what?" Robert responded with furrowed brows. As far as he knew he was clean, no misdemeanours, nothing to bring the law down upon him.

"You've done your time, lad. Twenty-third of July. You're free to apply for your Certificate".

Robert, of course, knew that the seven year term was up in July but, like so much in this system, he was never totally sure what would happen and the confirmation by the Constable that it was finally, really over felt like chains being lifted from his shoulders. He was speechless. Thoughts flashed across his mind, much like the thoughts that are said to flash across a dying man's eyes; of being sentenced to death, the interminable wait on the appeal, the loss of his family, the *Georgiana*, *Trafalgar*, that awful month on the road gang, and now; this would be his last muster, he could even return to Cambridge if he could find the money or work a passage. What to do? The possibilities milled around in his head.

That evening he was taken by three of his friends to their 'local' in Evandale to celebrate. The inn had the unusual name of *The Patriot King William IV*[1] (although the friends' choice was driven not by their respect for the late monarch's patriotism but because no-one could approach the inn without being seen, which allowed anyone who didn't want to be caught 'improperly tippling' to escape before the police arrived. The landlord's known 'intimacy' with the local constabulary was an added benefit).

Robert and his friends sat at a table with a jug of foaming ale in front of them, there was laughing and joking and he was happy, but he was not relaxed. The strictures and constraints of the last seven years had left their mark on him and despite the urging of his companions, he drank in moderation. Deep down, he felt that he would never again feel totally clear of prying eyes, never again be free from restrictive rules. And he didn't intend to cross swords with the System again – one month on the road gang had been enough, let alone seven years little more than a slave. He would enjoy tonight, yes; tomorrow he would lay plans for the future.

FABRIC

G len Dhu
    Launceston, 1839

THE KENNEDY HOME, Glen Dhu, stood on the outskirts of Launceston town, a thirty minute walk south from the Factory. The family consisted of Kennedy himself, his wife, a young son and two teenage daughters. They lived in a two-storey house with ten fertile acres of policies that belied the 'dark valley[1]' epithet with farmland beyond where dairy cows grazed contentedly. Michael Kennedy had a green thumb and, in his spare time away from the courthouse, he worked tirelessly on an orchard, vegetable and flower gardens that he valued greatly. He had even won a prize for 'best melon grown in the open air' with his cantaloupes at the Launceston Horticultural Society show and aimed to do the same with his roses.

To Mary Ann it was another impressive dwelling that dwarfed her home in London . The ground floor consisted of a drawing room and a dining room, each 20 feet by 16 feet, a store room, a pantry, kitchen, laundry and wash-house. There was also a dairy and an underground wine cellar as well as four bedrooms on the first floor. Outside, the house was fed by a well of spring water complete with a stone wellhead and a wooden superstructure from which a bucket was strung to haul up fresh water. There was also a large brick reservoir to hold rainwater.

Upon being brought to the house by Michael Kennedy at mid-day on Monday, the 29th of July, Mary Ann was shown into the drawing room and handed over to her new mistress. Kennedy immediately disappeared, leaving the two women on their own.

She began, "Mr. Kennedy has a position to maintain in society, Goulding. As an officer of the court, this household must be above reproach and that includes you. I expect you to bear that in mind and, provided you do so, things will be fine for all of us." She didn't say what would happen if things weren't fine, but Mary Ann had no trouble understanding the implied message.

She replied demurely with head bent, "Yes Missus"

"You have a room over the wash-house. That is to be kept clean and tidy. Now let us go over your duties"

Mrs. Kennedy showed Mary Ann the house, her room (where she left her meagre possessions), went through the daily routine, being asked regularly if she understood, until she had been shown everything, and everything had been thoroughly explained. Laundry on Monday, ironing and mending on Tuesday, assisting with baking on Wednesday and Saturday, daily sweeping, dusting, cleaning and tidying, bringing water in, clearing and preparing the fireplaces, emptying chamber pots each morning and evening. The introduction complete, Mary Ann was told to make herself some bread and cheese for her dinner and then to report to Mrs. Kennedy in the drawing room for her afternoon assignments.

Left on her own in the kitchen, Mary Ann cut a hunk off a

block of cheddar and helped herself to some bread from the pantry. She poured a glass of water from a jug and sat at the kitchen table, a knife in one hand, mouth steadily chewing the bread and cheese and sipping the water. She looked around at her new 'home' and wondered how things would work out this time. A clock ticked like a metronome in the hallway and she could hear a man outside stacking logs. The sun peeped between the clouds and peered into the kitchen through two small windows. A dog barked. But otherwise the house was still. Hushed.

Over the following days she met the other Kennedy servant, a rusty guts[2] as one person described him, shabby, grizzled, gruff, a middle-aged Irishman by the name of Brendan O'Neill. He was uncommunicative, preferred his own company and seemed to be wary of everyone and anyone. As he spent most of his time working in the gardens or the stable, Mary Ann had little to do with him, which suited them both just fine.

She also met the Kennedy children. The young boy, Brian, was rather spoiled by a doting father and the fussing of his mother. There were also two daughters, Mary and Siobahn, younger versions of their mother with long black hair and somewhat dumpy figures, both in their early teens. Although Mary Ann tried, she couldn't form any bonds with them. Brian was too aware of his role as the heir and the need to act beyond his age, sometimes with comical effect, but always requiring him to 'talk down' to the servants. The two girls were already bound up with the need to prepare themselves to someday find a husband. This involved time at a 'School for Young Ladies' during the week and concentrated efforts knitting and practicing their embroidery skills when not being coached by their mother in skills such as music, deportment, drawing and dancing.

Their efforts at embroidery and the consequent appearance of different fabrics in the house caught Mary Ann's attention.

When bolts of fabric were brought into the house as each new project was begun or when a dressmaker arrived to collect samples that Mrs. Kennedy and the girls had been examining, she felt a pang of regret, recalling walking as a child with her father to Mr. Dorrington's warehouse with their freshly manufactured bolts of cloth.

THE DAYS PASSED BY, one after another and another in monotonous drudgery.

One day in September, Mrs. Kennedy called Mary Ann over after breakfast, "We are going into town this afternoon. I need you to come with me to help carry. Be ready after dinner. O'Neill will drive us in." This was the first time she had been asked to accompany her mistress and Mary Ann found herself rather anticipating the outing as she toiled with the iron in the laundry.

With the clock striking twelve, she put the iron away and folded the last of the washing. She took the basket full of clothes and went up to the bedrooms to stow them away before returning to the kitchen.

Dinner finished and the plates and cutlery washed and restowed, Mary Ann went to the drawing room, knocked on the door and told Mrs. Kennedy that she had finished her chores and was ready to go when she was needed.

O'Neill had already brought the carriage to the front door and was standing by the horse, holding its reins and eyeing a clouded sky that threatened rain. Mrs. Kennedy rose and, wordless, walked to the front door. Mary Ann followed behind.

The past week's weather had been cool and unsettled and today was no different. Indeed, Mary Ann had overheard Kennedy grumbling about the cost of heating the house just a few days earlier, "Heaven's above, they're asking thirty shillings a ton for coal and fifteen for firewood. It's scandalous". Consequently the house had been noticeably cooler with only the drawing room heated and Mrs. Kennedy was now bundled up and carrying an umbrella. Mary Ann followed her example as best she could.

It wasn't long before they were at their first destination, a milliner's shop, where Mrs. Kennedy fussed and preened herself over a selection of hats, finally buying one that the milliner insisted 'suited her perfectly' and, with the hat box in her arms, Mary Ann followed Mrs. Kennedy back to the waiting carriage. They then went to the other side of town to a dressmaker where Mrs. Kennedy was shown bolts of fabric while Mary Ann remained quietly in the background.

She was fascinated by six wooden 'adult' figurines sitting on a bench, about 21 inches high, that the dressmaker had clothed in designs that she showed to her client, "And this is the latest fashion in Paris" she explained, holding up one of the dolls as she teased the skirt into shape. "You will see that it is unbelted and note that the bodice now tapers to the waist. I do adore the puffed sleeves off the dropped shoulder and we can of course provide the white gloves that are de rigeur, very fashionable.

She babbled on, the words spilling out in a well-rehearsed torrent, "Of course, we can change the fabric, perhaps make it up in the green silk that we were looking at to set off your beautiful hair. You will note that all the evening dresses these days reach the floor, ankle-length hemlines are so yesterday. But we still will need starched petticoats to maintain the exquisite shape." She continued in this vein without interruption; it almost sounded like a foreign language to Mary Ann, but she found it all fascinating, as did Mrs. Kennedy who was enjoying the attention.

As the presentation continued, the two women moved to another part of the premises to examine other fabrics and Mary Ann cast her eyes over the rest of the room. Bolts of fabric were stacked on shelves; on a cutting table a pattern was pinned to a beautiful width of red silk with scissors waiting to do their work; on a shelf was arrayed a selection of cottons that reminded her of her own days working with her father winding the silk onto bobbins. She could almost hear the clack of the loom again and a veil of sadness fell over her as she imagined her family again working together in their London home.

She was awoken from her reverie by Mrs. Kennedy, "Goulding! Take this out to my carriage while I finish up here" and she pointed to a large cane basket filled with different cloth samples that the dressmaker was holding out to her.

Mary Ann took the basket and left the shop, the handle of the basket under her left arm, her hidden right hand stroking the fabric. It was a sensual feeling, the cloth almost had a life of its own and she grasped a beautiful green silk sample in her hand and let the fibres caress her skin. She reluctantly handed the basket to O'Neill who secured it under a tarpaulin to protect it from the rain that still threatened but so far had held off and then Mrs. Kennedy left the shop too with obsequious pleasantries from the dressmaker accompanying her short walk to the carriage. With everyone on board, O'Neill shook the reins and the placid mare took off, hooves striking the ground and the wheels rumbling beneath them.

* * *

MRS. KENNEDY KEPT a tight rein on Mary Ann, but allowing her time off on a Sunday afternoon after church and also time off after she had reported at the police office in Cameron Street at the monthly muster. Nevertheless, she was expected to be back at Glen Dhu before nightfall. It was after reporting to the police office at the end of September that Mary Ann decided to make a detour on her way back to the Kennedy home. She hadn't seen Emma for quite a while and thought she would surprise her and perhaps take a walk together before she returned.

She arrived at Emma's lodgings with a spring in her step and knocked on the door with anticipation. There was a scuffling sound and soon the door opened with young William peering from behind his mother's skirts and Emma's daughter, Margaret – a reticent 3-year-old - watching from the back of the room.

"Mary Ann! How wonderful to see you!"

"It's been too long so I fought I'd say 'ello"

"Come in. Would you like some tea?"

"Oh Emma! You 'ave become the perfect mum. 'Ow old is William now?"

"He turned five in August. Takes after 'is Dad" and turning to reach out to her daughter, "Margaret's the shy one, but she's no trouble"

They caught up with what had been happening in their lives and Mary Ann suddenly jumped up and said, "Let's all go fer a walk. It's a nice day for it". After a little hesitation, Emma agreed and within fifteen minutes the four of them were outside the rather shabby lodging house. "Where shall we go?"

"Ow about the market, we can pretend we're off to Covent Garden and the kids can stretch their legs" Mary Ann replied. So, in good spirits the little band headed towards the docks, passing amongst a busy throng of people making about their business and watching out for passing horses and carriages.

They stopped at the corner of Cameron and St. John's Street to watch the 'Morning Star' coach load its cargo and passengers in front of the London Tavern readying for their journey to Perth and Longford. The two children enjoyed the spectacle and wanted to stroke the horses (but were restrained) and, after five minutes watching this sport, they continued on their way.

The market resonated with the normal hustle and bustle, hawking, shouting and organised chaos and, although it was but a pale shadow of Covent Garden, both Emma and Mary Ann recalled how they had met and they talked about Liz Diamond, wondering where she was now.

They came to a row of stalls with clothes and fabrics displayed. The clothing was basic workmen's trousers, jackets, caps and such like and there were also displays of fabric and samples. The fabric was mostly plain calico, but there was finer muslin on display and some printed cottons. There was also a selection of handkerchiefs. Mary Ann couldn't resist making her way to the stall and started examining the goods with Emma, holding on to both children, following behind.

As they were browsing, shouts broke out behind them, "You only gave me a florin! Now 'and over the sixpence you owe me, mate." One of the stall-keepers was shouting angrily at a well-dressed, ruddy-faced man standing in front of the stall.

"I gave you half a crown! I'll not be cheated" his customer replied with exasperation.

The stall-keeper walked from behind the stall and strode up to the other man, "Gimme my sixpence or it'll be the worse for you".

The stall-keeper was taller and looked stronger than his customer, but the smaller man was having none of it, "You'll not cheat me, sir. I'll have the police on you"

"You will, will you?" the stall-keeper shouted back, becoming more enraged with each exchange and, before another word could be spoken, he swung a clumsy haymaker punch at the smaller man who stepped back, leaving the stall-keeper unbalanced and striking air. In a moment a crowd had gathered around the two men who were squaring up to each other. Emma turned anxiously to Mary Ann, "Let's get out of 'ere. This is no place for us". Mary Ann nodded her agreement and the four of them retreated, heading away from the boisterous, noisy and increasingly aggressive crowd.

They had only gone a block when they heard running footsteps and the rapid, whirring *crack crack crack* of a rattle before a constable turned the corner, making for the increasing noise of the crowd, a truncheon in one hand and a rattle[3] in the other that he was swinging to sound the alarm. Mary Ann hugged herself tightly as he ran past.

"What's wrong, Mary Ann?" asked Emma, noticing that she was walking with arms folded to her breast in an unnatural manner. Mary Ann looked around her and seeing that they weren't observed, unfolded her arms to reveal a swatch of calico fabric hidden beneath her shawl.

"You didn't?" Emma exclaimed.

She explained with an impish grin on her face, "Yeah, I couldn't 'elp meself. It was just lyin' there on the ground. Dunno 'ow it got there but wiv all the argy bargy going on I picked it up. It didn't belong to anyone else so I fought, why not me?"

Emma shook her head, "It'll only get you into more trouble. You should leave it 'ere."

"That doesn't make any sense Emma, I dunno who it belongs to, maybe no-one, maybe they just tossed it away, and I can make somefing nice out of it. Just needs a wash. God knows I deserves it after everyfing that's 'appened to me."

Emma just shook her head doubtfully and they continued on their way, the children beginning to show signs of tiredness. Emma picked little Margaret up, freed her hand to take hold of William and before too long they were back at Emma's lodgings.

Anxious to examine her treasure and aware of Emma's concern about stolen goods, Mary Ann decided that it would be best to bid her friend goodbye and make her way back to her room where she could stash the calico for the time being. They hugged each other and, with promises to meet again soon, went their separate ways.

ROSETTA

Rosetta, south-east of Launceston
1839/40

THAT NIGHT MARY ANN lay on her bed with the calico draped over her, imagining what she could make from this treasure. The calico was undeniably of poor quality compared to the fine silks worn by the ladies and it was only a plain beige colour. But it was HERS and maybe she could find some dye? Anyway, it would allow her to make up a new dress or something. Frankly, it didn't matter what she made. It was HERS. She could find a needle and cotton – Mary and Siobhan had plenty, they were always embroidering something. She ran her fingers across the cloth, folded it, placed it against her cheek and, after hiding it under her bed, went to sleep with a smile on her face.

The next few days descended into the ongoing routine drudgery, although Mary Ann was able to 'borrow' a pair of scissors, a couple of needles and some cotton while cleaning the house. She would return the scissors and needles when she was finished. These, too, she hid in her room as she thought further on what she was going to make. She had concluded that she would need to work on her creation after she had finished her work. But she couldn't work too late as candle light into the wee hours might raise questions.

She had designed a dress in her mind and was ready to start on her project when calamity steamed in on an irrepressible tide. It had never happened before, but today Mrs. Kennedy had decided to make an inspection of her room while she was working in the laundry. With steam from the hot water rising, Mary Ann's arms wet and her hands wrinkled from the soaking clothes, Mrs. Kennedy made a grand entrance at the doorway of the laundry holding the calico, imperiously accusing, "Where did you obtain this fabric, may I ask?"

Mary Ann replied without hesitation, "Its mine. I found it, someone 'ad got rid of it at the market".

"Got rid of it?" Mrs. Kennedy snorted, "Got rid of it? Stole it more likely".

"I did not!" she replied, stamping her foot, with tears beginning to well up in her eyes.

"We'll see about that" Mrs. Kennedy said without compassion, "I told you when you came here that this house must be above reproach. And you betray us! Mr. Kennedy will hear of this" and with a thudding finality she left Mary Ann impotently standing by the wash tub, tears beginning to slide down her cheeks and a strangled sob in her throat as the black, swishing skirts of Mrs. Kennedy disappeared into the house.

* * *

IT WAS the 4th October and once again Mary Ann found herself at the police office on Cameron Street in Launceston. She protested her innocence in vain but the situation was unclear; until they could find the owner they couldn't prove that she wasn't telling the truth. The calico was nevertheless confiscated by the constable, his assurance to Mr. Kennedy being that he would attempt to find the owner and if not, the fabric would be sold as unclaimed.

Kennedy was adamant that she could not stay in his house, he feared for his reputation, so the constable undertook to speak to the magistrate and find a new assignment for her. So it was only a matter of days before Mary Ann found herself with a new master, a Lieutenant Thompson who ran a farm nearby at Paterson's Plains.

The loss of her prized fabric as well as the injustice of it all burned inside her but there was nothing she could do about it. She just bit her tongue and simmered under the iron fist of Governor Franklin's oppressive regime. She argued to herself that the year was almost done, which meant that she had another four years to serve out her sentence, counting the two years added on to her original seven. Time was passing and, if she kept her nose clean, she could try for a Ticket of Leave in the next year. It was time to play the system and obtain her freedom. Once that was accomplished she could rebuild her life.

Lieutenant Thomas Thompson, an ex-soldier who still paraded his rank, rented Rosetta[1] a small estate about one and a half hour's walk from the Cameron Street police office to the south east of Launceston in Paterson Plains. It housed Thompson, his wife Eliza and their children plus a governess and three assigned convicts who helped Thompson work the land. It was essentially a farm with a basic timber-built house and out-buildings and grounds where they cultivated crops such as wheat, oats and barley and ran a small herd of dairy cattle. However, it was not being run very well and the family only made ends meet with the support of bank loans, tolerant creditors and government-supplied free labour.

Mary Ann's role was to be the housekeeper and general dogsbody under the direction of Mrs. Thompson. Life at

Rosetta began much as it always did and she bent herself to her chores with as good an attitude as she could muster.

It wasn't long before she realised that things weren't going well for the Lieutenant.

It was Friday, the 8ᵗʰ November. She had not slept well with heavy rain, thunder and distant flashes of lightning during the night. Waking to a morning sky pregnant with moisture that promised more showers, if not rougher weather, she had started her chores when she heard someone banging energetically on the front door. She opened it to find a tall, solidly-built man wearing a cape and a hat dripping with the rain that had only recently stopped. "I am here to see Lieutenant Thompson, get him for me" he demanded with little civility.

However, before Mary Ann could respond, Mrs. Thompson appeared and told her to go about her business. Mary Ann retreated to the end of the hallway, not paying attention to the conversation, when the man raised his voice and angrily demanded, "I will speak to your husband. I am not leaving until I do. This has gone on long enough!".

Hearing the commotion, the Lieutenant surfaced from one of the rooms and made his way to the door, "Samuel, Samuel, there is no need for this. Please come in and let us talk things over like gentlemen"

This seemed to placate the visitor somewhat and he took off his hat, following Thompson into the drawing room, on the way handing the hat to Mary Ann who was transfixed by the situation. She took the hat, unsure of why she had been given it, but decided the best thing to do was to simply place it on the hatstand by the door.

Returning to her task, she could hear agitated discussion from behind the closed door although she couldn't quite make out what was being said and then Mrs. Thompson hurried up to her and told her to see to the bedrooms.

"But I've already cleaned the bedrooms, missus"

"Well, do them again" she snorted, obviously keen to get Mary Ann away from the increasingly heated discussion breaking through the closed door.

She did as she was bid, only to witness the drawing room door open as she was about to enter the main bedroom one floor up and she watched the visitor stalk out with a grim, determined expression, "I will see you in court, Thompson. I have been more than patient. And this is how my generosity is repaid".

Thompson followed him out, spied the hat and returned it to his rapidly departing visitor with a plaintive, "I will service my obligations, Captain. I just need a little more time. You know how difficult it's been with the drought, I promise you; on my honour".

But the angry man was already outside, mounting a magnificent black stallion. He left with an urgent flourish, his horse rearing a little before galloping away, breath steaming from its nostrils into the damp air.

Mary Ann quickly entered the bedroom, keen to avoid an upward glance from her master or mistress and keen to keep out of the way until emotions had cooled. She reflected that it wasn't just poor buggers like herself who had problems with money, or the lack of it. Shaking her head, she started cleaning the room for the second time that day.

The other servant in the house was the children's governess. She was about the same age as Mary Ann and had emigrated to Van Diemen's Land, a free settler with her family several years before. However, Miss Campbell was too concerned with her status and too busy with the children to be too familiar with a convict servant. The best that could be said was that, unlike others in a similar situation, she treated May Ann with civility.

Later that day when Mary Ann 'bumped into' her on her way to her room, she asked Mary Ann about the incident with Captain Tulloch.

"Captain Tulloch?" Mary Ann responded.

"Yes, the gentleman who came this morning a-banging at the door".

Mary Ann told her what she knew, which wasn't much and the governess leaned into her fellow servant and said quietly, "Lieutenant Thompson is in some trouble I believe. I hear that he's been to court and unless he can agree something with his creditors he will lose everything".

"What will that mean for us?" Mary Ann asked with a worried frown on her face.

"I don't intend staying around to find out" she replied, "But it probably won't make any difference to you if he can agree something. Anyway, I will be leaving tomorrow so I just wanted to say goodbye and wish you well. You are a good soul. I hope things work out for you". Mary Ann was quite taken aback by what she saw as a kindness and courtesy to her and returned her best wishes. With that she was gone. And indeed Mary Ann never did see her again.

* * *

THE OLD YEAR wound its way down and the new year entered with blue skies, brilliant sunshine, singing birds. It would have taken a hardened pessimist to have started 1840 without a spring in their step unless, of course, you were a small, virtually bankrupt farmer like Thompson. But Mary Ann was not a farmer and as the new year broke she took the opportunity of walking in the countryside and breathing in the clean, warm, fresh air when she was not busying herself with the household chores.

However, the 'feel good' factor disappeared when she was back in the house; it was clear that things were not going well for the family. Thompson would spend hours in a brown study as he pondered his plight and Mary Ann noticed that he was drinking more as he tried to put his problems to flight.

On the 24th January he rose early and left the house, pale faced. Mary Ann found out later that he had been called to a meeting of his creditors at the Exchange building on Charles Street in Launceston to agree a plan to settle his debts in order to avoid insolvency.

He returned late in the day and disappeared into the drawing room, his wife joining him, and the pair remained together talking for a good hour thereafter.

* * *

AT THE BEGINNING OF APRIL, a brilliant sun shone constantly from clear skies on the Rosetta household but it didn't lift the gloomy spirits and, with an easterly wind, the night temperatures plunged and frost accompanied most mornings. She would rise at dawn and watch her breath billow into the morning air as she rubbed her hands and stamped her feet to warm herself before staring her chores. She was now the only house servant and Mrs. Thompson kept her busy from dawn to dusk except on Sundays when she would attend the local church with the family and have a couple of hours free to escape the gloomy atmosphere of the house.

Good Friday fell on the 17th April that year and Mary Ann attended St. John's in Launceston on the Sunday with the family.

She saw Emma at the church but only had a few minutes to exchange news before she had to hurry away.

On the Tuesday after Easter, Mrs. Thompson told her that there was going to be an auction at the house that Friday. They were putting up their wheat, oats, barley, livestock as well as household furniture and valuables. Mary Ann would be required to assemble things downstairs for the day of the auction.

She felt sorry for Mrs. Thompson. Despite the obvious blow to her pride, she and her husband were standing together and she did not take out her frustration or anger on Mary Ann. Well, not in any serious way.

Tuesday, Wednesday, Thursday saw the house in a hiatus as items for auction were separated and placed in the drawing room and hallway. The children had been shipped off to a friend or a relative and Mary Ann and her mistress laboured together with the Lieutenant overseeing work outside. She collapsed into her bed each night extremely tired and slept soundly before waking at dawn and starting all over again.

THE FRIDAY FINALLY ARRIVED. At 9 o'clock sharp the auctioneer and the Permanent Assignee, Mr. Palmer, arrived and closeted themselves with the Lieutenant. First, they would auction the crops and farming equipment, then – probably after lunch – they would commence with the household items. All going according to plan, by the end of the day enough would have been raised to settle with the creditors and the insolvency proceedings would be extinguished.

Mary Ann was left to herself most of the morning so she unobtrusively observed the goings on. About a dozen people arrived in ones and twos and at 11 o'clock the auctioneer began his sing song act, knocking down bushels of wheat, oats and barley " Now gentlemen, what am I offered for this fine store of wheat? It's going for eight shillings a bushel in town. Do I hear seven and six?" he waited with no response, "Seven shillings then, do I hear seven shillings?"

And so it continued, the wheat finally selling for seven shillings and sixpence, the oats for three shillings and sixpence and the barley for five and ninepence. A number of tools were next put up for auction including a threshing machine that Thompson had bought anticipating better times. It was worked by one or two horses harnessed to a pole that they pulled round and round on a cogged wheel which in turn revolved a threshing drum. Mary Ann had not seen anything like it before and was spellbound when Thompson had one of his men demonstrate it for the assembled buyers.

At one o'clock everything had been completed outside and about half a dozen of the potential buyers followed the auctioneer to the house. Mary Ann scuttered into the house through the kitchen door and, seeing Mrs. Thompson standing in the hallway, asked if she could help. Mrs. Thompson turned and, with tearful eyes, thanked her but said no, Mary Ann should go to her room now and leave her to deal with this.

Mary Ann almost started crying herself. She knew not why, but the evident anguish was almost too much to bear and she wanted to hug and comfort her mistress, but knew that she couldn't. It wouldn't be seemly. With sadness, she left her and decided to go for a walk, decided to get away from this awful, miserable scene.

* * *

THE DAYS immediately following the auction saw carts pulling up to the house and furniture and paintings and ornaments being loaded and carried away. Mary Ann spent her time sweeping and cleaning the spaces that had once been sheltered by rugs and chairs until it was all finished. The house still held the bare essentials but it was so very strange, like an emptied warehouse rather than a living space where a man and wife and their family could grow. It was still more grand than anything Mary Ann had lived in back home, but she was older now, had seen more of life and she, like the Lieutenant and his wife and children, felt some of the despair.

As the weeks passed, the Lieutenant became more irascible, more unreasonable. The news that an assassination attempt had been made on Queen Victoria as she was being driven by Green Park[2] in London had him ranting about 'the world turned upside down'. To anyone that would listen he would try to blame his own situation on the breakdown of society where 'good and true men like himself' could suffer and he would point to the attempt on the Queen's life as an example of a topsy turvy world, conflating, no matter how unreasonably, his situation with the Queen's misfortune.

He would explode angrily at Mary Ann for the most silly of reasons until she started to feel more anger and less pity. After being berated by Thompson for taking too long to clean the hallway floor one day late July, she couldn't help herself, "I'm working as 'ard as I can. Bloody 'arder than you are. It's time you pulled yersef togevver and got on wiv life instead of moping 'round like a church mouse what's lost its church".

Thompson could hardly believe his ears. He had lost everything, he wasn't going to lose his dignity in front of a convict servant and he almost struck her for her insolence before drawing back. He knew that physical violence would likely not go down well with the authorities and instead, drawing back his fist, through clenched teeth he ordered Mary Ann to her room.

* * *

ON THE 24TH JULY, Mary Ann found herself standing in front of the constable in the police office at Cameron Street yet again. She had been charged with disobedience of orders and she knew better than to waste her breath disputing the charge. She was conducted to the cells and sentenced to four days solitary confinement.

She sat herself down and pondered on the events of the last few months. It was an eye opener to see how her supposed betters could be brought so low. It occurred to her that perhaps you were better off with nothing, that way you had nothing to lose. It had been a remarkable lesson and the more she thought on things the more calmly she faced the future, more assured than she had ever been before.

REDISCOVERED

*K*ing's Meadows
1840

TWO MONTHS after Mary Ann's run in with the distraught
Lieutenant Thompson, Robert Bright was lying in his bed,
thinking. He had grown into a man, with muscled arms and
shoulders and a solid frame, his auburn hair swept back from a
pleasant face. A face with strong, grey eyes and a complexion
weathered by the sun and wind and rain. About five feet six
inches tall, he was of average height but friends and others had
learned that, while not by nature aggressive, indeed essentially a
kind man, he could take care of himself if the occasion
demanded. He was a valued friend to those fortunate enough to
call him such.

He had found steady work with a Mr. Robert Marlow, a
licensed carrier and sometime farmer, who had built up his
business by supplying the growing town of Launceston and the
government with firewood, fresh vegetables, grain and other
goods as the need arose. He was thankful for his situation

because the colony's economy was coming under pressure and good jobs were hard to find. Robert was now one of Marlow's men, considered to be a reliable, steady worker in the fields and forests and a good driver, with the added benefit of being someone who took good care of the animals in his charge.

The Marlow property was about 1½ miles south of Launceston on the Paterson Plains road, near King's Meadows where Marlow owned a few hundred acres of land and where he occupied a simple house with some outbuildings that he used for storage and accommodation. This had become 'home' to Robert.

Like James Cox at the nearby grand Clarendon estate, Marlow had also implemented the 'Scotch' method on his farmland, one-third of the land kept fallow and green crops, potatoes, peas and turnips all in drills which allowed him to scarify between the drills with a horse or bullock-drawn plough, creating a clean trough to receive his seeds. Robert's experience in England had been put to good use and he was a valued member of Marlow's team of hired and assigned convict workers.

But Robert was not happy. He was in his mid-twenties and he could see men around him making good and starting families. He wanted the same. And inevitably his thoughts turned to Mary Ann.

It had been months since he had seen her. He had attended St. John's on some of the Sundays even though there was a closer church, simply on the off chance that she would be there, but each visit had been fruitless. He wondered where she might be, but couldn't think of any way to track her down other than hope that she was still in the district and that she would eventually turn up at St. John's. So he simply fretted and buried himself in his work, putting aside a few pennies each week to boost his savings for an uncertain future and resolved to attend St. John's regularly until he found out one way or another.

* * *

WITH SPRING TURNING TO SUMMER, Robert set out for St. John's once again. It was the second Sunday in November, the 15th, a fine morning with blue skies and a few fluffy clouds but the freshness of the day compared poorly with the underdeveloped hay-grass in the fields and patches of clover wilted and dried up. Everyone prayed for rainfall to breathe life into the planted crops and the apple orchards but, despite the lack of rain - or perhaps because of it - Robert breathed in the fresh air deeply and revelled in the warmth of the day. He walked steadily along the Paterson Plains road, humming a tune to himself and taking pleasure in the hardy crimson waratahs and yellow wattle growing wild, all the while hoping that maybe this Sunday Mary Ann would be there.

He could hear the St. John's church bell tolling as he made his way into town, calling the good folk of Launceston to Divine Worship. He arrived at St. John's Square by half past ten, a good half an hour before the service would begin as he was hoping to see her if she arrived, but his hopes were unfulfilled. Eventually, with some resignation, he finally entered the church himself and sat at the back by the aisle. The minister, Dr. Browne, began the service and Robert drifted, idly scanning the backs of heads in the pews stretching before him.

He rose with the rest of the congregation to sing the first hymn. He didn't know it, so he just opened and shut his mouth like a stranded fish and sat down when the rough harmonies were finished. The sermon droned on while Robert's mind wandered. Then, looking to his right, halfway down, he could have sworn that he saw someone who looked much like her, although, granted, it was difficult making out any woman from behind with heads encased in bonnets and an obscured view. But it might be her and his heart jumped.

Almost another hour passed before the final benediction and

Robert waited anxiously for the minister, his acolytes and the rows ahead to empty until the row with *the* woman filed out and the congregation made its way towards the exit doors.

Mary Ann was only three yards away when Robert caught her eye and they both flashed wide, toothy smiles at each other. Robert indicated that he would see her outside and she looked back over her shoulder as she made for the door with a coquettish half smile. Robert was smitten. Head over heels. His heart thumping and his palms sweaty. He felt like a ten-year-old again, uncertain of himself but unable to contain his desire to touch her, to feel her hair, to hear her voice, to bathe in her smile.

He soon joined the file of exiting worshippers, exchanged a few words with the minister at the door and burst out into the fresh, Spring-time air looking left and right to find her. At first he drew a blank and then, by a tree in the church grounds he saw her. She was wearing a full length light blue dress without frills or fripperies, buttoned up to the throat, a cloth bonnet tied beneath her chin and a light shawl over her shoulders.

Mary Ann was now a pretty young woman. Small and slim, about 4' 8" tall, she wore her brown hair long under a simple cloth bonnet. She had a pale complexion, understandable as she spent most of her days working indoors, wide eyes under a high forehead and a winning smile. A small scar on her left cheek was the only blemish on a pleasing visage. She had also matured and was no longer the uncertain girl who had arrived on the *Edward* but a self-assured young woman. Robert was entranced.

"I've been looking for you for months" he volunteered as he came up to her.

"There's been a lot of fings going on" she replied with a smile.

"It's wonderful to see you again. Can we walk together?" And Robert took her arm, without any objection, and steered her towards the Square.

They walked together, talking animatedly, ignoring everybody around them.

"Where are you staying now?" He asked.

"At a farm on Paterson Plains – I've been assigned to a Lieutenant Thomson but I dunno 'ow much longer that'll last. We don't get on too well. Where are you?". Robert told her about the Marlow farm and they soon realised that they were actually living quite close to each other – at most a mile apart. Certainly close enough to be able to meet relatively easily provided they could agree on a time and a place.

"Do you know the Sir William Wallace Inn at Franklin village?" Robert asked.

Franklin village was roughly midway between them both and could be reached in half an hour or so on foot. Mary Ann said she hadn't been there but could find it, so they agreed to meet the following Saturday afternoon – the earliest that both of them could get away. "Alright, I'll see you outside the blacksmith's shop at the inn" he confirmed.

Mary Ann looked over to where the Thompson family was engaged in conversation with other church members and explained that she had to go. He knew it was pointless protesting and, instead, took Mary Ann in his arms and kissed her fiercely, despite the disapproving frowns of the citizenry nearby. When Mary Ann looked up she saw his eyes staring urgently at her and she put her index finger to his lips, saying, "There *will* be more time. Robert. I 'ave to go now but I'll see you at the blacksmiffs". Robert nodded his head and said, "Yes. There must be. Lots of time. Until next Saturday".

After another hug, Robert smelling the fragrance of her hair and Mary Ann's arms holding him tight, they parted. She hurried away to rejoin the Thompsons; Robert remained in the Square, butterflies in his stomach, with a feeling that there was no place that he would rather be right now.

The rest of the week Robert was not totally engaged with the world around him, musing on the Saturday to come and beyond. Mary Ann likewise found it hard to concentrate and would find herself daydreaming about Robert, the urgency of that kiss, imagining his hungry eyes. Where was this leading she wondered and she too counted down the days.

The Saturday finally dawned. Mary Ann had chores to perform in the morning but had agreed with Mrs. Thompson to have the afternoon free, Indeed, with much of the furniture sold, the occupants rattled around like dried peas and the work-load had consequently eased somewhat. Thompson himself had settled into a surly demeanour after Mary Ann had returned to the house and she had little to do with him, taking instructions from Mrs. Thompson most of the time. She wondered how long this would go on, but guessed that free labour was all they could afford and Thompson was too embarrassed to raise his head above the parapet until he regained some of his reputation.

At noon, she finished her work, went to her room, cleaned herself up, brushed her hair and changed into her other dress (the blue one that she kept for Sunday and special events) and, packing some bread and cheese into a cloth, she left the house and set out for the village of Franklin.

A mile away, Robert likewise finished stacking firewood and at noon made his way back to the house where he washed himself, carefully shaved off the stubble on his face, discarded his work clothes and put on his Sunday best; brown trousers, a clean shirt and a brown jacket with leather reinforced elbows and sleeves. He only had one pair of boots and there was little point in cleaning them as he had unpaved roads to travel. He felt the coins in his pocket to make sure they were still there and almost ran down the stairs as he set his course for Franklin. On his way he stopped to pick some red and white wildflowers and tied them into a bunch, before carefully stowing them in his jacket pocket.

He arrived at the blacksmith's shop before Mary Ann, deliberately so, and watched with interest as the blacksmith worked red-hot steel at his anvil, the metallic clamour and the fiery sparks free entertainment for the passers-by. A sign outside the inn showed a red-bearded giant of a man, wearing tartan cloth and wielding a large double-edged sword with a flag in the background displaying Scotland's blue and white saltire. He was tempted to enter, he was certainly thirsty after his walk, but he waited for Mary Ann, all the while a fluttering in his stomach and a palpable sense of anticipation building.

And then, around the corner of a building, she appeared and, waving at him and smiling, she came on. Robert, immediately started walking to meet her, trying to keep his eagerness in check, trying to appear unruffled, in control and assured while, all the time, battling those damn butterflies. Mary Ann kept her pace, hoping that all would go well, wanting everything to go well and almost terrified that this moment couldn't be as good as she hoped it might be.

They met on the dusty street, halted for a moment as they looked at each other, trying to gauge if things were all they hoped they would be, before stepping close and, with arms entwined, kissed. A deep, long, endless kiss – a release from all the thoughts, questions, desires, anxieties over the days and hours that they had been apart.

Breathless, Mary Ann disengaged and offered the bread and cheese she had brought for their lunch at the same time as Robert pulled the bouquet of wildflowers from his pocket and proffered it to Mary Ann. For a second or two no-one said or did anything and then they both laughed together. A happy, unrestrained, joyous noise that blew away any concerns and uncertainties that might have existed before that precious moment.

"Let's have a drink" Robert eventually said and the couple walked hand in hand into the Inn to refresh themselves after their journeys. Robert had a thought, "My Dad used to tell me about another blacksmith in Scotland in a place called Gretna Green. He said that lovers would go there, just across the border from England, to get married". Mary Ann raised her head, suddenly senses afire.

"Of course, this isn't Gretna Green and the smithy outside isn't a church" Robert added, looking hard at Mary Ann. Then he said softly, uncertainly, "I love you, Mary Ann, will you marry me?" She grasped both of his hands across the rough wooden table and said deliberately, seriously, "Yes, Robert Bright, yes I will. I'd love to be your wife".

ST. JOHN'S

Launceston
1841

THE PRACTICAL ASPECTS of a marriage dawned very quickly. As an assigned servant, Mary Ann would need permission to marry and then there was the question of where would they live? Also, would Mary Ann be assigned to Robert or have to stay with the Thompsons?

Robert and Mary Ann talked through their situation. They agreed that the best solution would be to bring Mary Ann to Marlow's farm where she could keep house and live with Robert on the farm. But first they would need to obtain permission to marry and, to put this into motion, Robert paid a visit to the local police office. The constable there directed him to the local magistrate.

After providing him with their details, on 30th December a request for permission to marry was sent to Hobart for the Governor's approval. The constable had told them that he thought it was likely to be approved and, anticipating this,

Robert approached Marlow and Mary Ann approached Mrs. Thompson with their news.

Marlow was immediately positive, Mary Ann could work in the house and he would settle them a living area in the outbuildings so long as Robert remained an employee.

She anticipated greater difficulty but was pleasantly surprised when Mrs. Thompson readily agreed to transferring her to Robert's custody. It seemed that they were thinking about packing up and moving to the mainland anyway, so this was not an inconvenience at all. Mrs. Thompson even smiled and wished her well. So it was all now about waiting for the response from Hobart.

Mary Ann managed to call on Emma the following Saturday to break the news to the accompaniment of hugs and celebratory kisses and even a little jig in Emma's lodgings as the two young women rejoiced. Emma suggested that they marry in St. John's as she had done, "Reverend Dr. Browne is a good man, I'm sure he'd be happy to do it" she assured her, "But you need to speak to him soon to get the banns read. It'll take at least three weeks before you can marry".

THE MONTH OF JANUARY 1841, however, crawled by. Robert and Mary Ann would meet each Saturday afternoon and on Sunday and spend time talking about their future together. Now their decision had been made they were anxious to get on with it, but had to wait for the permission to come through before they could ask the minister to read the banns and name the date.

FEBRUARY, too, began to run its course and Robert started calling in at the police office every few days to see if the permission had arrived.

On Monday the 15th of February Robert called in once again

and was told by the constable that he had received a notice from Hobart. He handed the paper to Robert.

"Can you read it for me?" Robert asked, handing the paper back.

The constable unfolded the sheet and perused it for a few seconds.

"What does it say?" Robert asked petulantly.

"It says that you and Mary Ann Goulding off the *Edward* are permitted to marry. Congratulations".

Robert's face transformed with a wide grin; he raised both arms and shouted, "Hallelujah!" to which the constable responded with a little laugh and a 'hallelujah' of his own. Outside, the sun poured down its honeyed sunbeams onto the scene below and Robert skipped along the road bathed in its happy warmth. He wasn't going to wait until Saturday. It was a little over a mile to Rosetta and he wanted to break the news to Mary Ann immediately. He part walked and part ran the entire way, finally arriving at the farmstead late afternoon, a little breathless.

He walked up to the kitchen door and knocked. Mary Ann was just coming in to the kitchen and heard the summons. This was unusual. She went to the door and opened it cautiously. At first she didn't recognise Robert, he had his back turned to the door, but as soon as he turned she saw the happy face and then noticed that he was also waving a piece of paper at her, "It's come! We can get married now!"

Robert thrust the paper into her hand and, despite the fact that she couldn't read, Mary Ann carefully examined the hiero-glyphics – especially the bold signature at the bottom, not quite sure that this was really happening. But Robert had no doubts and he stepped close, wrapped his arms around her and sought her lips. They embraced and kissed for happy seconds before Mary Ann broke away, straightening her hair and her apron, "That's wonderful news, Robert, but Mrs. Thompson might see

us. Stand back you silly man". She laughed at her last admoni-
tion for she was just as excited as him and wanted to shout out
loud and bury herself in his arms again.

"What is going on here?" Mrs. Thompson asked, having
heard the commotion and gone to the kitchen to see for herself.

"This is me 'usband ter be, Mrs. Thompson, Robert Bright,
He's just 'eard that we're gonna get married".

Mrs. Thompson actually smiled and said, "Pleased to meet
you Robert. Let me congratulate you both".

Robert bowed his head and thanked her.

"So when is the big day?" she asked.

"We need to get Reverend Dr. Browne to set the date,
missus, but as soon as we can if that's alright wiv you and the
Lieutenant" Mary Ann responded.

"Whatever you and Dr. Browne agree will be fine with us,
Mary Ann. Just let me know when you know".

It was the first time she had used Mary Ann's first name and
somehow that little gesture meant more than Mrs. Thompson
could ever had understood. Almost as if with that simple token,
for Mary Ann, the chains of her servitude had dropped away
and the possibilities of a new, married life opened like a flower
welcoming the new day.

* * *

MARY ANN and Robert went to the church on Saturday the 13th
February and arranged to speak with the minister the following
day after the morning service. Dr. Browne turned out be a
caring, gentle man and he talked them through the process,
spent time ensuring that they understood the commitments
entailed with marriage and even quickly ran through the service
of marriage, promising to do so again when they met with him
in the run up to the big day. He even noted that it was St. Valen-
tine's day today and commented that it was an auspicious sign.

Neither Robert nor Mary Ann knew what an auspicious sign was, but assumed it was good.

"I will publish the banns next Sunday and the two Sundays following that which means the wedding day could be some-time the week of the 8th of March if that suits" he explained.

"As soon as we are able" Robert volunteered.

"Let me check my diary" he paged through a leather bound book on a table next to him, "Tuesday the 10th of March?"

Both Robert and Mary Ann nodded their heads in agree-ment. The date was set.

They left the cool and quiet of the manse and rejoined the rest of Launceston. Horse-drawn carriages rumbled down the street, footsteps of people walking back and forth drummed on the pavements, shouts of hawkers, the crack of horsewhips, even the call of seagulls swooping in from the sea mingled into the sounds of the city but Robert and Mary Ann heard nothing but 'Tuesday the 10th of March' echoing in their heads. It was a beautiful day, sunny with an azure blue sky, rather warm, and for both of them, smiling as they walked hand in hand, this was a day they would never forget.

MARRIAGE

Launceston
1841

MARY ANN HAD ASKED Emma (who was now six months pregnant) to attend her at the wedding when they had all met for a celebration at their lodgings in the High Street, on the southern edge of Launceston, a couple of blocks away from St. John's. Emma joked that she and Bill had been married there by the same minister, so they 'knew the ropes' and could teach Robert and Mary Ann, who were 'beginners'.

The Saturday night before the wedding, Edward Bromes, one of the other Marlow drivers and two of his other work-mates had taken Robert out to celebrate his last night as a bachelor with toasts in his honour and ribald jokes and laughter.

Fortunately he had been able to recover in the interim.

Mary Ann had a quiet night, wanting to be fully prepared for the big day – and night – to come. She also had to pack. This, after all, would be the last time that she would sleep in this bed and she had to pack her things to take to her new home. Mind you, her things made a pitifully small bundle; some work clothes, personal items; a brush, a comb, a mirror, the beads Robert had given her and the dried wild flowers from his bouquet that she had carefully preserved.

Robert met Mary Ann at Rosettta and Mary Ann said her farewells to Mrs. Thompson and the Lieutenant and they smiled and wished both of them well before they stepped out of the door and headed into town to begin their new life. Edward Bromes also came with them. He was going to be Robert's best man. Robert had given him a shilling and charged him with obtaining a ring to put on Mary Ann's finger at the church and he had done him proud, finding a small band of what looked like gold (although he rather suspected it was actually brass or bronze).

They went via the High Street to collect Bill, Emma and their children before they walked the short distance to St. John's church together, walking at an easy pace because of Emma's condition. It was another fine autumn day. The sun shone from a sky speckled with clouds, a gentle breeze ruffled Mary Ann's skirts as she crossed the square and the trees lining the grounds of St. John's stood at attention to honour them, fluttering their leaves with the excitement of it all.

Reverend Browne was waiting for them at the entrance to the church and smiled as he saw the bridal group. They were all wearing their Sunday best. Mary Ann in her bonnet and a white shawl draped across her shoulders with her blue dress - as she always did for church. Emma had picked some wildflowers, fashioned it into a pretty bouquet and given it to Mary Ann to carry. Robert had tried to polish his boots and some of the shine had even survived the walk. He wore a blue neckerchief with a freshly laundered shirt, a brown jacket and trousers.

St. John's Church, Launceston

They followed the Minister into the church and down the aisle without further words, Mary Ann and Robert leading the way, Emma and William with their children and Edward as well behind. With each measured step Mary Ann took in the surroundings, the sunbeams filtering through the windows breaking into the shadows, the still, warm and peaceful atmosphere, the sound of footsteps striking the bare floor and the overarching sense that here was a special place, that at this moment in time they were together, about to be united in God's presence.

The service began. The Minister gave a short sermon extolling the virtues of marriage and asked if anybody had any objection to Robert and Mary Ann marrying. At that point William coughed which made Robert start but there was no further comment and Reverend Browne continued. They repeated the vows after him and then Robert placed the wedding ring on Mary Ann's small finger.

With Mary Ann looking up at Robert and Robert gazing at her, the Minister opened his arms and pronounced them man and wife.

"You may kiss the bride" Reverend Browne said with a smile. Robert smiled too, an all-encompassing smile that radiated happiness and gently placed his hand on the side of Mary Ann's head and caressed her lips with his. There were no words spoken but at that moment Mary Ann put all of the heartaches of the years leading up to this moment behind her, revelled in the joy of the moment and, despite all the trials and tribulations that she knew would come, faced the future happily. Robert just couldn't keep a broad grin off his face and kept on smiling.

They completed the paperwork in the vestry. Robert and Mary Ann putting their mark on the document and one of the vergers, William Jones, witnessing the entry. Edward was unable to sign his name, so he too put his mark on the document as a witness. It showed Robert Bright, labourer and Mary Ann Golding, convict married in the parish church according to the Rights and Ceremonies of the United Church of England and Ireland by Banns with consent of Government.

"Well, Mr. and Mrs. Bright, let's go celebrate" Emma said with a giggle and the party stepped out from the church into the bright autumn sunshine and a welcoming world.

AS ONE

Launceston
1841

THEY WENT BACK to Bill and Emma's lodgings for a 'wedding breakfast' of a meaty stew with vegetables, bread, cheese and beer and talked and planned and laughed until, with dusk about to fall, Robert and Mary Ann made their farewells and escaped. Their new home was just under an hour's walk away and Robert was keen to make it before dark.

It was a strange feeling to be walking together as man and wife. They relived the service as they walked, Mary Ann laughing when Robert recalled Bill's awkward cough, and in no time at all they had reached the Marlow farm.

Edward had left earlier and taken Mary Ann's belongings on ahead and, when they entered their room, Mary Ann was delighted to see that he had put her bouquet into a vase with water. She looked around the room. It was a little smaller than her London home with a bed in the corner, a table and two chairs, a kitchen area. A window overlooked rolling hills. She thought, but didn't say, that it needed a feminine touch but time enough for that. And this would be their home. It was a very strange, but very comforting feeling.

Robert poured them both a mug of water to slake their dry mouths after the walk from Launceston and handed the mug to Mary Ann who had placed her shawl on a chair and removed her bonnet. Robert took of his jacket, loosened his neckerchief and, sitting on another chair, took of his boots, stretching out with a sigh.

They looked at each other. Didn't speak for a minute. Smiled at the delicious intimacy.

"Well, Mrs. Bright, welcome to your new home" he said as he replaced the mug on the table, "What do we do now?".

"Well, Mr. Bright, I can't begin to imagine" she replied with a teasing smile as she looked at him with a sideways tilt of her head.

Robert took the bait and stood up, walking around the table to come over to Mary Ann. He took her head with both hands, leaned down and kissed her, broke away and kissed her again. Then he bent down and scooped her up which caused Mary Ann to squeal and giggle. She put both of her arms around his neck and he carried her over to the bed, placing her down on the covers before sitting beside her. He looked at her and raised his eyebrows with an inquiring look.

"This won't do" she said, and stood up beside the bed in front of Robert and reached for her throat to begin unbuttoning her dress. Slowly.

Robert placed both hands on her hips, his legs apart and watched, breathless. With her bodice free, she reached behind her back and untied the overskirt which dropped into Robert's hands. He let it fall to the floor. She turned around so Robert could remove her underskirt, which he did, fumbling as he did so.

They were not speaking now, both entranced by the game

they were playing and he stood up, nestling his body close to hers before reaching to cup her breast beneath the shift in his right hand while he turned her head with his left hand and kissed her with a passion that had been building and building and building…

Mary Ann could feel his desire as he pressed into her body and turned back towards him, "My turn".

She pulled his neckerchief away and then slipped his shirt over his head before pulling it free of his entangled arms. She ran her fingers down his chest, felt the strong, firm body built from years of hard manual labour and kissed his chest before she reached for his belt, pulling it to release it, freeing his trousers which slid to the floor, Robert helping them on their way with two kicks.

They kissed again. Hungry, needy. Then, more hurriedly, Robert removed the rest of Mary Ann's clothes before doing the same for himself and they sank to the bed, entwined in a passionate embrace, hands exploring, touching, caressing,

He felt the smooth softness of her breasts, kissed each nipple and then moved his hand to the small of her back before bringing it round to her stomach and down her leg before stroking her inner thigh and then cupping her between her legs. Mary Ann gasped and uttered a small moan. She dug her fingers into his back and they kissed again.

Gently spreading her legs, he moved his body on top of her. He could feel her moistness and Mary Ann reached down to guide him now that the time had come. They both moaning now as Robert entered her and with a desperate urgency drove into her, caressing her breasts, stroking her hair as Mary Ann held his head close then grasped his shoulders, digging her fingers into him once again.

She climaxed with a series of groans and then Robert's whole body shuddered as he joined her, exhausting himself in a paroxysm of pleasure that rippled in waves through his body.

And then they collapsed together, relaxed side by side. Bodies damp with sweat, limp, exhausted.

"I love you Mary Ann" he whispered as he lay beside her. She turned her face to his and, with a breathless tremor replied, "I love you too Robert. I've never been so 'appy".

NEW BEGINNINGS

Launceston
1841/44

IN JUNE 1841, Emma gave birth to a son who they named Edward. They celebrated with Robert and Mary Ann, but in subdued style. Work was becoming harder to find and there wasn't the money for anything but the basics. Nevertheless the four friends made the best of it and even found a beer to 'wet the baby's head'.

Soon after, Mary Ann announced that she was pregnant with their first child and this was the trigger for Robert to seek other work. With business getting more and more difficult, Marlow had been reducing his labour force. The general economic malaise forced Robert to cut back on their spending, not that they were extravagant in the first place. But Marlow had laid off other men and was himself struggling in the anaemic Van Diemen's Land economy.

They saw out the year pretty much hand to mouth but happy nonetheless – the only stain on those happy months being the reminder that Mary Ann was not a free woman when she had to attend a muster, heavily pregnant, on 31st December with Emma. But Robert and Mary Ann settled into married life happily enough. She became a house servant for Robert Marlow and Robert continued in his job as driver and farm labourer, although his wages had been cut with the slow-down of business.

With the end of transportation to New South Wales, there had been a substantial increase in convicts coming to Van Diemen's Land but come 1842 it was no longer policy to assign them to private settlers. Governor Franklin was implementing the so-called new Probation system mandated by Lord Stanley in England whereby male convicts would now work in government gangs and, at one stroke, he removed the free labour on which the colony's economy had prospered[1].

* * *

ON 16TH MARCH, 1843 Mary Ann was delivered of a healthy boy and they decided to name him James, after Robert's father. The arrival of their son made them both think on the life they had left behind in England and there were moments of sadness when they realised that their children would never see their grandparents and their grandparents likely never know that they had a grandson. However, the thought of seeking to return never seriously crossed their minds. In England they knew that their lives would be one of grinding poverty with no hope for their children. In the colonies they were not wealthy, it was laughable to even think of such a happy state, but they had a roof over their heads, they eat regularly and Robert earned just enough to keep them whole.

Finally Robert found work at the Launceston hotel and moved his family to lodgings in York Street, not far from his new place of work. With people leaving the town because of the tough economy, rooms and buildings were standing empty so he was able to find something with a very modest rent and figured that provided he could keep in work himself, they could make a go of this new situation. He continued to put in long days but still found time to fuss over his wife, expressing concern that she didn't overwork herself and fussing ever more as the due date inched closer.

* * *

THE YEAR of 1843 was notable for several reasons. The flow of immigrants dried up. The year before 2,446 had arrived but this year was to see only 26. By year end, in Launceston alone, 264 houses stood empty, abandoned by owners fleeing to the mainland to escape economic hardships. In August the new Governor arrived with three sons who immediately secured lucrative government posts. He was Sir John Eardley-Wilmott, a man who had not given a moment's thought to the colony before being awarded the post. He was said to have been described by Lord Stanley (his superior) as being 'a muddle-brained blockhead" and he was not long in office when he learned that there was only £800 left in the treasury, which forced him to borrow £20,000 from banks and the military chest to pay government wages. It was into the hands of this financial and administrative 'genius' that Van Diemen's Land's future was to be entrusted.

In September, the ninth anniversary of Mary Ann's sentence, she, like Robert and Emma a few years earlier, applied for and collected her prized Certificate of Freedom. Upon receiving that little slip of paper, she clutched it to her breast and said a silent prayer before falling into Robert's arms in tears. The sufferings and pain were over. She and Robert could now make their own way in this world, wherever it took them.

At year end, on a warm December evening after a day of

sunshine that made you feel good to be alive, Robert and Mary Ann were talking after she had put James to sleep, "D'you 'member crawling outa bed early on a winter's mornin' an' tramping the foggy streets to find somefing to eat?" Mary Ann mused.

"I remember the dampness of the fens and how cold it could get" Robert replied.

"Yeah, I 'member those days too. It's better 'ere" Mary Ann responded.

"Mm. It is, but I want to make it better than this, Mary Ann. I see some men around me who've done well. Some of those who were sent here before us even own land and buildings and their own place. Why not us?"

Mary Ann looked thoughtfully at Robert, "It was easier for them, Robert. When they came there was land grants and ways to work the system. It's 'arder now". Robert nodded his head in agreement, "I know, but that mustn't stop us trying. For you and me and little James".

* * *

By 1844 the colony was virtually bankrupt. All sources of public revenue, especially land sales, shrivelled. The trade depression had brought most colonists close to insolvency and yet, at the same time, they were being asked to pay taxes. They objected particularly to paying all police and judicial costs – a substantial expense given the extensive system that had been put in place to manage this island prison. The colonial revenue amounted to £100,000 and judicial and gaol charges of £22,0000 and the police at £31,000 absorbed more than half the revenue.

Taxes to pay for this were equal to about £1 for every man, woman and child. In print and with outspoken anger the colonists insisted that these costs came about because Britain chose to use the colony as a dumping ground for their convicts and so should be for the account of the British Treasury. Feelings ran very high and talk in the clubs and bars lambasted both Eardley-Wilmott and his masters in London. Not that Robert frequented such places. There wasn't the money for such frivolities.

In March of 1844, Mary Ann fell pregnant again which added to the prospective financial pressure on the family. Robert started to look for work to supplement his wages, picking up a few coppers selling his labour 'on the cheap'. Mary Ann had started to take in laundry to add to the family's coffers, but it was poorly paid and hard work and there was only so much she could manage being pregnant with a young child to care for.

In Hobart, Eardley-Wilmot struggled to hold things together. He wrote dispatch after dispatch arguing that police and judicial costs were Britain's responsibility. He suggested that an 1842 Act, which had set £1 an acre as the minimum land price, should not apply in Van Diemen's Land. He also proposed that ex-convicts be granted smallholdings and that gentlemen settlers be granted larger estates. He encouraged irrigation works and urged London to fund them. He argued that conditionally-pardoned convicts should have free movement throughout Australia, not just Van Diemen's Land.

It all took time for this to be heard or acted upon of course and in the interim, to meet immediate financial demands, he used the funds supplied directly from Britain for convict and military needs to keep the colony's financial head above water. The blockhead may have 'muddled along' but he was not totally incompetent.

And on the last day of the year Mary Ann gave birth to their second son. They debated what name he should have and considered William, after Mary Ann's father, but in the end decided on George, after Robert's elder brother.

TURMOIL

*L*aunceston
1845/6

Where would be our roads and bridges and public buildings? Where would be our trade and commerce? Where, in short would be the free inhabitants who depend upon the exercise of their various mercantile agricultural and trading means for their subsistence if transportation was to cease?

Extract from article in the Cornwall Chronicle, 31st May, 1845

Is not the free mechanic and day labourer already deprived of fair wages? and as the market becomes crowded with more hands eager for employment, must not many be left to the sad alternatives - steal or starve?

Extract from Launceston Examiner, 7th June, 1845

THE PETITION AGAINST TRANSPORTATION: Notwithstanding the extraordinary exertions of those persons who have placed themselves prominently before the public, as the leaders of the party opposed to the future removal of prisoners from England and other places to this Colony, — the petition has obtained few signa-

167

tures; it lay at the Mechanics' Institute for many days, and was after-
wards submitted to the notice of the inhabitants, at their residences,
and has attached to it only about two hundred signatures.
Extract from Cornwall Chronicle , 21st June, 1845

* * *

IN 1845, Eardley-Wilmot's efforts finally produced a response. Land prices were reduced with the suspension of the 1842 Act and the geographic restriction of conditional pardons was liberated to allow free movement to any Australian territory.

It was around this time that Bill and Emma started talking about relocating to the mainland because it was becoming increasingly difficult to make ends meet. They now had three children, William, Edward and Charlotte, and Emma was expecting their fourth child in August that year. Bill had heard good things about opportunities in Melbourne and beyond and life was becoming increasingly hard in Launceston, "I canna see a future for a young family in this place, Robert" he ventured one day as they were visiting with Robert and Mary Ann.

"I agree times are hard, Bill, but how will you get there? And where will you go?" Robert replied.

"I dinna ken yet. But I'll find a way. It'll be better than hanging aroond here a-scratching for work".

"What about Emma?" Mary Ann interjected, "She won't be in any state to make that sorta journey 'til your newborn 'as arrived".

"It'll take time to plan, so that's no problem" Bill quickly responded, patting Emma on the belly as he did so. And they continued to dream about what the mainland might hold while mutually worrying about the prospects for work in Launceston.

In late August, Emma gave birth to another girl who they named after her mother.

* * *

1845 SLIPPED into 1846 and all the while the colony slipped further towards bankruptcy. In London, Lord Stanley continued to view Van Diemen's Land as a vessel whose sole purpose was to receive criminals from the mother land. But it was also becoming apparent that his new Probation system was failing and, with his eyes firmly fixed on his political career, he prepared the way to make Eardley-Wilmott take the blame, ensuring that the increasing chaos in the colony would be nailed to his Governor's door and not his own.

Back on the island, six of the governing council's members resigned over the police tax. Although they were replaced, the Governor couldn't keep demands under wraps for true representative government rather than the 'rubber stamp' that it had been heretofore, nor could he control the rising chorus calling for the end to transportation, notwithstanding the equally loud calls from industry and commerce on his doorstep to maintain the supply of free labour.

Although Robert and Mary Ann felt the backlash of the political turmoil in lower wages and the need to scrape and save to make ends meet, they generally ignored the comings and goings of the 'elite' and the politics of the time. Neither of them could read so newspaper articles and 'penny flyers' passed them by. Nor was there leisure time to idly gossip or discuss anything more than simply surviving.

* * *

ON THE FIRST Friday in April, tragedy struck Emma and Bill. They awoke after an unusually peaceful night's sleep to find baby Emma on her face in her cot, suffocated. Emma was completely distraught and it was all Mary Ann could do to comfort her in her loss. Bill, too, found it hard to handle, asking himself over and over 'how could this have happened'. Mary Ann and Robert took William, Margaret, Edward and Charlotte with them for two days to give their parents room to grieve and it was a sad, sad day when the four of them and their children stood by the pitifully small grave as they buried their baby, not yet nine months old.

* * *

WHILE EVERYDAY PEOPLE like Mary Ann struggled to make ends meet the colony's elite continued to thrash around the subject of transportation. Since the imposition of the Probation system there had been a constant narrative about the collapse of morals on the remote island, led particularly by Bishop Nixon of Van Diemen's Land. He believed that all convicts, without exception, left the probation gangs in worse moral state than when they joined them. He also coruscated the Female factories – they 'swarmed' with lesbians apparently. Eardley-Wilmott protested, providing evidence to counter these extreme claims in vain.

The Colonial office was about to dismiss him when Stanley quit the Colonial office, resigning in a dispute over the repeal of the Corn Laws, and he was succeeded by the young William Gladstone. Then, in July most of the island's Anglican clergymen petitioned the Prime Minister in England for an end to the Probation system, as 'an incubator of homosexuality'. The sanctimonious Gladstone's reaction was predictable. He was outraged and at the end of 1846 he dismissed Eardley-Wilmott[1] and transferred Charles La Trobe, the superintendent of Port Phillip, to Hobart to take over until a new lieutenant-Governor could be named.

Meanwhile, Bill had been busy. The death of their baby had released a new energy born of emotional despair and the need to cleanse everything. He started asking anyone and everyone about going to Melbourne or Sydney to start again and one day he pulled Robert aside and showed him a flyer. It contained lots of words including Pound signs and numbers.

"What does it say, then?" asked Robert.

An excited Bill pointed at a list of numbers on the sheet and replied, "It's looking for men on the mainland, they need tradesmen and labourers tae work the land and service the towns and villages. They're paying guid money too".

The flyer was being promoted by the Geelong, Portland Bay and Port Fairy Emigration Society to bring in labour to the Port Phillip colony, which was desperately short of tradesmen and labourers and it promised that wages of £22 to £25 a year was the going rate for Farm Labourers. Bill had spoken with one of the recruiters and he had given him the details of the scheme.

EMIGRATION TO GEELONG, PORT PHILLIP.—Wages according to the following scale are now current in this district, for persons of the description mentioned : —

Ploughmen	£25 to £30	per year	
Bullock drivers	23 .. 28	,,	
Shepherds	22 .. 25	,,	
Hut-keepers	20 .. 24	,,	
Farm labourers	22 .. 25	,,	

Shearing for 100 sheep, 10s. to 12s., with rations.

EDWARD WILLIS,
Chairman of Committee of the Geelong and Portland Bay Immigration Society.
Geelong, July 11.

Launceston Examiner

"I hae to find twa shilling for oor passage, but the rest is paid by merchants and farmers in Geelong. When we get there I'll be hired for at least £22 a year with somewhere tae live. It's a damn sight better than here".

Robert took the flyer and examined it.

It looked real, maybe there really was a scheme that could set them up, "Have you said Yes?" he asked.

"I've told them I'll think on't. I need to talk it through wi' Emma o' course and we'll hae to find the two bob. But I'll get that one way or anither".

He was clearly excited about the prospect, and why not, thought Robert. A cheap passage and a job waiting at the other end with pay higher than he'd earned in the last two years. And a chance to shake off the 'convict' tag and start again. What was not to like.

Robert returned home to Mary Ann and told her what was in Bill's mind, but rather than echoing the excitement, her first thought was the loss of a friend if Emma were to leave. Robert decided to let things rest. Clearly another move was not something that Mary Ann viewed with interest at the moment and he too, wasn't sure if he wanted to launch out into the unknown with two young children to care for.

However, Bill and Emma had made their minds up and in July they announced that they were on their way. They had secured passage on the *Henry* leaving Launceston in just over two weeks on Tuesday the 4th of August. Bill was clearly excited, Emma less so, but ready for the challenge.

Robert and Mary Ann wished them well of course and told them to send them news once they had settled down. But Mary Ann went to sleep that night down in the mouth. Friends weren't easy to find and keep. Losing one was a blow.

GO NORTH!

Ⓜelbourne
1849

THE NUMBER *of persons who left Launceston for Port Phillip and the other neighbouring colonies last week amounted to about 130: and we are told that about as many more are ready to go by the Shamrock and other vessels within a few days. The superior inducements held out to emigrants at Port Phillip, &c. partially account for the emigration mania. None will, in fact, remain here whose circumstances enable them to get away — what with His Excellency's worse than military rule, and his persisting in principles of Government utterly opposed to the Constitution and Liberties of the Subject, added to the oft-repeated and oft-reported baseness of the prisoner constabulary (in which Mr. Burgess Takes such peculiar delight), we do not wonder at the whole-sale emigration referred to.*

The Cornwall Chronicle, 15th March, 1848

* * *

IN THE AUTUMN OF 1848, the talk in the Launceston Arms was all about the gold rush in California. Fortunes were there to be picked up from the soil and people were travelling from across the world to share in the spoils. Robert listened hungrily to the stories being told in the bar as people read the stories in their newspapers. If only. He still harboured the ambition to make more of his life and striking it rich on a goldfield sounded quite wonderful to him.

He had heard rumours of gold being found near George Town at Nine Mile Springs[1] a couple of years back, but it had just been rumours. However, the thought had stuck with him. There had also been recurring stories about occasional gold strikes in New South Wales at Bathurst and other places, even Port Phillip, but nothing like the stories he now heard of the riches in California.

However, For Robert and Mary Ann, the big event that year was the birth of their third child, William. Much as it had registered on Bill Watson as his family grew, so it did on Robert. He started to think seriously about opportunities on the mainland for him and his children and, like Bill, he started asking around about assisted passages to Port Phillip and work opportunities there.

He came home a couple of months after the birth of William with news, "I've found us a passage to Port Phillip and a job there on a farm". Mary Ann looked up at him quizzically.

"I haven't said yes. Should we?"

Mary Ann had been expecting something like this. Talk since the birth of their new son had often turned to wondering about Bill and Emma and talking about the new land, new opportunities.

"What is it they're tellin' you, Robert?" she asked.

"There's a big shortage of skilled men so they're trying to get people who know the land to move. We get our passage paid for and when we arrive I'll have a job lined up on a farm. They were impressed by what I know about working the land and said I'd have no trouble getting work. It'd be good to finish with the odd jobs I get here and get back on the land, feel the dirt, smell the fresh air again. They also said I'd have no trouble pulling down a steady £25 a year at least, maybe more. That's £5 more'n I get now, Mary Ann and no risk of getting laid off!". His enthusiasm was catching and Mary Ann soon caught the bug.

Before the week was out they were both making plans for a new life. With the decision made, there was no point in hanging around. Robert presented himself at the commissioners' office the very next day and signed on to the scheme. Within the next couple of weeks, they had been assigned passage on a ship leaving in January.

Mary Ann and Robert with their two toddlers and a baby in arms presented themselves at the docks with their belongings wrapped up in two canvas bags and some food for the voyage. Robert had been told that they would be able to find water on board. As they walked onto the gangway, both Robert and Mary Ann thought back to their first and only previous sea voyage and reflected on the very different circumstances. This was a voyage of hope, not despair. A chance to make a new life, a leap into the unknown once again but a leap made with excitement in their hearts.

There were many others boarding at the same time, most of them emigrants like themselves seeking a new life but also the well-to-do dressed in their finery who were given preference by the officer standing by the gangway.

Stepping onto the gangway, Robert slung two bags over his back and held the hands of James and George while Mary Ann carried William. She had not gone more than two or three steps before she felt the gangplank sway with the movement of the boat on the water. For a moment she was scared, the thought of toppling into the sea with her baby flashed in her mind. She stopped and recovered her composure - and her balance -

before going further. Seagulls wheeled and cried, the sun smiled through an azure sky littered with wispy clouds, the smell of the sea was powerful and the calls of sailors making ready and the clamour of passengers clambering aboard smothered the senses.

Once on board, the journeymen like Robert and their families were marshalled into the steerage area and told to settle into whatever space they could find. Two barrels of water were secured against a stanchion in the middle of the area together with drinking gourds. The heads were at the far end and Robert was pretty sure that it would not be long after they were at sea before people would be using them regularly.

The two boys thought it a great adventure and, like other children in steerage, were running around exploring everything and making new friends. A couple, much the same age as Robert and Mary Ann, settled themselves against the timbers alongside the Bright family and introduced themselves as John and Eliza. One man had settled in early and was strumming a banjo. Around them was the noise, movement and palpable excitement of people readying themselves for a new start.

"What plans do you 'ave once we reach Port Phillip?" John asked.

"We're going to look for work on a farm" Robert replied, "And you?"

"We 'ave family there, so we're gonnna join 'em and see where it takes us" John replied.

"Have you been in Launceston long?" Robert asked.

"Long enough" John laughed, "it's been 'ard finding decent work for the last few years; we figured to change fings and me bruvver sent back good stories about Port Phillip, so 'ere we are. What about you?"

"Much the same, Robert replied. Some friends of ours moved there a year ago and, like you, we decided there was a better life to be had over there than in this dump".

Robert consciously found himself talking as a free man

rather than a freed convict. One of the advantages that he had seen in making the move was the opportunity to throw off the shackles of past history; no one needed to know or had the right to know that they had been transported or served any sentence. This was the very first time that he had talked to somebody in this frame of mind and he found it liberating.

"It looks like the children are gonna 'ave a good time" Mary Ann remarked and John's wife, Eliza, laughed in return, "They're certainly 'aving a good time at the moment but I wonder 'ow it will be once we're underway?"

Mary Ann grimaced at the thought and, with William wriggling in her arms. decided to put him down to give him a chance to crawl a little. The ship lurched, the timbers creaked and the sound of orders above deck told them that they were getting underway. Robert called James and George over, wanting to have them under his wing until they gained their sea legs, worried that they might hurt themselves. About fifty people huddled together and silently listened to the new sounds of sea, sail and shivering timbers as they gathered way and observed the changing motion as their ship headed up the Tamar and out to sea. They were on their way.

* * *

THE VOYAGE WAS UNEVENTFUL, other than for the inevitable bouts of seasickness that overcame the majority of those in steerage, but that was the worst they experienced and most disembarked thankfully, happy to stand on terra firma once more. On disembarking, they were impressed by the scene. Many large ships were in the harbour, some being loaded with goods, particularly bales of wool, some were being unloaded and some stood off from the docks at anchor in the bay. Impressive warehouses surrounded them and they could see passengers, dockers, sailors, merchants, a good number of Chinamen labouring on the docks. There was even a party of six aborigines who were demonstrating their prowess with a bundle of spears that they aimed at a target some thirty feet away, much to the delight of a small crowd of white men looking on. Gigs, phaetons and carriages with livery servants were everywhere. They saw a boy with a board carrying the picture and name of the society that had arranged their passage and went over to him, "Is this where we are to report?" Robert asked.

"Yessir, I'm to take youse to Mr. Entwistle wiv all the uvver ladies and gennulman off the ship".

It was the first time that Robert had ever been called sir. Yes, the salutation was from a raggedy urchin, but he stood up straighter, puffed out his chest and for a brief moment felt very important. He called Mary Ann over with the children and they waited while other passengers joined them until there were perhaps a dozen or more families and several single men in their twenties and thirties standing by the youngster under the punishing sun. About twenty minutes later the boy moved off and they followed, like the pied piper of Hamelin in reverse.

They made their way to a building not far from the docks and the men were separated by their trades, mostly farm labourers, but also ploughmen, a shoemaker, a blacksmith. Robert was introduced to a craggy Scotchman with striking red hair and a bushy red beard by the name of McCallum who still carried the evidence of his birth with rolling 'r's as he spoke. He asked him about his experience, about his family, his age, his religion. He also asked if Mary Ann could do laundry, sew and 'mak hersel' useful' to which Robert answered 'yes' without consulting Mary Ann, "Ten shilling a week for yersel' and five shilling for yer guid wifey and you'll hae a wee cottage for the baith o' ye and yer bairns. It'll be hard work but I'm a fair man and ye'll dae no better, I'm shair o' that. Do we hae a deal?"

Robert liked the farmer and upon answering in the affirmative, the Scotchman spit on the palm of his right hand and extended it to Robert to shake. Fifteen shillings a week and a cottage seemed like the land of milk and honey had been laid out before them.

The farm was a little to the north of the growing city, past Eastern Hills, by the Merri creek, a tributary to the main Yarra river at Abbotsford. It flowed for some fifty miles from the foothills of the mountain range to the north. Robert and his family were taken there by McCallum in a cart that he had brought down with him that morning.

As they were drawn out of town at a steady pace by the passive roan mare they cast their eyes with interest at the this rapidly growing town. The broad streets were clean and kept in good order, the houses on each side of the streets were well-proportioned and the shops appeared to be well stocked. New building appeared to be underway everywhere. As they trundled along McCallum, who was talkative if not always understandable, pointed out a carriage that passed them by, "Would ye believe, yon carriage belongs tae a man who cam here a convict and noo, sae rich that naebody kens the size o' his income nor cares tae ask either!".

A little further on he also pointed out a house under construction that was owned by another ex-convict who had made good somehow, "Folks say he's worth a hundred thoosand poond if he's worth a penny" he announced, richly extending the 'r's in each word.

They left the busy streets before too much longer and rumbled along dirt paths amongst open fields interspersed with the occasional tree. Soon, up ahead they could hear the sound of a church bell and then made out an imposing, brick-built church that McCallum said was the new St. Peter's[2] church. It stood tall and seemed to send a message about the wealth of its parish. As they passed nearby they could see people walking in through the main door.

St./ Peter's Church, Eastern Hill

Robert wondered if there was a wedding or a baptism or something of the sort underway, watching with interest the well-dressed people as they trundled on by.

Mary Ann had less time to observe her surroundings as William was beginning to get agitated and James and George had found something to argue about, requiring stern words from their mother to rein them in.

Soon after, they drew up at the McCallum homestead and within the hour were being settled into their new home.

SNOW

$\mathcal{M}$ elbourne
1849

ROBERT WAS SOON HARD at work. McCallum had him acting as a supervisor, showing younger labourers how to clear the fields of weeds, maintain hedgerows, sew the seeds. The beginning of Spring was soon upon them with the warming days promising a hot summer but this changed dramatically when, after a day of heavy rain on the 30th August, people went to their beds and woke up with amazement.

Mary Ann was the first to rise and she ran excitedly back to Robert, "It's snowing. Come look, it's snowing!". Robert rubbed his eyes and sat up. It was still dark but there was a glow from the snow and through the window he could see snowflakes drifting steadily, some had even piled up on the windowsill. He pulled on his trousers, put on a shirt and boots and followed Mary Ann to the front door which she threw open dramatically as if revealing a conjuring trick.

Outside they were greeted by a carpet of white as far as the eye could see. The snow was still falling and it looked like it was already several inches deep. Robert took a step outside and the snow crunched as his boots sunk into the un-compacted, fluffy white carpet. They were so surprised that the cold had failed to register but now Mary Ann noticed the change in temperature and her teeth started to chatter. Robert turned and laughed then went inside to find a blanket to put around her.

"Bless my soul, I never thought I'd see the day here" he said with a sense of amazement.

"The boys are going to have some fun today" he added as he shut the door and went to the fireplace, quickly creating a pile of tinder and logs and applying a flame to take the chill off the room.

Within the hour dawn had broken and the snowfall had ceased but not before they had woken the children up. They had, of course, never seen snow before and weren't quite sure what to do with it but their father and mother quickly dressed them and took them outside.

Robert bent down and picked up a handful of snow, compressing it into a snowball before aiming a direct hit at James. James tried to do the same but was unable to figure out how to turn the loose white fluffy flakes into a hard ball until his father showed him, and George too.

Then battle commenced. William was too young to play but he and his mother scrambled around, laughing as they fell on the slippery surface. Robert tried to make a snowman, rolling a snowball along the ground to create a larger and larger ball and instructing the two boys to do the same to make a head and to find twigs to make a nose and arms which they finished with two black stones for eyes. The two boys stood back to admire their prowess and ran excitedly into the house to bring Mary Ann out to see their creation.

Their work on the snowman completed they all went back inside to eat a bowl of porridge and, for the adults, down a mug of steaming hot tea. As silence fell over the table, memories flooded back to both Robert and Mary Ann and they quietly revelled in the experience.

Such a heavy fall of snow had not occurred since the founding of Melbourne. It began to dissolve about nine o'clock and as the heat of the sun strengthened about half-past eleven green patches started to appear with the acceleration of the melting process.

With the rapid change, water started flowing and, in Melbourne, despite the efforts of workmen to divert some of the water from Elizabeth street into the Yarra along Queen and Swanston streets, it quickly became a torrent. The inundating surge rushed from curb to curb down Elizabeth Street, at some points even threatening shop entrances. For more than two hours it almost seemed as if the town was divided by a rushing river and all communication across Elizabeth Street was suspended unless you were able to traverse it on horseback or in a carriage. Indeed, one cabman was taking advantage of the situation, charging an extortionate one penny a head to carry passengers across Elizabeth Street at its junction with Collins Street.

In the town, by about half-past one the snow had disappeared, and the flood gradually subsided but the Yarra river was rising considerably with the snowmelt and the preceding heavy rain, such that the citizenry were anticipating and preparing for the Yarra to overflow its banks. Those living close by the river had been removing their property to escape the expected inundation. The road to St. Kilda and the beach was covered with water at an early hour and the force of the flood had even washed away several large stacks of firewood.

On the Merri Creek, in the country, the melting snow and the wash from the hills following the non-stop rain the day before was also turning the creek into a tortured, writhing animal, carrying severed limbs from trees in its wake, its greedy fingers climbing up its banks, breaking over them by late afternoon. By dusk, the snowman was nothing more than a patch of ice, twigs and stones, a memory only, much to the disappointment of the boys.

Fortunately, the McCallum buildings sat above the floodplain and no one, including the Brights, had to take action to safeguard themselves. As evening came, some of the fields resembled rice paddies more than agricultural pastureland but there was little that the farmhands could do other than to move livestock onto higher ground. Everybody went to bed that night wondering what the morning would bring. As a precaution, McCallum charged four of the men to stand watch during the night in case there was need for an alarm to be raised.

But the morning broke without further alarm and – despite the creek still challenging its banks – the water in the fields began to slowly drain away and the violent thrashing of the Merri creek became a more manageable, if hurried, flow.

The heat of the sun combined with the ubiquity of the water made for a humid day. Robert and the rest of the men sweated copiously as they attended to the after-effects of the strange weather, spending most of the day searching for and collecting a quantity of posts and railings that had been scattered across the land by the water and Mary Ann too spent an uncomfortable afternoon at the laundry tub while she kept a wary eye on her boys, worried that they might steal away and fall into some waterhole left by the receding floods.

Melbourne suffered too and the flooded plains and roads wreaked havoc, in one case more than fifty bullock teams with shearing supplies and their shearers and labourers were unable to leave the town because of the flooded state of the creeks and rivers up country. But life, as it always does, gradually returned to normal as the sun re-established its preeminence and, while September and some of October saw extensive repair and re-instatement activity, November hove into sight and Summer eventually made its welcome appearance.

* * *

THE NEW YEAR, or Hogmanay as McCallum called it, was ushered in with celebrations, especially as it marked the mid-point of this vibrant century but in one way was quite novel for Robert. He had spent the day up country on the 31st and was heading back home. On the way he and one of the other farm hands, a Jim McAlister, stopped at the Pilgrim's Inn[1].

The inn had been built a couple of years before on a dusty track known as Plenty Road which ran north through the Plenty valley. It was mostly frequented by shepherds and other farming folk but to a thirsty Robert it was a welcoming sight. Outside the shingle-roofed wooden building a sign hung with a picture of a pilgrim hunched over a staff and the doorway was crested by a low-hung roof.

One drink lead to another and they were still there at 7 o'clock when there was a commotion outside. Several of the men at the bar, including Robert and Jim, took their beers and went to the entrance to see what it was all about.

Outside, a scruffily dressed group of six young men, already a little the worse for drink, were making a discordant attempt at harmony. Two of them had kerosene tins that they rattled with "drumsticks", there was a grasping concertina accompanied by a battered tin whistle, yet another man blew energetically into a croaky comb that made a wheezy, nasal tune of sorts and another twanged vigorously on a Jewish harp. The cobbled–together bush band played with vigour and soon had the onlookers clapping along and even singing when they attempted a song that they knew, especially 'Auld Lang Syne[2]' although it seemed most didn't know all of the words.

After about half an hour of this, the band stopped and

jovially "demanded" recompense from the publican, "Come on Mr. Robert Duff, time to pay up for this wonderful entertainment" they called out, laughing and the publican, who had been watching from the doorway, laughed too and invited them in for a beer each, this being the going rate apparently.

Robert did not stay any longer. It was perhaps thirty minutes to get back home and, even though it was the eve of 1850, he needed to get to his bed for he would be up early in the morning; it was after all a Tuesday, just another regular day.

GOLD?

Merri Creek
1850/2

OUR GOLDFIELD.

Eureka! We have gold – – gold in abundance. The verification of floating rumours has come, and we feel now in a position to state decisively that which we have long hoped to lay before the public. In area, depth, and richness of yield, the Pyrenean goldfield promises to be of first importance. Mr. Davis, of Avoca, brought to our office yesterday, a beautiful sample of pure gold dust, varying in size from a pin's head down to the most minute particles, found on Donald Cameron's Station, at a spot known henceforth as "Clune's Diggings."

Geelong Advertiser, 25th July, 1851

* * *

THE NEW LAND brought with it the experiences of new sights and sounds. In May, Mary Ann and the children were mesmerised by a flock of hundreds of sulphur-crested cocka-

187

toos in the trees making an awful racket and blotting the sun as they wheeled about. On another occasion, Robert and Mary Ann were out walking with the children one summer's evening when they came across dozens of green tree frogs within the space of a few yards. Their rattling cries of crawk...crawk... crawk filled the night air until the boys began to run excitedly back and forth as they tried to catch one, without success.

The wildlife also presented challenges. The farm had its own hens to provide eggs for the farm and to provide an income at times of surplus. But the native cat[1] and particularly falcons were picking them off to the point that something had to be done about it. McCallum issued four of his men with shotguns, including Robert, and told them to keep the guns with them as they went about their work. If they saw a falcon, they were to shoot. Over the following few weeks, the haul amounted to almost fifty birds and the hen coop settled back into relative safety.

Although money was never plentiful, they were putting a shilling away here and there and when their church started a part-time school to teach children the basics of reading and writing they signed James up, being the eldest but too young to do any meaningful work at the age of 7.

News of the gold rush in California had been part of the regular currency for a year and there had been some who had sold up and taken ship to America to dig for their fortune. And then, in the winter of 1851 a steady trickle of news started to be shared over a drink at the pub or after church or during tea breaks on the farm about gold being found in Australia.

"I hear that they've discovered gold near Bathurst. Hundreds are arriving every week they say" claimed one of the men standing at the bar.

Another chipped in, "It's true, a Digger named Austen turned up in Sydney with an eight ounce nugget of pure gold last month that he'd picked up from the ground".

"That'd be worth more'n thirty-five pound" exclaimed someone with wonder in his voice.

"You're telling tall tales, mate" another responded only to be shouted down by several others with equally outlandish stories, although all second or third hand.

IN FEBRUARY OF 1851, Mary Ann broke the news to Robert that she had fallen pregnant again and as the months advanced she had to cut back on her workload as things progressed. While Robert relayed the gold rush stories to her she was busy preparing the boys for a new brother or sister. When they were asked which would they prefer, James and George said a sister and William said he didn't want either – he was quite happy being the spoiled younger brother it seemed.

AS THE WEEKS WENT BY, more rumours surfaced about the New South Wales gold rush. At times, cold water would be poured on the stories; that five or six hundred men were working the diggings but very few were earning more than they would at regular trades and numbers were leaving in despair after labouring for days without any success. This notwithstanding, prices had been rising rapidly for shovels, pots and pans and the most ordinary of basic consumables. Word had it that the Governor was going to proclaim that by English law all gold found belonged to the Queen. And as the months passed without easy pickings, prices declined somewhat but still the diggings continued to attract both locals and immigrants, including Chinese eager to make their fortunes.

BACK IN MELBOURNE, despite the intense interest in what was happening on the Bathurst goldfields, things were more subdued and people, by and large, focused on living their lives day by day. The harvest had come and gone and now the farm was in maintenance mode. Robert with two others under his supervision were renewing and repairing fences, which made him recall his first job at Trafalgar, although this time others were undertaking the backbreaking work of drilling the post holes and Robert was overseeing the construction of the fences in addition to cutting and sizing.

THEN, in August, news spread like wildfire that gold had been discovered not one hundred miles away in Clunes. Gold had been found by a shepherd a couple of years earlier but it was viewed then as a random event rather than something of substance but now there was credible evidence and the newspapers were even giving directions and instructions for those who wanted to try their luck. At three guineas an ounce, it was easy to get excited.

One of the men at the bar was holding court one evening, "On this one field there are eighteen men working and it's no more'n eight miles from the spot where that shepherd found the nugget a few years back".

"So, when are you going?" Asked another with a laugh.

"Well, it's useless going up there without the right equipment – cradles, spades, stores, blankets, rugs. And you don't want to buy them at the diggings, they cost a fortune there. I've heard they're selling spades at a pound a piece at the mines!

You need to buy them in Geelong afore you go".

"And how do you get there?"

The man holding forth picked up a newspaper and read, "From Geelong to Boninyong, it's fifty miles and the Clunes diggings are another twenty-seven miles further. Once there, at Clarke's outstation you turn off to Coghill's and there you are -

the bloomin' goldfield laid out before you - just waiting for you to make your fortune."

Eyes widened at the thought and one or two even licked their lips in anticipation at the easy pickings although others expressed doubt but it is fair to say that no-one left the bar that evening without images of gold nuggets floating before their eyes.

Robert naturally thought about the opportunity but he was far too busy with the farm now that Spring had arrived. Mary Ann was also well on with her pregnancy and late at night on 27th September, 1851 after a relatively quick delivery, a new son arrived.

Robert wanted to call him Benjamin after his brother and Mary Ann was happy to acquiesce. A couple of days later little Benjamin, lustily announcing his presence, was baptised at St Peter's Church at Eastern Hill along with three other babies. Although they had not requested that the bells ring, they rang nevertheless, probably because one of the other parents had made an appropriate contribution to the church funds.

They left the church with the three boys in tow and Benjamin in Mary Ann's arms under a brilliant sun to the sound of the bells – it all seemed to promise much for the new addition to their growing family. James particularly. Although he had been unwillingly enrolled in the church school, he had proved to be a reasonable scholar and after a year was able to write his name and had a basic grasp of reading, much to the pride of his parents to whom reading and writing remained a mysterious art.

* * *

News from the goldfields continued to excite everyone. The latest news was that gold had now been found at Forest Creek and at Yuille's diggings by Buninyong and Ballaarat. By year end, Bendigo Creek had joined the list and the gold fever became palpable amongst young and old alike in the region. Robert too found himself sorely tempted.

In the winter of 1852, Robert was drinking at the Pilgrim Inn when a gnarled man in travel-stained clothes with wild grey hair sprouting from beneath a battered hat and a bushy beard came up to the bar. He put a rucksack down by his feet with a thud and stood next to a pensive Robert before ordering a beer. He then took out a bundled cloth from his pocket along with some coins, paid for the beer and, in sorting out his change spilled some chips of gold onto the bar from his bundle. He quickly scooped them up, looking nervously to his right and left and returned the treasure to his pocket.

"Where are you headed, mate?" Robert asked, although he really wanted to ask where he had come *from*.

"Who wants to know?" The Digger responded without taking his eyes from his beer.

"Bright, Robert Bright. And what your name?"

The Digger took a moment before replying then said, "Ethan Harrison, glad to meet you" holding out a hand to shake. Robert took his hand, shook it and looked him in the eye. The man had piercing eyes that made Robert want to look away but he forced himself to maintain eye contact.

"Glad to meet you too. Are you stopping long?" Robert asked.

"No, just on my way to town to get some supplies" he replied as he took another draft of his beer.

"Are you working the goldfields?" Robert finally asked him, unable to restrain his curiosity.

"Well, I guess that's pretty obvious from what you just saw. What about you?" the Digger enquired.

"I work on a farm nearby but it's impossible not to hear about what's happening at Castlemaine and Ballaarat at the moment. Is it really as busy as they say?"

"Busy and getting busier. There's people coming in from everywhere, including the Chinese. There were even some Americans from California turned up last week. Still, at least for the moment, there seems to be room for everyone" Then he chuckled to himself and added, "But I'll be heading back as soon as I can to work a claim, just in case".

They ordered two more beers and continued talking. Robert wanted to know how he had become involved in prospecting for gold and what was involved. The Digger became more talkative as he drank his beer and it was a good hour later before Robert bade him farewell.

At home that evening, after the children had been put to bed, Robert relayed the story of the Digger at the pub to Mary Ann. She could see where it was leading and was sceptical, "And just 'ow much money 'as 'e made on the goldfields?"

Robert responded defensively, "He had maybe £10 worth of gold in his pocket and he said that he was going back to properly work the claim – he really has only just begun and people are flocking there for the easy pickings".

"Yeah, yeah! Easy pickings. I'd bet our savings that it's only the lucky few that will make anything out there".

"Maybe so, but people will make fortunes from what I hear and that's something we'll never do labouring on the farm and washing clothes".

"Robert, we've got four youngsters to look after as well as ourselves. 'Ow would we manage on the goldfields?".

Robert conceded that it wasn't straightforward and insisted that he wasn't proposing to do anything, but that it was something that they ought to keep in mind if their situation changed, without describing how that might happen. The conversation petered out and, with the night closing in, they both made their way to their bed, falling asleep with hopes and troubles and indecision swirling around in their heads.

GEORGE WILSON

*M*erri Creek
1852

....Bendigo Creek Diggings have been whispered about very myste-
riously for the last few days as something better than anything yet
discovered.

Geelong Advertiser and Intelligencer, Monday 22 December 1851

* * *

THE FOUR BOYS, James, George, William and now Benjamin were a handful, often quarrelling, sometimes fighting, always mischievous. At nine years old, James was the eldest but still not old enough to seriously contribute to the household, although he would often accompany Robert on his chores and would help his mother with the laundry and pushing a wheelbarrow around the farm to pick up and drop off clothes that Mary Ann had repaired and or washed or pies she had baked to add to the family income.

News of finds at Bendigo Creek was the talk of the town and Robert eventually couldn't hold back. Why, only a couple of weeks ago a nugget weighing over 100 ounces was said to have been found by a mere boy surfacing on the rise on Bendigo Creek.

It was February. The day had been pleasantly warm as the season changed from the harsh heat of summer to the more gentle autumn. Robert came home after a particularly rowdy evening at the Pilgrim Inn with a dozen Diggers who had called in on their way to the goldfields. He opened the cottage door and immediately began to talk with ill-concealed excitement about the fortunes to be made, "Mary Ann, we have to give it a go. I mean, even if we only find a few ounces it will set us up. It won't last forever and Bendigo is only a few days walk north, it's not as if we have to sail to California!"

"I dunno, Robert. It seems such a risk. To frow away all we've worked for 'ere". The frown on her forehead showed the pain this was causing her and Robert stopped talking and pulled her close, kissing her on the top of her head and hugging her tight, "I know, I know. It is a risk. Perhaps I should go first to see what's what. You can stay here while I'm gone. We've got savings to add to your wages and I can be back in two or three weeks. I've already cleared it with McCallum. If it doesn't work out, we'll be able to keep on here just as we are. What d'you think?"

They talked on for another forty-five minutes before Mary Ann finally realised that she really didn't have any choice, so reluctantly agreed with the plan. Robert would take £3 of their savings and see what could be done.

The next week, Robert journeyed to Melbourne and back to buy basic supplies, including a spade and a trowel, a pan to sift dirt and a blanket. All things he had been told he would need. He wrapped it up in a bundle together with some food, ready to strap onto his back before leaving early the following morning for a journey that would take him perhaps five days, four if he pushed it, sleeping rough on the way.

He left before Easter as dawn was breaking after Mary Ann had made him a bowl of steaming porridge. It was a clear sky and being autumn, he would avoid the fierce summer heat and it wouldn't be too cold at night. He just hoped it wouldn't rain. Mary Ann kissed him with a tear in her eye and James, who had risen before the other boys, stood by her trying to put on a brave face.

"Mind you look after your mother, James. I'll be gone a few days so you're the man of the house while I'm away" Robert instructed him as he knelt down in front of his son. James nodded his head but couldn't find words for the occasion.

Robert hefted his pack onto his back and, with a final kiss and a promise that he would be back soon, he began the long walk north for Bendigo, full of hope and a little uncertainty too. But, he had rationalised to himself, nothing ventured, nothing gained.

Mary Ann and James watched until he reached a clump of trees. He turned and waved and she waved back, then he was gone.

SHE CLOSED the door and started on the children's breakfast. Salted porridge with a glass of milk for them all except Benjamin. She was weaning him off her breast and had mashed him some rice with milk. She woke the other boys and presided over a messy, argumentative table then made some tea for herself. Once everything had been cleared away and washed, the boys helping, she sent James, George and William with a wheelbarrow to McCallum's house to collect the laundry that she would work on today.

The cottage seemed emptier than normal. Benjamin was happily playing on the floor with some wooden bricks. Otherwise it was quiet and almost lonely. She shrugged her shoulders. She'd experienced worse in Launceston at the Factory in solitary and she smiled grimly thinking about how she'd beaten the system. It would just be a few weeks. And there was more than enough to keep her busy.

* * *

ROBERT SET A STEADY PACE. His objective was to get near to Sunbury that day and he reckoned that if he forced it, he would reach the Bendigo Creek goldfields within the week.

The sky was clear and, being early in the morning, it was cool. Ideal weather for a brisk walk. As he walked, he imagined the riches resting in the earth waiting to be discovered. His head had been filled with stories of people just like himself who had already stumbled across not just ounces but pounds of gold. He reasoned that even if he was only able to dig out just eight ounces, for example, that would be worth what he would earn in a year as a farm labourer. It seemed like a reasonable gamble. So he kept walking, the road generally sloping up a gentle incline, with his footsteps eating up the miles as he dreamed on.

With the sun at its zenith, he decided to break for a few minutes and rummaged in his supplies, taking out a mutton pie that Mary Ann had baked. He sat at the side of the track, over-looking a dribbling, muddy creek that meandered across the fields. After chewing for a couple of minutes, he clambered down to the creek and, straddling the bank and a stone in the water, he bent down, cupped his hands and drank deep from the cooling, if muddy water. He splashed some water on the back of his neck and his face, straightened up, clambered up the bank, hefted his pack onto his back and stepped out again with renewed vigour.

As he walked, he was passed by two horsemen moving at a steady trot, spades and other equipment tied to their saddles. They didn't stop, just passed him by as if he wasn't there. He had been walking for an hour or so after his dinner, when his eye caught a flash in the distance, something reflecting the sun. As he kept walking he saw that there were two men perhaps half a mile ahead who were also heading north.

In less than an hour he had caught up with them. They were also carrying mining equipment, which was what had reflected the sun earlier. One of them, like Robert, had a spade on his back and the other carried a saw in addition to their packs. They appeared to be about the same age as him, one a little taller with scraggly brown hair and the other about the same size as him and sporting a trimmed black beard. The taller man walked with a slight limp, which was keeping their progress in check. They both wore straw hats to shield them from the sun, like Robert.

"Where are you heading mate?" Robert asked as he drew up alongside the pair.

"Looks like the same place as you" the man nearest to him replied, pointing at Robert's spade.

"Bendigo Creek?" Robert asked.

"There or thereabouts" the Digger responded.

Robert fell in with them and asked if they had worked any other claims or whether this was a new expedition. They, like Robert, were novices and were heading to the goldfields to make their fortune. Before long, though, with Robert's pace slowing to match theirs, and the appearance of more men coming up behind them, he decided to move on and said his goodbyes, striding ahead with a "See you in Bendigo" as a farewell.

The further he walked, the more people he saw – all heading north. He passed another five men marching north and was passed by three on horseback. There was also a cart being pulled by an old nag, piled high with the possessions of a family, the man's wife and children perched on top and holding on grimly as the cart navigated the rutted track with tree roots and holes adding to the difficulty. In places the track was no wider than a garden path, hemmed in by trees that scratched the side of the cart as it juddered its way forwards. He walked with the man leading the horse for about half a mile, exchanging pleasantries, then said goodbye and moved ahead.

The scenery was unremarkable but it was a fine day, a few clouds chased each other across the blue sky and he reflected on his life at Dunn's farm in Burwell. While he missed his family and the familiar environment, the fairs, the pubs, his friends, he had to admit that the grey skies, the cold of winter and the hopelessness of life was no match for the 'good to be alive' feeling he had at that moment. Fresh, warm air and the lure of a fortune to be made. He continued walking with deliberation – 'Bendigo here I come' he said to himself and he smiled.

With the sun slipping below the horizon and painting the sky in hues of orange, red, yellow and gold, Robert started looking for somewhere to sleep for the night. He had brought a blanket with him and intended to find a dry, sheltered spot where he could make a fire, line the ground with brush and leaves and sleep rough.

Walking on another half hour, ahead he saw a cluster of trees and he made for them. About fifteen or twenty other parties had already made camp in the vicinity. As he scouted for somewhere to set up his own camp, he said hello to one of the two men camped nearby and received a brusque response, their English was broken and he assumed that they were European prospectors, perhaps German or Dutch or Polish?

A small creek ran through the copse and the trees offered some cover in the unlikely event of rain. He set about collecting material for a fire and his bed, and after checking the ground around him for signs of any unwelcome wildlife, he lit a fire and made a bed for himself in a hollow near the roots of one of the trees. As he was making camp, other travellers arrived and began to pitch their camp for the night too.

Although he couldn't see any sign of rabbit burrows, he

thought there would be no harm in setting a trap on the off chance that a rabbit might stray his way and supplement his food supplies. As he was whittling sticks that he had collected, he thought back to doing exactly the same thing as a boy and nodded with satisfaction when his trap was in place, knowing that there would be no gamekeeper to bundle him off to gaol in this deserted place.

Once he had set the trap, he collected some water from the creek and mixed it with some oats that he had packed, heating it over his fire to create a basic porridge in his billy can which he wolfed down before he settled in for the night with a warm belly. With the temperature falling he put extra logs on the fire and watched with satisfaction as the hungry, flickering flames caught the logs in their embrace. Then, sighing contentedly, he laid back with his arms clasped behind his head.

After a full day walking with a pack on his back, it was good to be still, feeling the inevitable aches and pains ease their way out of his body. He had passed through Sunbury some time ago and figured that he must be somewhere south of the settlement of Gisborne because he could see Mt. Macedon in the distance.

He had done well. The empty sky with sporadic stars and the Southern Cross pre-eminent contrasted with the crowded, star-encrusted northern hemisphere skies and Robert yearned to trace the Plough and the Little Bear, but that was another world, another life. He gazed skywards for a few minutes more then closed his eyes.

For a while, the night was broken by the sound of other camps talking, shouting, arguing, drinking, singing and gunfire as weapons were cleaned or gave warning to others or perhaps hunted game but as the night wore on it quietened, everyone tired and readying themselves for the next day's efforts. As he listened to the sounds of the night, he thought of Mary Ann and the boys and hoped that they were doing well. He smiled as he realised that they would be sleeping in a bed tonight while he would be sleeping on the ground with a blanket wrapped around him. Yes, they would be doing well compared with him! Finally, he prayed and settled back on the pack that he was now using as a pillow. As the blackness of the night enveloped him, Robert drifted off to sleep with the comforting crackle and fluttering of the fire to keep him company.

He woke twice during the night and both times rekindled the fire to keep it going. As dawn broke, other camps stirred and he woke to stretch a stiff body before checking his rabbit trap – which was undisturbed – dismantling it and stowing the sticks and rope away before making more porridge for breakfast. He then washed his face in the remnants of a creek, water puddling on its bed, kicked the fire out and, heaving his pack on his back and hanging his spade from his shoulder, he struck north once more, eager to be on his way, one of the first to break camp.

OVER THE NEXT two days he travelled through a rural landscape with substantial flocks of sheep grazing on the homesteads established by earlier settlers and he also noticed aboriginal shepherds in the distance and, of course, like a trail of hurrying ants, the tramp of prospectors heading for Bendigo. The road was busy with fellow travellers and every now and then he would notice the remnants of previous travellers who had passed this way, broken wheels and axles, abandoned trunks and clothing, carcasses of horses and bullocks that hadn't made it.

By mid-morning on the third day he was approaching the edge of the busy settlement of Gisborne. The town appeared to be prospering, no doubt because of the traffic to and from the goldfields, with a brewery, two wine saloons, several hotels, grocery, grain and hay stores, harness makers, blacksmiths, butchers' shops and many cottages and tents. Outside the *Bush*

Inn[1] hotel, an enterprising resident had set up a stall under a canvas shade and was selling tea, pies and other bits and pieces to the irregular procession of people like Robert heading to and from the goldfields. A dog barked and he heard the sound of hooves and neighing from horses coming up behind him.

Robert decided to dig into his pocket and treat himself to a pie and some tea. Two Diggers had just left the stall and another man, about his age, wearing a slouch hat and sporting a black mottled grey beard was just leaving the stall with a billy and a pie. His dusty clothes and the bulging backpack mirrored Robert's. As Robert walked up, he sat down on steps leading up to the veranda, shaded from the sun in front of the wooden building and he drank his tea while picking crumbs out of his stubbled beard. The sun shone brilliantly.

"Good morning, mate" Robert called out to both the stall owner and the Digger.

"G'day yerself" the seated man replied and the stall-keeper flashed a smile at Robert with a "G'day, what can I do for you, mate?"

"I'll have two of your meat pies for later and a billy of tea" Robert replied.

"Right you are" and he poured Robert a steaming cup of tea and handed it to him together with the two pies, which Robert stuffed into his pack for later. Robert paid the man.

"Where you heading?" the seated man asked.

"Bendigo Creek" Robert replied, "And you?"

"Same. Done any digging before?" he asked.

Robert ventured that this was something new for him but that he was ready to learn and he was keen to try his luck.

"What's your name?" the man asked Robert.

"Bright. That's Robert Bright" he answered and he held out his hand.

"George Wilson" he replied and he took Robert's hand with a firm grip and shook it in greeting.

"Take the weight off your feet, it's a long walk yet" Wilson said, gesturing to his right.

Robert took him up on the offer and settled down, resting against an upright post supporting the tin roof and hiding from the sun that was flitting in and out of the clouds,

"What are you expecting to find?" Robert asked.

"Same as Forest Creek, I guess" Wilson replied.

"So you've tried your luck before?" Robert asked.

"A little, but I plan to get in early at the creek".

They talked some more and once Robert had finished his tea, Wilson stood up and suggested that they walk the rest of the way together, "Safer together, if any bushrangers try to bail us up on the way" he said before adding with a smile, "Not that I've got anything worth having". Robert laughed and agreed with him.

The two men bid the stall-keeper goodbye and walked north out of Gisborne into the countryside, looking to reach Five Mile Creek[2] before nightfall. As they left town, two men on horses with tools strapped to their saddles rode past them in a cloud of dust and soon disappeared over the hill. The sky was clear and the sun was relentless – it had been a very dry summer that year and the ground was iron hard. Their boots kicked up dust as they walked down the track.

* * *

THEY WALKED STEADILY, talking every now and then but more often walking in silence, breathing heavily as they made their way over the mountain range through the notorious Black Forest between Macedon and Five Mile Creek. They kept a watchful eye as they worked their way through the trees because this was the haunt of Captain Melville[3] and his gang and other bushrangers. Unlike the rest of the road north, this part of the journey was heavily forested and the road wound in and out of the trees creating obstacles for the traveller and ideal cover for an ambush. In wet weather, it became a mass of mud-holes – indeed, hardly a road at all. But, despite its reputation, the mountain crossing was thankfully strenuous but uneventful.

The following morning they broke camp after the sun had risen and were quickly on their way, passing through the small hamlet of Carlsruhe with its hotel and police station and making Kyneton about an hour before sunset. It was a busy place. Perhaps 300 people lived there and there was a miscellany of housing from slab huts and tents to wooden establishments including the appropriately named *Gold Diggers Arms*[4] that was in the process of construction.

They made camp a mile or so beyond the village, well off the road north along a creek bed that had all but dried up and, as before, spent a rough night under the stars but without any other campfires nearby. At least there was no chance of rain tonight, Robert thought and, again after saying a prayer for Mary Ann and the boys, he tried to sleep with George on the other side of the fire snorting and snoring as he dreamt of gold.

He had been asleep perhaps for an hour or two when he was woken by something stirring. He opened his eyes lazily, taking a few seconds to focus, then raised himself on one arm. The fire was still dancing and the embers glowed brightly. Then he felt something nudge him in the back, "Don't move or it'll be the last thing you do" he heard in a soft whisper. He turned his head and saw a shadowy figure holding a musket pointing straight at him. He froze, unable to make any part of his body instigate the action his brain was urging.

"What do you want?" Robert finally managed to say.

"Don't be funny, mate" the figure replied, "Give me your gold".

"I don't have any gold. I haven't even gotten to the fields yet" Robert replied with a sense of rising anger.

"I'll give you to the count of three to find it or it's curtains for you, mate. So stop being a silly bugger".

Robert began to get up.

"Hold it, there" the bushranger ordered.

"How am I to get anything if I'm lying on the ground?" Robert replied.

That made him think, "Alright. Slowly. No sudden movements"

Robert did as he was bid and was surprised to see that George Wilson had disappeared, he was on his own. His thoughts were spinning like a weathervane in a storm. How was he to disarm this man? Would he kill him if he couldn't produce any gold? What kind of idiot would hold him up when he obviously had nothing of value – bloody hell, he didn't even have a tent!

"I'm waiting. Get a move on or I'll drill you, I swear I will" the bushranger was beginning to sound a little desperate and Robert wondered if that was a good thing or not.

He was about to say that the gold was hidden under the tree in the hope that he could catch him off guard when another voice came out of the dark, "Drop the musket or I'm gonna put a bullet in yer back".

The bushranger started and began to turn to face the voice. Robert took his chance and leaped on the man, shoving the rifle away with his left hand while throwing a venomous punch with his right into the surprised face that had turned back. The gunman stumbled with the force of the blow, tripped over a tree root and fell backwards, discharging the musket into the air as he fell.

George Wilson then appeared out of the night and rushed up to the fallen gunman and placed his foot on the barrel of the musket. The assailant gave up trying to recover it; being a single shot weapon it was only useful as a club now anyway, and instead picked himself up and, waiting for George's attention to slip, ran away from the two men with an awkward gait as fast as he could, disappearing into the night with George shouting threats after him, warning him to stay away.

George picked up the weapon, "Hmm. An Enfield[5]. I wonder where he got that from?" and then he put it down, resting it against the trunk of a tree.

Robert suddenly felt drained of energy and emotion. He realised he had come close to death, "Where did you get to?" he asked.

George smiled grimly and said, "I heard him coming so melted away before he made camp until I could see what was what. While you two were talking shop I crept round the back and got the drop on him. Must admit, I wasn't expecting you to jump him like you did, but you really spoiled his game, the nackle-assed[6] scamp[7]. Just as well 'cos I wasn't armed – just hoped that he wouldn't figure that out".

Robert almost shouted, "What? You didn't have a gun?" Robert shook his head and picked up the musket, "Well, we're richer by one musket than when we started".

They made up the fire again and settled back into their beds, George Wilson putting the Enfield beside him, "Just in case I need to pretend again" he said and the two men pulled their blankets around them, laid back and tried to gather their strength for the next day.

THE DIGGINGS

Bendigo
    February, 1852

THE TWO MEN were up with the dawn and broke camp early to join the trek to the goldfields. Walking along the track they continued on through the settlement of Elphinstone and passed broken carts and other detritus. About three miles further on they reached the infamous Porcupine Inn[1].

They walked up to the hotel but couldn't see anyone about, which seemed strange, although there was shouting and a general clamour from nearby. The Inn itself was a ramshackle building with broken window panes and sun-parched paint peeling off the cracking wooden walls. Surprisingly, all the doors were locked. Wilson shouted through one of the broken panes, "Here are customers looking for a drink!" only to hear a voice from within shout back, "You can't come in".

"What d'ye say? A pub shut in the middle of the afternoon? You're 'aving a lend o' me, mate".

"We're closed, sod off".

Realising the futility of further talk, the two men made their way to the yard where it began to dawn on them what was happening. It appeared that a boxing match had been going on with the two contestants arraigned in opposite corners of a makeshift ring complete with seconds and hangers' on.

One of the outhouses in the yard had been turned into a rough bar where drinks were being served to a rowdy clientele. At another couple of rough forms, dinner was being served. The Post Office part of the building was closed and wherever you looked it appeared filthy and neglected. Drunks staggered around the yard and shifty, hard-looking men eyed them up, no doubt marking out potential targets.

Back in the ring the fight had finished, the victor, bare-chested with bloodied face and hands, surrounded by happy backers washing away the blood. The loser alone in the other corner but for two seconds who were likewise cleaning up his ravaged face as he cried out for a tot of rum.

Robert and George fought their way to the bar and bought a pot of beer and paid their half-a-crown for a serving of soup and roast mutton. They were keen to quiz anyone fresh from the diggings to hear the latest news about the finds. Gold had been taken at different locations on the Bendigo over the previous months and a major rush had been sparked by discoveries at Golden Point[2] along the banks of the creek.

At the table they sat opposite two brothers named Albert and Jack. Their surnames were not asked for nor given. They were, like Robert, new to the gold fields having arrived from England a few weeks earlier. Albert was about 25 years of age and his brother a year or two younger. They were from a middle-class family and had read about the fabulous wealth of the diggings and had decided to make their fortune.

It was impossible not to mark them as brothers. Albert and Jack both sported newly acquired beards and had outfitted themselves in Melbourne with moleskin trousers which they wore with flannel shirts, gaudy handkerchiefs tied round their necks and canvas jackets and (like Robert) cabbage tree hats[3]. Although they would not have admitted it, they had been working hard on their journey from Melbourne to dirty and roughen their clothing to make them 'fit in' more easily. They were eager and excited and Robert found them good company.

"How about we work together on the diggings?" Albert suggested after they had been talking for half an hour. Robert looked at George and George shrugged his shoulders, "If you like" he responded laconically. Robert did like the idea of sharing the toil and the risk so he wiped his right hand on his trousers and offered it to shake on the partnership, which initiated a round of handshakes amongst the four men.

The formalities of partnership concluded, George said, "We should be on our way" and with that the four of them hoisted their loads onto their backs and left the inn talking about the riches waiting for them ahead. They decided to find a spot to sleep a little further on within striking distance of Bendigo so they could rise early and make the diggings late afternoon the next day.

* * *

UP EARLY ONCE MORE, marching across the parched landscape, they saw many more men walking or riding to and from Bendigo, signalling that they would soon reach their goal. Despite their weariness, their mutual enthusiasm burned bright. Along the way George passed the time educating his companions on the technique of digging for gold. Robert, Albert and Jack hung onto his every word.

On approaching the diggings a day later Robert was struck by the rattling sound ahead. As they walked on he realised that this was the sound of hundreds of cradles being shaken and the rocks and dirt tumbling on and through them. As far as the eye could see men were working in holes with pickaxe, shovel, bucket and knife in search of the buried treasure. Each hole had its mound of dirt piled up with narrow footpaths winding through it all. Although some trees still stood amongst the frantic excavation, he could mark out tree stumps that stood like forlorn children of the earth, still, bearing witness to the slaughter of the erstwhile forest as the miners cleared the land. On the hills, tents ran into the distance, an infestation of canvas scarring the higher ground.

They were fortunate to come across a digger leaving for Melbourne who was selling up and so equipped themselves relatively cheaply with canvas, a cradle, a blunt pickaxe, a sledgehammer and some cooking pots and a fry pan for the princely sum of £5 – a bargain given that cradles alone were selling for £3 to £5 in the stores. They added this to the collection of tools they had brought with them. They also purchased some supplies from a canvas-roofed store flying a gaudy flag pitched above the creek near the Commissioner's quarters.

They walked on a little further, looking with not a little concern at the fierce-looking dogs chained by the tents and the occasional growling and barking warning off ne'er-do-wells. Coming across a blacksmith's shop – a roughly built, canvas-roofed edifice flying a white flag with a red saltire - they decided to sharpen their tools on a grinding stone for sixpence, then headed into the hills.

They were able to find a spot on the hill overlooking the Adelaide gully where they made camp for the night. George explained that regulations required each tent to be at least 20 feet apart and the same distance from any creek, "We'll make do 'ere tonight and make proper camp when we've staked our claim tomorrow" he added as he set about throwing the canvas over a surviving tree branch. It was dry. It hadn't rained for weeks. And some that they met expressed concern about the lack of water to wash the dirt while others said that there was more water than a month ago and still plenty of water for all purposes, so they dismissed the cautionary words and ploughed ahead.

The number of people coming and going, the line of tents housing government officers, soldiers and police and the sturdy log hut under construction for a lock-up, the smell of sheep offal and sheep carcasses lying about with the accompanying buzz of swarming flies and biting insects, the barking of dogs, the discharge of guns, the general clamour, the sense of urgency and excitement that hung in the air was all ridiculously intoxicating.

* * *

AT THE DIGGINGS, the higher ground had been turned into a campsite and while there were one or two slab[4] huts that had been roughly erected, most men (and it was almost exclusively men) were living in tents and some were simply sleeping rough. As night fell, campfires appeared like a swarm of fireflies and gunshots could be heard together with the noisy reloading of muskets.

When they heard the first shots, Albert turned to George with an enquiring look and George replied, "That's just the Diggers warning thieving buggers away during the night; it 'appens every evening, just keep off if you don't want a bullet". The fusillade of gunshots continued for a couple of hours, perhaps a thousand discharges until the noise receded into the background as they became acclimatised. They made camp for the night, adding to the myriad campfires that burnt across the hills, erecting a makeshift shelter with the canvas and the tent that Albert and Jack had brought with them.

As they settled down, they could hear the noise of Diggers drinking, singing, gambling, fighting; the frenzy of dogs snarling, barking and sometimes fighting – all the sounds of life in this unique environment. Robert had lost the toss and was sent to collect water for the billy, returning three quarters of an hour later to a generous campfire at the ready. They cooked their mutton over the fire, made some coffee and wiped their tin plates clean with the damper left over from the previous day. No alcohol tonight, but Albert had some tobacco to share and the four of them contentedly laid plans for the morrow,

The next morning they woke before dawn and, like many others on the goldfields, rekindled their fire and made some porridge and tea. Then they gathered their equipment and headed into the gulley. There were perhaps a thousand or more men there and Robert's initial thought was to wonder whether they would find space to work a claim amongst this chaos. It looked like a termite's nest with a constant movement of men attacking the ground, carrying and sifting dirt; all serenaded by the raucous, rhythmic rattle of cradles being rocked back and forth. The smell of decaying butcher's carcasses, dog and horse turds and the ring of pickaxes striking rock, shovels scraping earth, carts and wheelbarrows rumbling back and forth, oaths, curses and barking filled the air.

They spent a good two hours before they found a pitch for themselves, twenty-four feet square of hope. They pegged out their claim with generous paces by marking the line with their spades and hammering in a short stick at each corner. Inside the claim they piled two shovels, a pick axe, a couple of buckets, a puddling tub, two prospecting pans and a cradle to wash the dirt. Then George walked to the centre and, dragging his shovel, turned as he marked out a circle. This was to be the first hole. Then began the process of breaking into the dry earth to demonstrate that they were working the claim. Having 'christened' the claim, George sent Albert and Jack off to find somewhere to set up camp while he and Robert began the great adventure.

Initially they examined the surface soil in case there was

anything of interest under a rock, scraping back the turf to see if there was any easy gold caught up in the roots. After about an hour, Robert saw something glinting and called George over, "Is this gold?" he asked, holding up a nugget the size of a pea. "By God, it is" George replied and began scrambling with Robert to see what else he might have uncovered.

Robert placed the pea into a matchbox[5] that he had kept for the purpose. With another half-hour of scraping and sifting, they found more small nuggets and by mid-day had scrutinised the entire claim. They had been walking or working for the best part of six hours and figured that it was time to break for dinner, the sun now past its zenith and even their modest effort had them both sweating with the exertion. As if on cue, Albert and Jack appeared carrying some mutton and coffee and a billy with some tin cups.

"How goes it?" Albert called out.

"Fair to middling" George replied with a grin and Robert added, "We've found gold!".

They both rushed over and Robert opened his match box and poured out four peas of gold – at £3 an ounce, worth perhaps £25 – as much as Robert made in a year as a farm labourer. Albert 'whooped' with delight and Jack threw his hat in the air with excitement. "Let's 'ave some dinner and we can get organised" George broke in and the four men were soon sitting around a camp fire, under a sheltering gum tree toasting some mutton on sticks of loose brush and boiling the billy, the sun beating down. The meal was accompanied by the regular slap of hands on faces, arms and necks to ward off the flies and biting insects.

They were excited but George calmed them down, "We've been lucky, but that's the easy stuff finished. We're gonna start hitting rock soon. Hard as iron rock. We need to dig out this hole and with luck we'll find more and bigger nuggets or gold flakes that we can dig out of the rock or when we wash the dirt away. We'll take turns digging; one of us will fill the buckets with dirt and take them to the creek where another two of us will be rocking the cradle and feeding it with water and panning the remains in the cradle for gold. We'll take turns about doing the different jobs. Alright?"

"Alright!" they exclaimed in unison.

"Well" George said, getting up off his haunches, "Jack, Robert, you haul the first bucket loads of dirt; fill 'em up and follow me down to the creek and I'll show you what's what" and with that he walked over to their claim, handed a shovel to Jack and picked up the cradle, "Albert, you can get on with the 'ole while we're gone. It's the easy part right now. The 'ard yakka[6] comes when we gets to the rock".

They were perhaps a quarter of a mile from the creek and George strode away while his two companions quickly shovelled dirt into their buckets and followed him.

At the creek, George set up the cradle and when Jack arrived, he told him to pour a load of dirt into it, which he did. He told Robert to empty his bucket and fetch water – which was easier said than done as the creek had dried up into puddles and there were already dozens of men dredging buckets along the bed. But he did the same and returned with a bucketful of muddy water which he handed to George. "Now rock this cradle from side to side while I pour the water over the dirt".

So the process began. The water and the dirt without larger rocks (which were trapped in the sieve) fell onto slats in the cradle. The slats and wooden strips on the bottom of the cradle (called riffles) would catch the heavier gold nuggets and most of the flakes while the sand, soil and clay sludge was washed away.

Finally, the fine earth and gold flakes (if any) remaining in the cradle were separated out in a panning bowl, the water being washed with the dirt over the side by swirling it around gently, leaving heavier flakes of gold that were picked out one by one and carefully stored in their matchboxes.

That done, the process began again and again and again…

IT WAS DIRTY WORK, the clay soil caked on their arms and faces, mingling with the sweat. But, to Robert's delight, at the fourth attempt panning the fine dirt, he came across a flake of gold about one quarter the size of a fingernail and he called excitedly for George to look at it, " I think I've got a nugget of gold here" he called out and George stopped what he was doing to come over and look.

"Right enough, that's just what it is" he said as he examined it, "Fingers crossed there's more to come".

Robert whooped with joy and George patted him on the back, "Let's not make too much of it, Robert. If that's all we find it won't be anything to write home about and we don't want anyone around here thinking we've found anything special if and when we do".

Robert looked over his shoulder and took the warning to heart but nevertheless couldn't stop grinning through a muddied face as he got back to work.

At the end of the day they had accumulated several flakes and two very small nuggets of gold that weighed perhaps six ounces in addition to the nuggets Robert and George had found at the start of the day. At the going rate, that was worth about £12 each. And all that from just one day! With dusk approaching, they all returned to their camp with aching backs, weary but encouraged.

That evening, they were drinking tea and cooking damper[7] over a fire to eat with some fatty mutton that they had bought at the diggings from a vendor who had charged an extortionate price. Albert and Jack's hands were bloodied with their pickaxe and shovel work, blisters burst. They had cleaned themselves up as best they could and had bandaged their hands. Robert and George had escaped this problem, they were both used to such labour and their hands were well-hardened to the task.

"We need to keep a look out for the traps[8]" George commented as he stirred the fire with a stick.

"Are they are problem?" Robert replied, "I mean, a special kind of problem here".

"We're supposed to get a mining licence and if we don't they'll fine you five quid[9] or you can find yourself chained up or on a road gang. They're all bloody lags[10] and they can be proper bastards – just in it for themselves - so best we don't cross 'em".

"How much is a license?" Robert asked.

"Thirty damn shillings a month although they're trying to raise it to £3 a month"

"Between the four of us?"

"No, each"

"Fuckin' hell!" Albert replied, "Thirty shilling even if you don't find anything?" "Yeah. It's bloody unfair which is why 'alf the Diggers don't get one. At least not until they've found their ridge[11]" George replied, then added, "Mind you, the Diggers are 'aving none of it. Before Christmas last there was a meeting near the Commissioner's tent of more'n a thousand protesting against it and getting up a petition, even swearing they just wouldn't pay it. So it's still one pound ten, at least for now".

Robert mused on this as they chewed their supper. He certainly didn't want to fall foul of the police but it just didn't seem fair that they had to pay this tax; £6 for the four of them. He would just follow George's lead he decided and hope to have everything straight before the traps came around on a license hunt. In the meantime, they'd keep an eye open for trouble and be ready to scarper[12] until the coast was clear again.

OVER THE BALANCE of the week they worked tirelessly on their claim. Usually the panning produced a few flakes of gold but they also found more small nuggets. The cradle had to be washed thoroughly frequently because the clay would sink into the riffles and create a smooth surface, allowing the gold to wash away. But, like everything, the more they practised the better they became at the task. They were now driving through rock and the jar of the pickaxe as well as the blistered hands made for an unhappy initiation for the two brothers. On the fourth day Jack arrived back from the creek with a wheelbarrow, "I figured it'll be easier using this than buckets to get the dirt to the cradle" he explained, "And I got it cheap, only three pounds". They all agreed that it was a good idea and it certainly improved their productivity.

They used the gold to buy supplies and equipment and after ten days took their remaining gold to the assay office in Bendigo and received the princely sum of £10 9s 6d each for their trouble. From this, they grudgingly purchased a mining license and, with coins jingling in their pockets, looked at each other wondering what to do next.

Robert had never had as much money in his pocket before and he was constantly conscious of the fact, keeping his hand in his pocket and rubbing the coins together over and over again and patting his pocket where he had several pound notes stashed away. The privations of camping out, the discomfort, the aches and pains, the bites and stings, the smell with the lack of sewerage, all this was worthwhile.

He was eager to get started again but George was clearly not as motivated and as they stepped into the dusty path, he put his arm around Robert's shoulder, clapped Albert on the back and urged them all to have a drink before they made their way back. Robert felt that he couldn't object after all George had done and in truth a beer would go down very easily.

They went to one of the stores and George purchased some beef jerky and tobacco. As the storekeeper was totting up the bill he asked, "Anything else?" and George responded, "D'ye 'ave any liquor for sale?"

The storekeeper looked sideways at them and answered, "Not for sale, I don't[13]. but I've some patent medicine if you're thirsty, it's ten shilling a bottle". "We'll 'ave one each" George said and, with each of them paying for their 'medicine' they walked out of the shop clutching their bottles. Once outside, George opened the bottle and took a swig before offering it to Robert, who did the same and passed it on to Albert, who repeated the process and passed it to Jack. Although it was poor quality grain whisky and watered down, it was a welcome kiss on parched lips.

As they made their way back to camp, the sun slipping below the hills, they all downed more than perhaps they should have done but they made it without mishap and, feeling much less vulnerable with licenses in hand, Robert made up a fire. Then, with the night falling, the fire crackling and a contented buzz from the sly-grog, they told jokes, passed on news they had heard until eventually they crawled into their 'beds'. Exhausted after the day's effort, and despite the yelps and snarls and barking of innumerable dogs, the shouts and drunken laughter that floated across the hills, the tramping of hobbled horses, the croaking of bullfrogs and the discharge of what sounded like a thousand pistols, they were soon snoring under their blankets.

* * *

THEY QUICKLY FELL INTO A ROUTINE. They started their work at the break of dawn and finished up each day about half-an-hour before the sun disappeared over the horizon. For perhaps an hour the diggings were relatively quiet, if it could ever be called quiet, with dogs roaming the diggings and the volleys of gunfire, which was almost a tradition amongst the Diggers.

During this time the fry-pan would be put to work on an open fire and everyone saw to their tea.

After this, the Diggers began to settle down, usually in front of a campfire with a pipe of tobacco and listening to or telling stories sitting on logs in front of the camp fire. These logs, with their bark stripped to ensure no centipede or other insect could attack, were arranged between the campfire and the Diggers' tents. It would not be unusual to have half a dozen to a dozen familiar faces sitting on the logs, enjoying their pipes and chatting about past experiences and future hopes. Sometimes the stories became very "spicy" and at other times there could be earnest debate or raucous laughter from a well told story or practical joke.

Every tent had its campfire. And with thousands of Diggers on either side of the creek, Robert had once imagined that two tongues of fire were licking their way along the creek each night. As the night wore on, the firelight reflected in the Diggers' faces as they contentedly drew upon their pipes and cheroots.

Although liquor could not officially be sold, this was no hindrance to its availability and most every night a drunk would fall into a hole making his unsteady way home. Indeed, perhaps the hardest thing Robert found to ignore when trying to sleep was the loud swaggering talk, unrestrained laughter, swearing and general excesses of the drunks splitting the night air which could easily spill over into an unco-ordinated flailing of arms and legs that passed for a brawl between two or more inebriated Diggers. Late at night, with fires dying down, in the darkness they would blunder into mine holes, trip over the logs (which provoked drunken oaths), relieve themselves on the tents, alarm every dog within hailing distance and too, it was not unusual to hear the drunken wails of someone crying out for help and directions. The usual response was a discharge of a pistol to scare them off, which further added to the disturbances.

And the stream of hopeful Diggers from around the world kept arriving.

The back of the license added rules and regulations:

- *Regulations to be observed by the Persons digging for Gold, or otherwise employed at the Gold Fields.*
- *Every Licensed Person must always have his Licence with him, ready to be produced whenever demanded by a Commissioner, or Person acting under his instructions,*

otherwise he is liable to be proceeded against as an Unlicensed person.

- *Every Person digging for Gold, or occupying Land, without a Licence, is liable by Law to be fined, for the first offence, not exceeding £5; for the second offence, not exceeding £15; and for a subsequent offence, not exceeding £30.*
- *Digging for Gold is not allowed within Ten feet of any Public Road, nor are the Roads to be undermined.*
- *Tents or buildings are not to be erected within Twenty feet of each other, or within Twenty feet of any Creek.*
- *It is enjoined that all Persons at the Gold Fields maintain and assist in maintaining a due and proper observance of Sundays.*

DECISIONS

Bendigo
1852

The Bendigo Creek Diggings continue to be the most productive, yielding a much greater quantity of gold, and with much less labor than any of the other Diggings. Number of persons who have arrived in the colony this week : 1016, Number of persons who have left: 297, Addition to our population this week: 719.
Argus, Melbourne, Monday, 26 April 1852

* * *

ROBERT CONTINUED WORKING the claim until late March. It was hard, very hard work with sultry hot weather settling on the toiling men. The trees had by now mostly been cut down and the barren plain was a succession of countless gravel pits with the heads of men popping up and down from their holes. The air was filled with the sound of cradles rattling their stones, the harsh metallic clang of pick and shovel at work, the busy ceaseless hum of so many thousands. Innumerable tents stretched into the distance, including stores with large flags hoisted above sporting the lion, the unicorn, the Russian eagle and other devices.

The summer drought had added to the hardships with clean drinking water at a premium and increasing food prices. But still they persevered and still hundreds of people arrived every day like swarming ants looking to find somewhere to pitch their claim. After five weeks, Robert told his partners that he needed to get back to Mary Ann for a short while and they agreed that while he was gone they would retain any gold they found for themselves and would keep working the claim.

Reluctantly but with a sense of accomplishment and, for the first time in his life, real hope, Robert made his way back to Merri Creek - a wealthier man.

* * *

As HE WALKED UP to their cottage on McCallum's farm he could hardly contain his excitement. The thought of seeing Mary Ann again and of holding his boys filled him with a delightful sense of anticipation. The thought of sleeping in a real bed too was something to savour. But most of all, being able to show Mary Ann the money he had made, vindicating his decision to go to Bendigo, filled him with a certain pride.

"It's Daddy!".

George had seen him coming and he rushed out of the trees with James following, arms and legs pumping to make up the ground. They both leaped at him, one into each arm, and he hugged them tight, luxuriating in the unconditional expressions of joy at welcoming their father home. Mary Ann heard the commotion and came to the door of the cottage with William at her feet. She saw Robert and the boys the same time as William who took off, running with his little legs driving like pistons and crying out, "Daddy. Daddy!".

Mary Ann broke out in a huge, grateful, happy smile and she waved at Robert whose hands were too full to wave back, but he too was smiling and laughing at the antics of his boys who were now competing for attention.

In a few strides he was at the door and he put the boys down to embrace Mary Ann. They hugged for a moment, wordless, as if he had been gone a lifetime. It was of course the first time that they had been parted and the reunion was all the more emotional for that reason. Despite the children looking on disapprovingly they kissed. A long, needy kiss, holding each other tightly, urgently. Reunited again.

Robert disentangled himself and held Mary Ann at arms-length. She looked only at him for a moment before saying with a wry grin, "We need to get you into a bath!". With Mary Ann leading the way, holding Robert's hand, the family went into the cottage.

Mary Ann busied herself making Robert something to eat and drink while the boys questioned him about what he had been doing and where he had been. Robert took great pleasure in talking about the busy town of Bendigo and how the Diggers went about finding gold. That naturally led to Mary Ann's question, "And what did you find, Robert?"

He went to his hip pocket and pulled out several pound notes and then to his trouser pocket to pour shillings and sixpences and pennies and halfpennies on the table in a jingling, tumbling waterfall of money. Mary Ann stopped in her tracks. She had never seen so much money before, "Robert! Did you rob a bank?"

Robert laughed, "This came from our claim at Bendigo. There's more than twenty pounds here and that's just the beginning". Mary Ann sat down and began counting the notes. The boys wanted to play with the coins but Robert stopped them,

"Go outside and play, boys. Your mother and I want to talk a bit. And close the door on the way out".

The boys reluctantly left them alone and they heard the sound of James and George challenging each other to a race as they closed the door.

"What do you think Mary Ann?" Robert asked.

"Think about the money?" she replied

"No, the claim. I can earn much, much more on the gold-fields – at least while it's still young. I have to go back before it's completely swamped by fortune hunters".

Mary Ann looked up at him. She really didn't want to move on. They didn't have much here but it was home and a move with a baby and three boys would obviously be difficult.

"Are you sure it's the right thing to do?" she asked.

"I've already earned more in six weeks than I could earn in a year on the farm, even after the costs. And we haven't even struck a big find. This is just from bits and pieces. If we find something big we could really be set up".

"Who's 'we'?" she asked and Robert told her about George Wilson and Albert and Jack and how they were working the claim while he was gone.

"It's rough, but we can make camp there, I'll build up a slab hut for us so we'll be alright. I can work at the diggings and you can look after the children and keep everything neat and proper for us. I've got enough to buy a horse and a cart to get us over there and sell it at a profit once we're there. Let's give it a go, Mary Ann. I think it's worth the risk. There will always be work on a farm if it doesn't work out. But what if it does?"

Robert's passionate pleading couldn't be denied and Mary Ann finally nodded her head and said, "Seems like you've got it all worked out, Robert. Alright, let's do it. But first fings first. Time to shave that beard off – it spoils an 'andsome face - and get you into a bath, you smell!".

That night Robert and Mary Ann put the boys to bed a little

later than usual because of all the excitement and then, after sitting around the fire and talking further, they made their way to bed. Robert sank back into the straw mattress and sighed. It had been too long. He pulled Mary Ann to him and she looked down into his face and kissed him as he ran his fingers through her hair. The physical effort, the tension, the excitement, the fear, the hope – all had exhausted him and before he knew it, almost immediately, he had closed his eyes and was fast asleep in her arms.

Mary Ann kissed his brow, pulled the blanket up over his shoulders and laid back on the bed. Her mind was turning over what the future might bring. She was sure that many hardships lay ahead but that was the way life had to be lived, wasn't it? At least it was unless you were one of the nobs or somehow ran into a lucky strike. And maybe they would. With these thoughts buzzing around in her head she closed her eyes and tried to sleep.

* * *

OVER THE FOLLOWING few days Robert and Mary Ann were busy organising their move. They had broken the news to the boys tentatively, unsure how they would take it, for they had made friends with some of the locals, but the thought of their own horse and a journey to a fabled land (as Robert described it) quickly won them over. McCallum wished them well and offered that 'There'll aye be a place back here on the ferm if things dinna work oot" and they were off before dawn, on the road with all their meagre belongings in the cart, James sitting up front with his father and Mary Ann and the boys sprawled in the back, sitting on the few belongings they owned, all covered by a tarpaulin that would double as a roof or a groundsheet when they camped, braced against the jolting of the wheels over the rough ground.

. . .

THE JOURNEY in the cart was slower than walking because of the state of the road. Robert kept eyeing the sky with threatening clouds in the distance, hoping they could make it before the rains came because this track would turn into a quagmire if it did and then what? It took them a strenuous two days and they were within reach of the Black Forest by nightfall.

Finding a place by the road to settle, they slept rough in and underneath the cart with a fire burning nearby, which the boys heartily endorsed as a great new adventure. Robert made sure that the wheels were properly chocked and that there was no danger of it moving or collapsing on those underneath. A bed of brush and leaves under canvas and unstitched flour bags stretched on top of all served as a mattress and blankets which provided some elementary ability to stay warm during the night.

The next four days followed the same pattern before they reached Bendigo Creek itself. Robert hobbled the horse and secured the family in a wood, bark and canvas-roofed shelter on a rise above the creek that he spent the rest of the day constructing about half an hour away from the diggings. It was very simple but they had a roof over their heads for the night and he would improve on it over the coming weeks. It gave them somewhere to sleep. While he had been doing this, the boys had built a small stone fire-pit for cooking.

It may have been rough, but many lived a lot rougher back in London thought Mary Ann. It was enough to get them started. She set about making the place liveable as best she could while Robert went over to the claim to let his partners know that he was back.

He approached the creek with a little trepidation, half worried that they would not be there but he needn't have worried. He found them working away beside a hole that had grown wider and now more than six feet deep and he shouted out his greeting as soon he saw them. George looked up and returned the wave, "About time you came back, you bugger, you're missing all the fun!"

Robert told George that he had brought his family with him and that they were staying in a hut about half an hour's walk away. He asked how things had been going and George advised that they had broken through the rock and confirmed that they had continued to make small finds and that other Diggers on the goldfield had discovered sizeable nuggets too, "Now we're through the rock, with any luck we'll find the good stuff".

He wanted to get to work straight away but they agreed that Robert should take the day to get his family settled, sell the horse and cart and return after this to get started once more. Clapping George on the shoulder and bidding Jack (who was in the hole) good luck, he left the claim in an enthusiastic frame of mind.

Preparations for wintering on the ground started to become evident with slab huts and stores being built on many of the rises above the creek. Forty tents housed the government officers, police and soldiers and the strong log lock up was complete and had already housed its first 'residents' – a distinct improvement from chaining men to logs, especially with the colder winter nights in prospect.

COME MAY, with chilly winter approaching, the rain began to fall accompanied by blustery winds. Heavy driving rain in sporadic showers hammered down on the diggings saturating the earth, flooding excavations, softening the ground – all actually welcomed by the Diggers who relished the long-desired opportunity for intensive gold washing. Diggers could be observed running with abandon in every direction with cradles, puddling tubs and tin dishes to work the mountains of earth stored up besides every pitch. However it was less welcome on the road north which was becoming almost impassable, with the consequent impact on supplies. Prices of even the most basic of items like flour, rose alarmingly.

Excitement rippled across Bendigo Creek in mid-May after Diggers nearby discovered several large nuggets and, as the news spread, a rush started with hundreds more men arriving with spades, buckets and hope. With the new find, Commissioner Gilbert relocated his camp to a ridge overlooking the creek, almost in the centre of the valley. The news made Robert even more sure that it was only a matter of time before they too struck riches.

Digging continued, turning the flats into hollows and mounds that struck Mary Ann as resembling a vast cemetery with yawning graves awaiting the bodies of thousands. Even with the Diggers' vicious, unending attack on the valley, buttercups and snowflake-like small flowers timorously fought back and took hold here and there, cautiously poking their heads towards to the sun before a digger's spade or pickaxe struck once more. It was a slaughter of the greensward but William managed to pick a small bunch of the sporadic wild flowers and brought them back to his mother with a sheepish grin. Mary Ann hugged him and found something to hold them, cherishing the gesture.

Robert and his partners continued with their steady toil, moving to a different location when their hole appeared to have become exhausted, and while never making a big find, they were doing well enough. Robert could look after his family, pay the license fee and even add to their savings.

And Mary Ann soldiered on. She took charge of Robert's share of the gold and the money, doling out pocket money to Robert each week. She was thankful that Robert wasn't a gambler or heavy drinker – unlike his friend, George who was a bad influence in her opinion. And the children were coping. James, George and William made themselves useful – if there wasn't work to do at 'home' they would make pennies turning the smith's grinding wheel or carrying and fetching or standing guard or they would play with other children at the diggings. James would also help out at the cradle at times.

At home one night, the children abed, Robert and Mary Ann went for a short walk, "What's gonna 'appen, Robert?" she asked.

"What d'you mean?"

"I mean 'ow much longer are we gonna be doin' this?"

"Well, I don't see this as a job for life" Robert replied, "We just need to make enough to set ourselves up, then we can decide what we want to do and where we want to do it"

"And what do you wanna do, and where?" Mary Ann asked, looking up at him, his eyes glinting in the reflection of campfire light above a shaggy beard that was the mark of a seasoned digger.

He turned the question around,"What do you want?"

Mary Ann had indeed been thinking about this very topic. The enticement of sudden riches let most people on the gold-fields indulge in flights of fancy and she had thought about returning to England perhaps. Then she had wondered whether she really wanted to go back to that life.

"I don't want us to be 'ere wiv the nippers forever. Maybe get back on a farm wiv clean air, a clean 'ouse and somewhere for James and the others to build a life?"

"If we struck it big, we could get a ship back home" Robert said with a lack of conviction.

Mary Ann bit her lip then replied, "Would you really wanna go back? I mean, do we want that life again? At least 'ere we can be what we wanna be, we can be really free, can't we?"

Robert stopped walking and took her two hands in his, "Yes. We can be really free. If we strike a seam we could make enough to even buy our own land, build our own farm. The sky's the limit".

Mary Ann squeezed his hands and laughed. A tinkling, happy sound that made Robert's heart melt.

"Then that's what we'll do" he said with finality and the two of them continued walking, thinking their own thoughts.

RED RIBBONS

Bendigo
    1853

ON 18ᵀᴴ JANUARY, 1853, Governor LaTrobe announced that the township would be called Sandhurst but, notwithstanding its shiny new name, the new year broke with drought, causing problems for all. The four of them struggled to wash their gold deposits with the creek now a trickle and drinking water too became a precious commodity, often requiring a long walk to fill a bucket and bring it back home.

Then the drought broke and now the diggings became a muddy quagmire. But life went on and sometimes – perhaps to alleviate the stresses and strains or boredom of life – strange things happened…..

The Diggers numbered in the thousands. They came from everywhere and countless tents lined either side of the creek. The dominant nationality was English and, with Queen Victoria's birthday coming up on the 24ᵗʰ of May it seemed that a spirit of competition had been sparked with each tent striving to create a bigger bonfire than its neighbour to celebrate the event.

English emigrants had been dragging parched gum branches from the bush to heap them into bonfires until, as sunset neared, many, many tents had an enormous pile ready to be set alight. Robert observed the scene around him but saw little sense in wasting a day's work and, like the 'foreigners'; the Irish, French, German, American, Chinese and others saw little reason to celebrate the birthday of this remote figure who headed a system that had caused him and his wife so much pain.

George shared his view but Albert and Jack entered into the spirit of things and on the Sunday afternoon before the great day they too piled up wood and brush in readiness.

On Tuesday the 24th, after the sun had slipped below the horizon and night had begun to spread its dark wings, the first gunshot echoed across the hills and thousands of bonfires flamed to life with the accompanying roar of fire seizing hold of dry logs and the machine gun rattle of burning tinder-dry gum leaves. Jack ignited their bonfire and it blazed merrily, the heat searing their faces and the flames creating ruddy reflections on the four diggers as they toasted each other and "the Queen". Robert felt it would be churlish to refuse the toast, but his heart wasn't in it.

Only the sullen tents of the foreigners remained in shadow creating dark gaps amongst the ribbon of light leaping along either side of the creek.

* * *

ROBERT HAD CONTINUED to improve their 'home' and they were now living in a two-room slab hut with a canvas roof, reinforced with bark and a side addition used for storage. They even had a very rude fireplace set against the wall with a clay and stone chimney. Tins were kept clean and bright as silver, four sacks had been sewn together to form a rug on the floor, and they had even acquired a mastiff named Bull who was normally tied to a long chain to add some protection. His bark was worse than his bite, but he had a fearsome bark!

The furniture consisted of a bed for Robert and Mary Ann and two more for the children. They were improvised stretchers about 12 inches above the ground made from opened-out flour bags nailed onto a frame of saplings resting on forked sticks sunk into the ground. Pillows were flour bags stuffed with eucalyptus leaves, feathers and worn out clothing. Each bed had two plaid blankets to keep in the body heat as they slept, although in the winter this was hardly adequate. The beds also served as sofas to sit upon and the remains of a wooden crate served as a table.

Mary Ann would wake first about 4 o'clock - light of dawn or the chill in winter would be her alarm clock. She would re-stoke or start the fire, coaxing the embers to life with a match and a combination of dry kindling and a patched up bellows that James had acquired from a smith for whom he had been working.

While she was doing this, James and George would go to the creek to collect fresh water (if they left it any later it would be a brown soup, muddy from the gold-washing). On Sundays, they could do it later because there would be no work on that day, but otherwise the creek quickly became a turbid slurry as the Diggers got to work. The boys took it in turn to empty the chamber pots every morning (or the 'gazzunder' as everybody called it), walking as far away from the tent and the creek as possible, usually tipping the effluent down a disused miner's hole.

Like many others on the goldfields, they had become accustomed to the underlying taste of eucalyptus in the water and Mary Ann had even started soaking gum leaves in the water before boiling it to flavour the tea. If finances permitted, they would have a little sugar added too. At first, when money had been really tight, it was not unusual to make 'Jack-the-painter' tea - a humorous name for 'tea' made from just boiled gum leaves.

Their morning meal would usually be porridge mixed with a mutton broth from dinner the night before – a recipe that she had gleaned from a Scotch woman in the Camp. She would also put the dough made the night before onto the fire to bake a hot damper to go with the breakfast. Sometimes they would have mutton chops or steak instead of porridge. They never saw eggs – there was nowhere for chickens to feed.

As the diggings awoke the clear blue sky turned a cloudy grey as thousands of camp fires struggled to take hold with damp and green wood.

Breakfast over, tin plates would be cleared away to be washed and Mary Ann would attend to other chores – including the daily task of making the dough for the damper.[1]

James and his brothers had also been given the task of establishing and maintaining a small vegetable garden (with Mary Ann's oversight) and they would help with other chores such as collecting water from the creek and tinder and logs for cooking or to set a fire during the winter months. They would also accompany Mary Ann into the growing township of Sandhurst to buy food and supplies at the stores on Camp Street – a path that followed the line of the creek bed - and help carry them back home.

The stores were set up near the Commissioner's compound, a ten acre site enclosed by a two-railed fence that also housed the Government post office, the Adelaide Escort office, Police magistrate's court, Officers' quarters, Pensioners' barracks etc..

These stores were actually large tents, square or rectangular, and most everything required could be obtained (if you had the money). The goods were all crammed together in no particular order; from sugar-candy to potted anchovies, from East India pickles to Bass pale ale, from ankle jackboots to a pair of stays, from a baby's cap to a cradle and every apparatus for mining from a pick axe to a needle. And all accompanied by confusion, noise. So much noise.

Walking around Mary Ann would see a pair of dripping herrings hung above a bag of sugar, a box of raisins, a bundle of ribbons beneath a couple of tumblers, bread and yellow soap, pork and currants, saddles and frocks, blue serge shirts, green veils, baby linen and tallow candles – all heaped indiscriminately together and surrounded by bawling children, swearing men, wary storekeepers and a surprisingly large number of women now, gabbling twenty to the dozen.

Most of the storekeepers would also buy gold either for cash or in exchange for goods and it was important to make sure that you were not being short-changed. Mary Ann had seen shopkeepers weighing parcels separately on the excuse that the weight would be too much for the scales and then, on adding up the grains and penny weights, the sellers would often 'lose' at least half an ounce of gold in the reckoning.

On one occasion, she had heard, out of a seven pound weight one person had lost an ounce and three quarters in this manner and, of course, there were a multitude of other ways to cheat including resting glass pans on a piece of green baize which itself was sitting on a wet sponge to add to the weight, thereby requiring more gold to level the scales. It was common for examiners of gold dust to grow long fingernails and, running their fingers about the dust, to gather some of it up under these fingernails.

There was a general perception that nine-tenths of the men

were honest and industrious while the other tenth were outcasts and transports; often described as 'the refuse of Van Diemen's Land' – even though Robert could by no means be compared to such. It was this black history that she sought to keep hidden and which governed Robert's interactions or lack of such with government officials and police.

Although the government would license a respectable public house on the road, it absolutely forbade the same on the diggings to eliminate the sale of spirits and wild behaviour. Mary Ann felt that this typically officious, short-sighted view produced the opposite to that intended with illegal sly-grog sales fostering unlimited drinking and riotous behaviour. A situation that would have been avoided with effective regulation.

* * *

WITH ROBERT WORKING the claim during the day, Mary Ann would pack him some damper and mutton from dinner the night before to take with him and she and the boys would have dinner on their own - usually mutton, boiled potatoes and at times onions or carrots. On Sundays, they had also dined off parrot or possum - which made an interesting change - and Mary Ann would also make a plum duff[2] for 'afters'.

Once a week, first thing, Mary Ann would do the laundry in the creek and the boys would help hang it on a line to dry. They would also buy grain and grind it themselves and there was always sewing, darning socks and mending tears in clothing, and knitting.

Unfortunately, James was no longer able to go to church school to improve his reading and writing as such community support just didn't exist, but Robert had bought James his own bible to practise his reading. Sometimes, of an evening, James would slowly read stories from the bible to the family who all sat enraptured at this young prodigy, enjoying the images of the walls of Jericho tumbling down and suchlike. The other boys, however, didn't have the patience to learn from James and besides, if Mum and Dad couldn't read or write, why should they bother?

Other nights, if Robert wasn't too tired after a full day working the claim or blowing a cloud[3] with other Diggers, they would sing songs or hymns that they had learned with Robert playing a comb and paper and the boys banging sticks on pots as accompaniment. They all really enjoyed those nights. Well, they tried, although the mosquitoes, ants, fleas and centipedes that haunted the night did their best to spoil the fun and the preventative remedies, such as burning cow dung or eucalyptus leaves at their door or Robert puffing energetically on his pipe were sometimes almost worse than the problem.

While the politicians, police and military went about their business, Robert continued to make a living from their small finds, and added to their savings, but still nothing substantial to make a real difference – especially with a monthly mining license to pay, which was increasingly being viewed by the diggers as an imposition too far.

And early in the new year, Mary Ann fell pregnant again.

* * *

THE MONTHLY FEE was causing real hardship on the Victorian goldfields and a groundswell of frustration and even anger was building about not just the fee but perhaps even more the arbitrary and repressive enforcement by way of regular police license hunts.

Victoria had seceded from New South Wales less than a year earlier and there was a feeling that the newly independent government should do more for those they served. It was seen as unfair that the fee was payable regardless of whether gold was extracted; it was bureaucratic and unwieldy and it was just too high, particularly given the lack of basic amenities and the inadequate protection provided with increasing lawlessness, robbery and claim jumping.

The perception of justice not being served also inflamed passions. It was impossible to escape the regular harassment of the traps on their 'License hunts'.

From 1852, the Diggers had been constantly harassed, arrested and persecuted. Troopers would appear without notice and summon the miner with the order to "Show me your license you Digger dog". This could happen several times a day. They would be arrested if they couldn't produce the paper on demand even if they were bathing or when the license wasn't actually on their person but a few yards off in a shirt pocket. Upon being arrested, the miner was typically handcuffed and chained to the trooper's horse then dragged to a rude cell or chained to a log for the night, sometimes being thrashed en route with the flat of the trooper's sabre.

* * *

LATE IN MAY printed placards began to appear on gum trees advertising a meeting that would take place on the first Saturday in June – they advised that 400,000 people would be thrown upon the colony in twelve months and it asked the question: "What is to become of them?" the placards also advised that Captain Brown of Sydney would address the meeting. The question on the lips of many was, "Who is Captain Brown?" and nobody knew.

Around the same time, at another smoke-o in front of a campfire with perhaps half a dozen others listening to stories and exchanging salacious jokes, talk turned to the meeting and the mysterious Captain Brown and then to the license fee. "I dunno about four 'undred fousand people arriving in Victoria but I do know sommat 'as to be done abaht the license" one of the hard-bitten crew commented as he spat out some tobacco. Another responded, "Unless the Guvner cuts it there's gonna be trouble, that's the rights of it".

Robert listened attentively and murmured his agreement, "It ain't just the cost" he added, "What about paying it every three months instead of each month? It's a whole day away from the claim to sort out their bloody papers".

"What abaht not paying nuffin'" another responded.

"Yeah, that would stop the traps. It just ain't right the way they pester honest Diggers" another added. His companions all vociferously expressed similar frustrations.

On the Saturday advertised, the diggings awoke to a day of rain and winds which had the effect of dampening the spirits of would-be protesters but Captain Brown addressed the few agitators who did turn up and they agreed to reschedule the meeting to the following Saturday at View Point, Bendigo when it was anticipated the weather would be kinder.

About six or seven hundred turned up at that public meeting, generally in good order, and Captain Brown revealed himself to be a witty, eloquent Irish-American. Rightly concluding that there was more interest in discussing the Poll tax affair (as he described the license fee) and that it would be folly to mix this question with the 400,000 new arrivals, the meeting was adjourned to consider these matters on Saturday, 25th June at Fifth White Hill and word spread around the Bendigo diggings rapidly.

On the 25th about 1,200 turned up, including Robert and George, and a lively meeting ensued. Captain Brown was in the chair and he proposed four resolutions:

- *1st. That In the opinion of this meeting, the prospective increase of population demands some energetic legislation to prevent an extensive pauperisation among the Diggers.*
- *2nd. That, as a consequent of the squatter land monopoly, the chief field for the development of labour is the diggings, a reduction of the licence is imperative.*
- *3rd. That the most legitimate means to obtain a reduction of the Licence, is by petitioning the Executive: a committee be appointed to frame one, subject to the approval of the Diggers.*
- *4th. That as it is desirable to secure the co-operation of our brother Diggers in this movement, an abstract of the proceedings of this meeting be sent to the colonial press to secure the fraternisation of the other Diggers at the various goldfields of the colony.*

There was loud, unanimous support for the resolutions and noisy condemnation of the police harassment of the Diggers in pursuit of an unjust tax. It was agreed to meet again the next Saturday to read out a petition to be sent to the Governor. Robert left the meeting a little hoarse with all the shouting and cheering as he was swept up in the general fervour.

On Saturday, 2nd July, at two o'clock, another public meeting was held on Fifth White Hill with Captain Brown again taking the chair (as Dr Jones[4] – the President of their recently formed movement - was unable to make it owing to a conflicting business engagement).

Captain Brown rose and eloquently reiterated all that had been done thus far before turning the podium over to George Thomson, a 27-year old firebrand Scotchman from Coupar Angus in Perth who had studied law and been active in the Chartist[5] movement before emigrating to the goldfields the year before. He continued firing up the crowd with powerful calls to end injustice.

Robert stood in the crowd, which must have been more than 2,500 strong, and felt his emotions flaring with a sense of injustice. His mind flashed back to the 'Swing' protests in Burwell and his unearned imprisonment in Cambridge and he yearned to do something to fight the system.

Dr Jones then climbed onto the stage and apologized for his late arrival. He then assumed the chairmanship and stated his objections to the present licensing system, "I am against it on two grounds. First, it is without question excessive. Does it not bear alike on both the fortunate and unfortunate Digger? And is this fair?" The meeting voiced its agreement with a multitude of cries and oaths before he quietened the gathering, "And second, it requires the armed power of the Government to collect this tax, a power that is exercised with brutality and against all the rights you have earned as free men going about your daily business. No, I am for the complete abolition of this penurious tax that creates misery and stultifies endeavour – my friends, it is simply not necessary in the present advanced and civilised state of the goldfields!"

The meeting roared its support with throaty chants of "No more mining tax" and "No taxation without representation" from a contingent of American Diggers, echoing their grandfathers' cry that won America's independence, before he called for calm and continued, "Even if this unjust tax were to be reduced by one-third it would still require extraordinary means to collect it but, notwithstanding my views, I acknowledge that complete repeal may not be practical or wished for at this time and, if that is so, if that is the wish of the thousands of Diggers on the goldfields of this colony, I would go along with it because I believe the time is fast approaching when this iniquitous tax will be swept away anyway."

Captain Brown then followed him, agreeing totally with the Chairman. He spoke passionately of the hardships endured by the Diggers, of their exposure to an inhospitable climate, of their frail huts and tents, on the ruinous cost of food and supplies because of the bad state of the roads. "And who is responsible for this? Why, it's the Government who wring a tax out of every honest man and then do nothing to earn it!"

He sat down amidst the voices of hundreds, perhaps thousands, expressing their determination to fight for their rights with cheers and fists held high. Many of those present wore red ribbons in their hats to express solidarity and they waved them wildly to reinforce their support.

Dr Jones stood again, called for quiet and read the proposed petition[6] to the meeting. It contained basically the same demand to reduce the license fee and calls to justice and fairness.

Throughout the reading it had been mostly quiet, interrupted at times by shouts of support where a particular clause caught the imagination and when he finished Dr Jones rolled the parchment up and tied it with a green ribbon before handing it to a man behind him.

He then called on any person in the meeting who wished to speak to do so, which saw a German Digger by the name of Gooble mount the platform and address the crowd in both German and English.

He called on his countrymen to raise their hands – they amounted to perhaps a hundred – and he went on in a strongly accented tongue, "My countrymen are ready with rifle and sword, ready to assist our English friends in this colony to stand up for their rights. All Germans here will do their duty, for if the English submit to this evil poll tax they cannot surely be part of the glorious English nation which rules the destiny of the world".

Several other speakers earned cheers of support with similar calls to duty when some traps made their appearance escorting an inebriated Digger between the Hills. When the crowd's attention was drawn to this their passions rose further and they began hissing their displeasure.

Then a few, then many more, perhaps a thousand in all, began charging down the hill onto the alarmed constables with wild whoops and angry shouts, some waving clubs in the air and all exhibiting a fury that promised vengeance. The constables looked once, looked at each other, then bolted for safety leaving their prisoner to the mob.

Order being restored, it was announced that they would meet again Saturday next at two o'clock and there began the process of many of those in attendance signing their name or their mark on the petition, including Robert who gave his name as William Bright, not wanting to risk future trouble if this all turned out the wrong way.

A subscription was also raised amounting to £30 to fund continuing agitation. The crowd gave a wild three cheers for Jones, Thomson and Brown and then it was adjourned with the Diggers streaming away in every direction, energised, animated and spoiling for a fight.

Robert returned home and sat down with a mug of tea that Mary Ann had boiled up on his arrival. He relayed the events to her and she, in turn, recalled her own experience of a public meeting all those years ago in Finsbury Square. She also recalled the dreadful public hanging she had witnessed and cautioned Robert against putting himself at risk. Her very obvious concern and agitated manner registered with Robert. He would weigh his actions carefully, he assured her, "Don't you worry, Mary Ann. I know I have responsibilities to my family".

FOOTNOTE:

The petition ended up being signed by 31,000 but Governor La Trobe replied that the he was "satisfied the diggers are mere grievance mongers. I know my duty, and I will do it at all risks. If the Diggers trouble the Government much more, I will let them hear how cannon can roar." He also dispatched more soldiers to Bendigo and the raids became more intense.

On the 27th August a mass meeting of some 10,000 Diggers took place at the present day Rosalind Park in Bendigo and many in sympathy wore a red ribbon as a badge, which gave the protest its name – the Red Ribbon Affair. At a meeting on 28th August shots were fired and then on the 30th August La Trobe appeared to cave in when he announced that he would abolish the licence system and replace it with an export duty and a small registration fee. He also suspended the license for September, which took a lot of the heat out of the protests for the time being.

EASIER PICKINGS

Bendigo
1853

IT WAS a few days after the meeting that George arrived for work a little later than usual and told Robert, Albert and Jack that he was giving up working on the claim, "I'm off. You're welcome to the claim, but there's better ways for me to make a living". Robert was surprised and urged George to stay on, as did Albert and Jack, but he was not for turning.

"What are you gonna do?" Robert asked.

"I ran into someone I know a few weeks ago and he's got sommat in mind"

"Anyone I know?" Robert asked, intrigued.

"I don't think so. D'you remember meeting Joe Grey the other night?"

Robert couldn't remember him and shook his head with a drawn out "No, don't think I do".

"Well, he's putting sommat together and he's asked me to join him. It's not anything that you would want to try with your family and all and anyway, you'll be able to keep everything to yourself now".

Robert, with Albert's and Jack's support offered to pay for those tools that George had contributed to the partnership but George would have none of it. And with this rather off hand, evasive and mysterious brushing away of their queries they parted company.

THE PRIVATE ESCORT CAPER

❦

*M*ia Mia
20th July, 1853

AN OFFICIAL GOVERNMENT gold escort service had been established to transport the gold from the goldfields to Melbourne but, in keeping with the entrepreneurial times, a private gold escort company had also been established which operated with rather less security but offered greater speed and less bureaucracy. The *Melbourne Gold Escort Company* provided a regular escort from the McIvor[1] diggings about 30 miles from Robert's claim, to Melbourne.

On the morning of 20th July, 1853 Superintendent Warner with Sergeant Duins, four troopers and a driver set out from the McIvor goldfields to Kyneton where it was to meet up with the regular Bendigo escort and continue on to Melbourne.

The sun was climbing into a clouded blue sky and all seemed well with the world as the party made their way from the gold-fields, a horse-drawn cart rumbling along with its cargo roped and secured on a bed of straw and troopers stationed either side and to the front and rear of the gold wagon..

At about the same time, further south, a group of seven men armed with pistols and muskets pulled up their horses soon after they had crossed over the Campaspe river on the way to Kyneton. The spot they had chosen was just past a bend with a hill on one side and the Mia Mia creek on the other. The group was led by Joe Grey and included George Wilson. They dismounted, felled one tree and scouted around for other loose branches, pulling the largest ones with some effort across the road to block any oncoming traffic. Once they were satisfied that the barrier was impassable, Grey ordered two of the men to hide behind the screen and two to watch for the escort up the road with instructions to ride back and warn them when they appeared. The rest of the group remounted and road back up the road about thirty yards to hide themselves on the hill over-looking the track amongst the trees, ready to block a retreat.

A half hour later, the scouts appeared and signalled that the escort was on its way. Grey called for silence. The gang pulled up woollen comforters or scarves that they had wound around their necks to disguise their faces and checked their weapons. It wasn't long before they heard the rumbling sound of a wagon, the jangling of harness, the neighing and drumbeat of horses coming up the road.

Sergeant Duins was leading the way and as they rounded a bend he saw a tree felled across the track, blocking the way. The hairs on the back of his neck rose and he looked anxiously around, "Halt" he cried, holding his right hand up and restraining his horse with his left. Grey decided to seize the moment and stepped out, shouting, "Put down your weapons! Put down your weapons, I say! Instead, before Duins could do or say anything, one of the troopers opened fire.

The country air was immediately split by the thunderclap

fury of gunshots and the thwack of bullets as they thudded into covering trees. For Grey and his men, the troopers were easy targets and they were quickly cut down, one trooper shot in the neck as he was trying to unstrap his carbine, another who lay injured and pinned down by his dead horse and three others lying prone with gunshot wounds. Warner and Duins struggled to control their panicked mounts and continued to exchange shots with the gang.

When Warner's horse was shot in the jaw he disengaged and then he and Duins urged their horses at the barricade, seemingly the least defended obstacle, trying to break through as best they could while shots flew by like angry wasps. Two bullets hit the flank of Duins's horse as he cleared the barrier and guided the injured animal away from the ambush. George Wilson and John Francis (one of the other men) now mounted their horses and galloped after the two escapees, shouting wildly for them to surrender.

But Duins and Warner were having none of it and instead turned and fired at their pursuers, although the distance was too great to have any effect, and they disappeared from sight. The quietness of the countryside reasserted itself with gunsmoke hovering amongst the box trees, its acrid smell polluting the air.

It had just taken a few minutes. Wilson and John Francis slowed and walked their horses down the road gathering up all the dropped and discarded firearms they could find before returning to the scene of the gunfight.

Meanwhile Grey and the other men had carried the boxes of gold from the dray into the bush so that they were hidden some twenty yards off the road. They broke the boxes open and began to hurriedly empty the gold into paniers. Wilson and Francis rejoined the gang in the midst of this rapid, urgent activity. They all worked in silence, breathing heavily. In the process some of the men discarded tin pannikins to make room for the gold. As they would later regret, tin pannikins with their names etched on them.

One of them, William Atkins, broke the silence, "D'ye think we killed any o' the troopers Joe?"

"Can't tell, Bill. And we don't have time to check them out with those two buggers escaping. They'll be bringing men back in short order. Let's just get this bloody well done and be on our way".

Once the gold was in hand, they threw all armaments in the river except for their pistols, these being more easily concealed, then all remounted and set off at a gallop before settling into a steady pace across country, travelling about seven miles that day and camping in the bush that night while a hue and cry was being raised across the countryside.

By the light of a campfire they divided the gold as evenly as they could and arranged for two of their party to keep watch through the night in turn. Grey was particularly worried that their pursuers might be using dogs or black fellahs to track them; he had seen how good they could be before, so he wanted to keep moving as fast as they could without exhausting their horses.

The following morning they continued, passing the second night by the side of a river on Mollison's Run before moving off in the same direction, always keeping to the bush, avoiding the road and potential search parties. The next night they camped out in the bush again, this time near Kilmore, and then on the Sunday morning they split up at Rocky Water Holes, making their individual ways to Melbourne or elsewhere.

Some of them, including George Wilson, had arranged to meet again at John Francis's house at Collingwood Flat by Melbourne. The plan was to then buy a passage to England on one of the many ships calling in at the entry point for the Victorian gold rush. The others made off on their own, intending to melt into the bush and the colony as best they could. George Francis (John's brother) returned to the diggings, hoping to lay low and escape attention.

* * *

ACROSS THE GOLDFIELDS there was an uproar. An extensive search was organized with Diggers from adjacent goldfields joining in, worried about the effect this would have on their fortunes, all looking to apprehend the gang. The sense of outrage and the fear inspired by the hold-up spread like wildfire across the colony. Not only was this escort at risk, but every other, and there was already resentment that runaways and ex-convicts were at large – especially from Van Diemen's Land now transportation had ceased.

There had already been another theft on the St. Kilda and Brighton Road as well as £30,000 stolen from the barque, *Nelson* while moored at Williamstown and although three men had been arrested, the gold had never been recovered. And now the Melbourne Gold Escort Company had been robbed. It was all too much. The government offered a £2,000 reward, the Escort Company added £500 and the police began rounding up miners for questioning.

* * *

AT THE BEGINNING of August two policemen appeared at Robert's claim, one an aborigine, the other a grizzled ex-convict, as Robert was shovelling dirt into the wheelbarrow. Albert and Jack were at the creek. Robert didn't notice them at first but as they announced themselves, Robert thought they must be checking on his license so he went to his pocket to pull it out for inspection.

"Oh no you don't!" the policeman with the gun called out

and raised his musket, taking aim at Robert standing below him at the side of the creek. Robert had no idea what was happening, but froze, "Don't you want my license?" he asked.

"You keep your 'ands where I can see 'em and come over 'ere" the policeman ordered.

Robert put his shovel down and clambered up the bank towards the policemen who backed away as Robert came closer.

"Empty your pockets"

Robert did as he was bid, the license being the only thing to show.

"Now turn around and put those 'ands up"

Robert did as he was bid, becoming more and more confused and more and more concerned with what was happening.

The aborigine now came up to him and patted his pockets and under his arms while his companion kept his musket trained on Robert before telling him to put his hands down, "We're gonna pay a visit to the Commissioner's office" and with that statement he pushed the muzzle of his Enfield musket into Robert's back, driving him towards the track that led to the rapidly growing centre of township activity on the ridge over-looking the creek.

They arrived there twenty minutes later, Robert none the wiser as to what was happening because the policeman had refused to answer any questions and, indeed, had cuffed him around the ear, drawing blood, with the instruction to "shut up and keep walking'. He was roughly pushed into what passed for the police office and bundled into a small room where he was told to sit down and be quiet. The door shut and he waited.

It was a good half hour before the door opened again and a small, balding man wearing a brown check suit and a black cravat entered, followed by Robert's captor, still holding his Enfield with his finger on the trigger.

"What's your name?" the bald man asked.

"Robert Bright"

"Let me see your license"

Robert pulled it out, looking at the guard as he did so to make sure there was no untoward reaction. He opened it, placed it on the table and smoothed it out.

The bald man examined it without saying a word then pushed it back to Robert.

"Where's George Wilson?"

Robert furrowed his brow, "I don't know"

"So you admit you know the man?"

"Yes, he worked the claim with me until a few weeks ago"

"Don't come the innocent with me, Bright. You two are partners"

"We *were* partners until he took off more than a month ago" Robert replied.

"And where were you on the 20th July?"

Robert looked confused, "Probably working my claim. I can't remember what day that was, but I'm always on the claim or in town getting supplies or at home with my wife"

"We know you and Wilson are working together. Stop playing the fool and tell me where he is"

"I tell you I don't know, I haven't seen him for weeks now. He said he was going off to do a job with someone called Green or Gray or Grant or something like that"

The balding man sat back in his chair and examined Robert through slit eyes, then pulled out a pipe and began filling it. He took his time, then put a match to the tobacco and drew a deep breath before puffing out a cloud of smoke.

"Last time, Bright. Come clean or it'll go badly for you"

Robert protested that he didn't know what this all about, that he had no idea where George Wilson could be and that he had done nothing wrong.

The balding man turned to the guard, "Lock him up. We'll see if a night in the cells improves his memory" and with that he looked hard at Robert and exited the room. The guard told Robert to get up and he marched him out and down a hallway to a door guarded by a turnkey who opened it with a jangle of keys then took Robert by the arm, pushing him into a cell already occupied by two other men.

Robert stumbled into the cell, straightened himself up and said, "Bloody 'ell. These pigs just can't leave us alone". One of his companions ignored Robert, he just sat on a bench in the corner examining his grubby fingernails. The other had been watching the entrance and said with an Irish accent, "Sean O'Neill, welcome to the cheapest hotel in town". Robert introduced himself but he was in no mood for levity and just paced up and down for a few minutes trying to figure out what had just happened.

He had heard of the robbery – you would have had to be deaf and blind not to - and he put two and two together figuring that George must have been involved, which explained his evasive departure, but that didn't help him. What could they do? Charge him as an accomplice without any proof? He knew full well that justice was a fragile commodity here especially with his record as an ex-convict from Van Diemen's Land almost condemning him out of hand.

O'Neill cut in on his thoughts, "Take the weight off your feet man, no point worrying; what will be will be". O'Neill was a larger than life character. At least 5' 10" tall he had a shock of unruly ginger hair, a ginger beard that had not seen a razor or scissors for a long time and a powerful frame. He looked like a man you would not want to mess with, yet his personality was so easy-going it was hard to imagine why or how you would cross him. Everything to him seemed to have a positive side and the hiccups and pitfalls put in his way were but temporary misfortunes likely to be corrected the next day.

In Robert's frame of mind, O'Neill's unwarranted optimism grated and made him even more anxious and angry at the injustice of it all. As night began to fall Robert started worrying about Mary Ann and the boys. He presumed that his mates would have heard about the arrest and hopefully they would have let Mary Ann know. But what would they do then?

Albert and Jack however had also been arrested and were being held in a separate cell and Mary Ann was beginning to wonder where Robert was, although she wasn't too concerned as occasionally he was late home if he stopped for a smoke-o with other Diggers. But when she had put the boys to bed and the midnight hour arrived she knew something was wrong. She spent a very restless night.

She woke early and busied herself with making breakfast after which she instructed James to go to the diggings and ask around to find out where his father might be. She was in no physical shape to be running around herself, being advanced in her pregnancy, and she needed to look after the other boys. James ran off, pleased to be entrusted with such an important task.

He returned a couple of hours later with the worrying news that his father had been arrested by a policeman and taken away in the direction of the Bendigo township. He hadn't been able to find out anything else so had decided to come back home and report.

Mary Ann dropped everything and placed her hands on James's arms, looking him in the eye, "Yer a good boy, James. Well done. Now I 'ave to go to town. I want you to stay 'ere and keep an eye on yer bruvvers. I won't be more'n two or free hours, maybe four. Can you do that?" James nodded his agreement and Mary Ann told the other boys that James was in charge while she was in town and she wanted no trouble reported when she returned. She then left the hut with a heavy heart and made her way slowly up to the ridge at the centre of the valley to Commissioner Gilbert's camp, hoping to find Robert, or at least news of him.

When she eventually arrived at the police office, in some distress, she asked after James and was told that yes, Robert was in gaol for questioning but that no charges had been laid yet. She asked to see him but was told by the duty officer that he would need to speak to the detective first and he wouldn't be back for another two or three hours. Mary Ann decided to wait, James would be able to look after things a little longer.

Robert was taken back into the interview room about mid-day. He had no idea that Mary Ann was a few paces away behind the wall. The detective entered again. This time without the guard.

"So, Bright, what do you have to tell me?" he began.

"I told you yesterday that I have no idea where to find George Wilson and I have no idea what this is all about, why am I being kept here?"

The detective sighed then asked again, "Where were you on the 20th of July?"

Robert grew exasperated but asked, "What day was the 20th July?"

"Saturday"

Robert thought hard. He recalled going into town to pay for his monthly license about that time, he had had a good few days in the middle of the month and had decided to buy the August license early as a result. But was it the 20th? He didn't think so.

The calm of the office was suddenly broken by the sound of a woman shouting and the duty officer trying to reason with her. Robert knew that voice. It was Mary Ann!

"That's my wife!" he exclaimed. "What are you doing with her here? She's almost due. You should be ashamed of yourself!".

The detective seemed to be taken aback and told Robert to wait while he went to see what was happening. He came back a minute later with a tear-stained, red-faced, clearly angry Mary Ann in tow and held the chair for her to sit down.

"You have ten minutes" he stated and then left the room.

They both spoke at once, reaching out to hold hands across the table. Then Mary Ann asked, "What's going on? They won't tell me anyfing".

"They seem to think that I know where George Wilson is. I think they believe he was involved in the Mia Mia robbery. But what are you doing here? You shouldn't be out and about in your condition. And what about the boys?"

Mary Ann told Robert that she was at her wit's end when he didn't come home and she had been told that he might be here so she came to help. As they spoke he told her that they wanted to know where he was on the 20th July.

"When was that?" Mary Ann asked.

"It was Saturday, three weeks ago"

Mary Ann considered, counting back in her mind the events of the last few weeks then she sat up excitedly, "That was the day you and James went into town for me 'cos I wasn't feeling up to it. I remember 'cos the Sunday before we 'ad gone to church and met Mrs. Callaghan and she came round on the next Saturday to see 'ow I was getting' on".

Robert recalled it now, "And that means that the shopkeeper should remember me and if not, then Mrs. Callaghan would because she was still there when we got back".

The door opened and Mary Ann stood up to face the detective with arms on her hips, "You wanna know where Robert was on the 20th July? Well 'e was shoppin' for me in town and Mrs. Callaghan also saw 'im at 'ome that afternoon. Tell 'im, Robert!"

The detective looked crestfallen but replied, "We'll check out the alibi". Then he opened the door and said, "You can go, Bright. Take your good wife home. But don't leave the diggings. We may have more questions and if you hear where Wilson is hiding you'd better let us know immediately if you know what's good for you".

Mary Ann flounced out of the door with an, "I should think so, too" over her shoulder and Robert followed, eager to get away and to return home. It wasn't until Robert returned to the claim after seeing Mary Ann back home that he caught up with Albert and Jack who had also been released shortly after him.

AFTERMATH

⬥

*M*elbourne
August-October, 1853

THE DISCARDED tin pannikins with names engraved on them were discovered at the scene and led the police to some of the culprits.

George Francis stayed on at the diggings and he, like other miners was arrested and later released but his behaviour aroused suspicion and the police followed him. The rest of the gang took different routes to Melbourne.

On the 10th of August, Melbourne police arrested John Francis and his wife on board the ship *Madagascar* in Hobson's Bay and George Wilson and his wife were arrested the following day. They also arrested George Francis the same day as he too was boarding the ship and, under interrogation, he agreed to give evidence against all the gang in return for his and his brother's freedom.

On 23rd August, clearly regretting snitching on the gang, George Francis committed suicide by cutting his throat.

While the death of the Duke of Wellington on the 14th of September captured the imagination of the whole British Empire, the Melbourne police were busy capturing other Private Escort gang members. George Melville and his wife were arrested on board the barque *Callooney* and William Atkins and his wife, who had booked a passage on the *Hellespont,* were arrested at a boarding house in Melbourne.

A total of £250 10s 0d was recovered from those arrested in bank notes, sovereigns and bank drafts in addition to seven bags of gold. However, the bulk of the gold was never recovered and the rest of the gang, including Joe Grey were never found. Grey had been in Melbourne but, unlike his compatriots, moved to a different address every day so was not apprehended and was able to escape, perhaps to Adelaide.

George Melville, William Atkins and George Wilson were all charged with the murder of Thomas Flookes and sentenced to death. They were publicly hanged on Monday, 3rd October 1853 before a large crowd and the bodies handed over to their families.

Having turned Queen's Evidence, John Francis and his wife were given free passage out of the colony to begin a new life in Cape Town.

* * *

FOOTNOTE

Mrs. Melville decided to make some money from the situation and arranged to put her husband's body on public display. She decorated it with flowers and ribbons and displayed it in the window of an oyster shop on Little Bourke Street, charging 2/6d to view it. The police swiftly heard about this act of entrepreneurship and reclaimed the body, returning it to Melbourne gaol where it was buried together with other executed criminals.

After this, the policy was changed and instead of being returned to their family, all subsequent executed prisoners were buried within the grounds of the gaol.

ELIZABETH

Bendigo
1853

WHILE THE CLOSING stages of the infamous robbery were being played out in Melbourne, Mary Ann went into labour. James was dispatched to alert Mrs. Callaghan and she and another neighbour arrived soon after to oversee a short, successful birth while Robert and the boys went for a walk amongst the trees, having been banished by a pair of well-meaning, officious but unofficial midwives.

Robert and the boys returned a couple of hours later with a rabbit that they had caught in a trap and Robert told the boys to stay back as he poked his head around the door, "How is it?" he called and was answered with a command to come in and greet the birth of his first daughter.

He stood at Mary Ann's side. Her brow was greased with sweat, her hair damp with loose strands plastered against her face and her face was red with the pain and exertion of childbirth. She held the swaddled baby in her arms and smiled wanly up at James. He sat down and kissed his wife on the forehead before tenderly pulling the blanket back a little to examine the wonder of a new-born babe. He smiled and said softly, "Well done lass, well done". Mary Ann attempted an exhausted smile and Robert said, "She's beautiful. What shall we call 'er?"

Robert and Mary Ann had played with names during her pregnancy, with Elizabeth and Sarah being the unconfirmed alternatives but they had not reached a conclusion, hoping not to prejudice the chances of a daughter by picking a girl's name.

"I think you need to make that decision, Mary Ann" Robert added while he continued to look at the infant.

"Well then, let it be Elizabeth, after your Mum, and our next daughter will be Sarah, God bless 'er, after mine".

Robert nodded his agreement absent-mindedly, his attention absorbed by the bubbles on the baby's lips as she gurgled contentedly. Their family was growing: James, now 10; George, 8; William a rumbustious 5, Benjamin, 2 and now Elizabeth. Another mouth to feed but also a daughter. He felt at ease with life for a moment.

"Enough of this". Mrs. Callaghan intervened, breaking the spell. "The mother needs her rest and the baby wants to sleep. This is no place for a man right now. You leave her with us". Robert didn't argue. He kissed Mary Ann again and smiled as he rose and left the room to tell the boys about their new sister.

NEW YEAR'S EVE

❦

*B*endigo
1853

THE INFLUX of prospectors had continued with a steady stream of people from Van Diemen's Land and New South Wales but also from around the world including Britain, Ireland, Holland, Germany, France, Poland, the USA and China.

News of the Australian gold-rush had reached China the year before – the country had been suffering from years of war and famine and the chance of digging money up from the earth was a powerful lure. Villagers borrowed for the fare and their wives and children stayed behind to provide payment 'in kind' if they were unable to repay the loan.

At the goldfields they kept to themselves and worked together in large teams - some worked the claim, others were responsible for cooking or growing vegetables. But unlike most new arrivals, they generally chose to work abandoned claims where alluvial gold finds had declined, collecting remnants that had been missed before. They also worked at other jobs in and around the diggings, such as washing clothes, selling vegetables they'd grown, selling cooked food or herbal medicines and so forth. As it ever was, their differences made them targets for abuse and discrimination. Bare-footed, pig-tailed, strangely clothed, carrying bamboo poles with heavy loads strung at each end and practising a 'heathen' religion - it all created unease.

One day Robert witnessed an all too familiar sight of a sailor arguing with a Chinaman by a claim. It quickly became violent and ended with the sailor's arm around his victim's neck while he cut the Chinaman's pig tail with his knife. This accomplished, he pushed the unfortunate man into a muddy hole to shouts of acclaim and laughter from the onlooking crowd as he held his trophy aloft. Robert turned away. Such rough-housing was not at all uncommon and although he was more than capable of looking after himself, he made sure that he steered clear of such pointless violence if he could. There was too much else to achieve and, being a transport, he was never sure about how he would be treated by the police. Better safe than sorry was his motto.

With George gone, the three men had teamed up with another digger that Robert had met some weeks before, William Begg, who had arrived at the diggings fresh from Scotland, green but hopeful.

As the flood of new prospectors arrived, fields were opened in quick succession - then, as holes were worked out, the diggers moved from gully to gully – Golden gully, then New Chum, almost simultaneously Tipperary and Spring Gully were pegged out and fully occupied. The discoveries at Long Gully, California, Eaglehawk, Devonshire and Peg Leg[1] had been opened in quick succession.

Eaglehawk Gulley, Bendigo, 1853

At first claims were worked over superficially, hurriedly washing the soil with tub and cradle and, because there was not much water, inevitably a considerable quantity of gold was left in the soil. Now the diggers were returning to previous diggings, this time teaming up to buy or hire a puddling machine to do a more thorough job.

Like everyone else, Robert and his partners had been moving from gully to gully as each hole played out, but they had stayed with the rich Eaglehawk field to the north-west of the Commissioner's compound in Sandhurst. Because these gullies contained a highly plastic, grayish-white clay soil – known as pipe-clay - it was hard, manual work with a spade or pickaxe. So they took note of the appearance of horse-drawn puddling machines that were being used to go over 'played out' holes, and they noted with interest the success others were having in making new finds and how much less effort was required. They began to think about possibly adopting the new technology themselves.

* * *

AFTER SWELLING with new arrivals through the year, it was noticeable in the run up to Christmas that the number of miners working the gullies actually fell as they left Bendigo to spend time with friends and family or to chase after a new find at Bryant's Ranges, twenty-four miles away.

Robert and his partners stuck to their task though, even today, a Saturday - which had been a particularly warm day. The intense heat had sapped energy and, adding to the general discomfort, the mosquitoes and little stinging flies had been particularly aggressive. William Begg had also been afflicted by the scourge of the goldfields, an infection in the eyes that had tormented him to the point where he was unable to see, unable to work. Whether it was caused by the dust or the sand flies or some other insect, no-one seemed sure but Mary Ann had fussed over him, cleaning and bathing his eyes with boiled water and a zinc sulphate ointment prescribed by a doctor at the camp, although the expensive ointment (at £5!) didn't seem to do much for the poor man and it was simply rest and time that produced a cure in reality.

Even though life was hard, there was also a time and a place for entertainment and, today being the 31st December and the Sabbath tomorrow, tonight was the time to do just that. It was George's ninth birthday today, so they would mark that when he returned home with a simple celebration, and then Robert was taking Mary Ann out on the town.

They had finished up early, about three quarters of an hour before sunset and, squatting by a waterhole, Robert had vigorously scrubbed the dust and mud off his body and face before returning home to watch a glorious sunset with Mary Ann. After they had finished their tea, Robert waited for Mary Ann to 'pretty' herself and then, kissing the children goodnight and instructing James to watch over them all, Robert took Mary Ann's arm and they stepped into the cooling evening breezes heading for a gathering nearby in the growing township of Sandhurst.

They arrived as a makeshift band struck up a tune. Albert, Jack and William were already there and Robert and Mary Ann joined them to the accompaniment of hugs and kisses for Mary Ann. The 'band' had between them fashioned triangles from a meat-hook, a horse-shoe and a spoon to ring out a 'melody'. They were accompanied by a penny tin-whistle and a dish-bottom drum. The voices of the bandsmen added to the cacophony, which was joyful if not musical and the crowd joined in to add to the festivity. Tonight, there was also a travelling band of notably untalented musicians to expand the repertoire.

Although officially prohibition was enforced on the goldfields, liquor was easy to come by. One particularly fat woman was particularly popular – as her girth was caused by strapping a tin 'hot water bottle' container under her clothes from which she dispensed brandy through a tube for a shilling a go. Others could be seen wandering with a kettle, pretending it was tea, but actually dispensing grog, and others had brought their own flasks. Robert and Mary Ann were no innocents and the release of inhibitions were a salve to the hardships of life.

The band struck up a mazurka[2] and Mary Ann dragged Robert onto a makeshift dance floor where other couples and some miners without female partners were cavorting. Albert and Jack among them. They joined a circle of dancers and began energetically cavorting themselves, stamping their feet more or less at the right time, clicking their heels with wide grins on their faces and throwing their arms in the air with abandon. The music ended and they left the floor to sit on one of the logs scattered around, breathing heavily.

Mary Ann's unrestrained laughter made Robert smile too, seeing a young girl come alive, throwing off the weight and burdens that had dogged her across the years, and his heart felt very full. He took her in his arms and gave her a long, tender kiss before disengaging and whispering in her ear, "I love you". Mary Ann looked hard into his eyes, "I love you, too Robert. I really do". For a moment the world around them fell away, the music stopped, the heat of the summer night framed a world in which only they existed.

And then the sounds and the gaiety returned and they both laughed together, almost embarrassed by their intensity.

They stayed long enough to see in the new year, singing 'Auld Lang Syne' lustily with a bunch of Scotch and English Diggers, which brought tears to Mary Ann's eyes as she thought of her mother and family on the other side of the world. But she kept her thoughts to herself and just hugged Robert extra close as they kissed to celebrate a new year of hope before making their way back to their slab hut, hand in hand. Robert's thoughts too had dwelled on his family and the 'green and pleasant' land of England as they brought in the new year, but he kept his thoughts to himself.

As they walked past the diggings and into the gum trees, Robert began to muse on their future, "I've been thinking Mary Ann. I haven't had much luck on the claim of late and I'm thinking of trying something new. Even the Chinese are digging next to me now and if that isn't a sign that the gold is running out where we are, I don't know what is".

He went on to explain that he'd been discussing possibly breaking new ground and perhaps acquiring a puddling machine to improve the yield. He was also beginning to wonder whether they should move on to one of the other goldfields in Victoria like Clunes or Ballaarat or closer to home at the nearby Kangaroo Flat[3] diggings, which sounded promising, or should he find work on a farm again because, with the allure of easy money on the goldfields, it had become more difficult to find labourers and farm wages had consequently increased.

Mary Ann listened carefully but was loathe to make a decision. They had a home of sorts, rude though it was, their little vegetable garden was producing, the children were settled and, while it was far from ideal, it was their place and their life.

"I fink we should sleep on it, Robert. You 'n me 'ave 'ad a drop or two and this needs a clear 'ead. It'll be clearer in the light o' day".

And with those words of wisdom, the hut looming up ahead in the darkness and the branches and leaves cracking and rustling under their homeward-bound footsteps, they put the matter aside and made their way to bed after tucking James in, who had fallen asleep while he was on watch.

PUDDLING

*K*angaroo Flat
1854

R<small>OBERT</small> <small>WOKE</small> early that Sunday morning. As it was the Sabbath, no-one worked the diggings so the day would be spent attending the local 'church' with the children, who would attend a rowdy 'school' alongside the service. The church was a tent set up by a Presbyterian minister, who dug for gold himself during the week. Afterwards they would attend to chores around the hut, mending, tending the vegetable garden, spending time with the children.

He and Mary Ann had agreed to return to their discussion of the previous night after dinner when the children would be out of the house at play.

Robert and his partners had heard of another major discovery at Kangaroo Gully, about three hours south of his current diggings and that yet another gold rush was under way. They had been talking about moving off their current claim, which had not yielded anything of note. "We can get in at the beginning rather than scratch for the leavings of others" Robert explained enthusiastically.

"Will we 'ave to move?" Mary Ann asked.

"Until we know that it's worth it, I can either camp out there during the week or walk there and back – I should be able to do it in, say, three hours. We're also looking at getting a horse to drive a puddling machine, so I could ride him there and back".

"I dunno Robert" she began, "Suppose, when you get there, it's all just a rumour? Can you trust what you've 'eard?"

Robert accepted that he had only heard about this by word-of-mouth but there was no reason not to believe it and surely the opportunity to get in on the ground floor was worth taking the risk when Kangaroo Gully was really no distance at all?

They continued in this way for another thirty minutes before Mary Ann accepted that his heart was set on going and, ever the pragmatist, she agreed that it was worth exploring the potential if they didn't have to set up a new home immediately. Robert was excited. Gold fever had been reignited and he resolved to set off the very next day.

* * *

IN THE END, Robert was only away for two days and he returned full of enthusiasm, "Must be a thousand or more there already" he gushed, "But there's still plenty of land that hasn't been broken yet. They're digging up nuggets the size of apples, Mary Ann. This big!" and he bunched his fist to show her, "William and Albert have pegged out our claim and I'm gonna speak to someone here to get a puddling machine set up and a horse to work it".

"If we strike it rich we can finish up here and buy some land to farm, what d'you say?"

Mary Ann looked at Robert sideways, "That'll be right" she

laughed ironically. "Good luck 'as always followed us so why should this place be any different?"

Robert looked pained and replied obstinately, "I know it's a risk but nothing ventured, nothing gained and it has to be better than scraping a worn out bed after all".

She accepted the strength of that argument and, in truth, the options as she saw it were either to go back to labouring on a farm (which was still a reasonable possibility with wages of maybe £25 to £30 a year on offer, although it offered no more certain employment than digging up gold) or striking out on another gully and she had to admit that the chances of fortune smiling on them were greater at the beginning of a rush than at the end. Robert was probably right. She took Robert's face in both hands, smiled and said, "Let's do it. Let's make a fortune!"

Robert kissed her hard, wrapped his arms around her and swung her around, much to the amusement of the watching children who started laughing at their antics.

* * *

ROBERT and his partners pooled their savings and bought a horse that Robert named Bess as well as a small cart on which he loaded the iron fittings that they had bought for the puddler. At the site they would fell a tree, saw slabs to line the hole or collect bark if that was easier and bore a hole in the stripped tree to make the puddler arm. His iron fittings would provide the central fulcrum on which the arm would turn. Then they would use slabs of wood or bark to line the hole.

It was clever but quite simple: they would make a circular trough in the ground into which they would pour water to mix with the clay. The horse would then be led in a circle pulling the puddling arm which dragged a harrow through the clay mixture. This would break up the soil into lumps and turn it into a runny sludge. Any gold would be released from the clay

Horse-driven puddling machine

and sink to the bottom. The watery clay would then be drained off from the top and the residue on the bottom of the trough cleaned up with a pan or cradle to collect the gold.

It took them a week to set everything up and when it was finished there was a real sense of accomplishment and anticipation as Robert took Bess's bridle and the harrow began digging into the clay bed. It was a darn sight easier than using a shovel, Robert thought.

At the end of the first two weeks they knew that it was going to work. They had found gold, not a lot, but enough, and the deeper they went the more they would find if the experience of others was to be believed. It was still dirty, back-aching work, especially the panning of the sludge after the harrow had done its work. But there was no question that they were more productive and the likelihood of missing gold was substantially reduced now that they were able to totally break down the clay.

* * *

However, there was much more than working their pitch going on around them. Despite saying that he was going to reduce the license fee, Governor La Trobe had reneged on his promise when he could not get the Victorian Legislative Council to agree to his proposal and this betrayal of trust added to the simmering discontent on the goldfields driven by heavy-handed policing.

It was later that year, in November, while Robert and his partners were relaxing around a camp fire that they heard about more trouble. A man they had never seen before had arrived from the Ballaarat field seventy miles to the south and he relayed the story of a murder at the Eureka hotel. Apparently a Scotch miner, James Scobie, had been killed by the hotel owner, a James Bentley. Everyone knew he was guilty but he had escaped the noose because he'd bribed a magistrate. The Diggers erupted, forcing Bentley and his wife to flee for their lives as his Eureka hotel was burnt to the ground even though the Commissioner, a man named Rede, and his troopers formed in a line in front of the hotel with swords and guns drawn to protect them.

But this had only inflamed passions further; an egg was thrown at Rede, bottles, stones, sticks and missiles followed, the sound of breaking glass encouraged more aggression and soon the hotel was ablaze at the back corner, the fire fanned by a dry wind. The police tried to save the building but the fire would have its ravenous way and, beaten, they retreated in some disorder.

A little later that month three miners were arrested and charged with arson even though two of them had been nowhere near the fire. This inflamed the sense of injustice prevalent amongst the Diggers further and the outrage resulted in a mass meeting of four thousand where they decided to form a Diggers' Rights Society to protect them from arbitrary justice.

Another miner then relayed another story he had heard recently from Ballaarat. "Apparently the servant of a local priest went to a nearby tent to visit a sick man. While he was inside a rough-looking trooper on a license hunt comes galloping up to the tent and shouts, 'Come out here, you damned wretches!' The servant, a hunchback, came outside, and he's asked if he'd got a licence. He was a foreigner, so didn't speak good English, but he tries to explain that he's a servant to the priest, not a miner. This just riles the trooper who gets angry and shouts, 'Damn you and the priest' and he dismounts to drag the servant along with him. The servant protests, says he can't walk over the diggings and this makes the trooper even more mad; he strikes him down, drags him about, tears his shirt and injures the poor fellow so much that all the diggers around start crying out 'shame! shame!'

At this point, Commissioner Johnson rides up and starts to tell the crowd that the trooper mustn't be interrupted in the execution of his 'dooty.' By now the priest himself has appeared and, to calm things down, hands a fiver to Johnson as bail for his servant's appearance the next day at the police-office.

Well, the following morning, the servant's charged with being on the goldfields without a licence. The poor man tries to defend himself, but we know how that's gonna go and he's fined five pounds anyway to the anger of people watching on. So now Commissioner Johnson stands up and changes the whole story, saying that the servant hasn't been charged with not having a licence, but with assaulting the trooper, if you can believe it!

This now changes the case so the magistrate has to call the trooper who repeats that old chestnut about doing his 'dooty,' which really means licence-hunting. A respectable witness then swears up and down on the bible that the servant's innocent and that he saw the trooper strike the foreigner and knock him down.

Well, you can guess the rest, the magistrate didn't give a fig, he'd made his mind up before the trial began, so he bangs his gavel and repeats "Fined five pounds; take him away.

That's justice on the gold fields."

"Isn't it just" Robert replied with a shake of his head and a swig from a bottle.

"So what's being done about it?" Albert asked.

"They've formed the *Ballaarat Reform League*[1] and they're saying that paying taxes if you can't vote for the law is tyranny and they won't stand for it. They even said if things don't change the Queen won't have a colony to govern anymore because they'll go their own way" the Ballaarat Digger replied.

"That sounds like fightin' talk" an Irish voice piped up.

"They mean it, I'm sure o' that" he replied.

* * *

OVER THE FOLLOWING WEEKS, while Robert and his partners continued to work their claim, Mary Ann and the children went about their daily lives and a delegation from the Reform League travelled to Melbourne to negotiate with Governor Hotham about a number of issues including freeing the arrested Diggers, the abolition of the license and democratic representation.

However, rather than negotiate, as soon as the meeting with the Diggers ended, Hotham[2] convened a meeting of his generals to organize direct action to nip this insurrection in the bud. If they wanted a war, they were going to get it, he mused at his desk after dismissing everyone. And he smiled grimly.

PRELUDE

Ballaarat
1854

The coming Christmas is pregnant of changes, for on next Wednesday will behold such a meeting for a fixed, determinate purpose as was never before held in Australia. The Australian flag shall triumphantly wave in the sunshine of its own blue and peerless sky, over thousands of Australia's adopted sons; and proudly will they think on that day that the sky, the earth, the flag, and everything Australian are well worth the price of their deepest devotion. The men of this country, on that day, will look up to the Southern Cross floating above their heads, and, invoking the Genius of Liberty, protest against their countless wrongs — the incarceration of their countrymen, now languishing in a felon's jail — their long exclusion from their own broad and fertile lands — together with the unaccountable prevention from unqualified appropriation, as toil would have awarded, of the boundless wealth with which these lands have been conceived by the God of Nature. And when the loud Paean of :

'Now's THE DAY AND NOW'S THE HOUR, SEE THE FRONT OF BATTLE LOUR.'[1]

280

*shall have pierced the blue vaults of Australia's matchless sky,
from the brave men of Ballaarat on next Wednesday, at Bakery Hill,
there will not be one discordant voice in the sublime and heroic
chorus.*

Ballarat Times, 24th November, 1854[2]

* * *

BALLAARAT HAD BECOME A RUMBLING VOLCANO, and whether it
would remain dormant or explode violently was impossible to
call. A hot wind blew across the Flat at the end of November,
both literally and figuratively. The Diggers' demands were
causing alarums in the colony's corridors of power and a decision was made to concentrate all available military and police
resources at Ballaarat to counter the threat.

The obvious reinforcement of government troops and police
only flamed the passions higher. Notices of a meeting of the
Reform League on Wednesday at 2 o'clock ramped up the
general sense of anticipation.

TUESDAY, 28th November

As troops from the 40th (2nd Somersetshire) Regiment from
Geelong neared Ballaarat, the officer in charge called a halt. The
wagons rolled to a stop, horses tossing their heads and pawing
the ground, soldiers in the carts sitting on ammunition boxes
wondering why they were stopping. The officer ordered the
soldiers in their red tunics out of the wagons and the sergeants
barked out orders to form up in marching order. A stentorian
command of "Fix bayonets" rang out, which was smartly
executed with accoutrements jangling and steel blades glinting
in the sun. "Forward march!"

The soldiers' red coats formed a choreographed phalanx as
they tramped down the main street, bayonets flashing, with the

wagons rumbling behind, their feet kicking up the dust while a hot sun rose in the blue sky. The insulting jibe of "Joe, Joe[3]" from the populace followed them.

Rumours flew about, false news being spread by both sides to influence the population, such as the ring leaders were all foreigners and therefore not trustworthy and conversely a rumour that the delegates sent to Melbourne had all been arrested.

4 P.M.

A detachment of the 12th (East Suffolk) Regiment, arrived from Melbourne. They were passing the burned out shell of the Eureka in their wagons and were trundling by a large number of diggers on the streets. There were more jeers as they passed by, spooking some of the draft horses pulling the wagons carrying soldiers and ammunition. They made their way through the angry crowd but the final wagon was not as fortunate.

Two of the diggers leapt out and cut the traces, then a dozen or more put their shoulders to the wagon and, as if it were a mere feather pillow, heaved it over, smashing it and spilling its cargo of soldiers and ammunition into the road. A swarm of Diggers seized the soldiers' muskets and began beating them with their own arms and seriously injured the driver, leaving him bloodied and battered on the dusty road before being dragged to safety. Bullets began to fly and a drummer boy received a wound in his leg before also being retrieved by his comrades who beat a hasty retreat.

7 P.M.

Some thirty troopers appeared on their way from Bacchus Marsh[4] marching to the bridge. As they marched by, the usual taunts of "Joe, Joe" were thrown at them and approaching the new road the verbal assault turned physical with stones thrown at the unwelcome arrivals. They kept marching until they reached the bridge when the officer decided he had had enough or maybe felt that he could retire across the bridge if needed. He ordered a halt, an about face, and then, "Charge!"

They cut left and right with sabres as they ran into the mostly unarmed Diggers and, with the red mist rising, followed the fleeing Diggers into the tented campsite by the road. A few of the Diggers fired on them with their revolvers and the fire was returned. Fortunately no-one was mortally wounded, but several on both sides were injured. Before he lost control, the officer recalled his men and they made their way back over the bridge to the safety of the Camp. It was a prudent decision, because several of the Diggers had gone back for their own weapons and, had they returned while the troopers were still advancing, the scene could have turned very bloody indeed.

10 P.M.

A squadron of mounted police followed the earlier military, galloping through the main street with a thunder of hooves pounding the hard ground, the officer in charge urging his men onwards as he dug in his spurs. As they tried to negotiate the exasperated populace, the diggers, who by now had been drinking for some hours, really lost their temper and grabbed any weapon available, sticks and stones in the main, and began to rain down blows on the troopers who by now had lost momentum and their formation. Despite sustaining injuries, the battered squadron broke through and eventually made it to the Camp.

Reproduced courtesy Public Records Office, Victoria

WEDNESDAY, 29th November

The town stayed quiet until 2 p.m. when the Diggers began to assemble on Bakery Hill. First hundreds then thousands until fully 4,000 assembled to hear a report back from the delegation that had presented their demands in Melbourne.

Meanwhile, Hotham had ordered all men that could be spared from the 40th and the 12th Regiments to march to Ballaarat. Three hundred men of the 40th and their officers – with their band – marched out of Melbourne that afternoon. With them they took two six pounder cannon and two twelve pounders. Virtually all of the officers and men of the 12th Regiment were dispatched likewise – another body of 300 men. Twenty four sailors from a man o' war in the harbour and twenty marines, as well as fifty horse and the same number of foot police joined them. In all nearly 1,000 heavily armed troops and police were being assembled at the Ballaarat Camp.

At Bakery Hill, history was being made. The sun was on its westward way, darting in and out of scattered clouds as the Southern Cross was hoisted up the flagstaff.

The pole was eighty feet in height and straight and true as an arrow. This was the maiden appearance of the Diggers' standard, displaying itself in the midst of sturdy, self-reliant, armed gold-diggers of all languages, black, brown and white faces, eyes fixed on the standard. One of the men said in a hushed tone, "There is no flag in old Europe half so beautiful as that".

The Original Eureka Flag

Captain Ross[5], considered the 'bridegroom' of the flag, posted himself, sword in hand, at the foot of the flag-staff, surrounded by his rifle division.

Calling the meeting to order, the Chairman, Timothy Hayes, proceeded to put the following resolutions to the assembled crowd:

1. A resolution disputing and decrying the government's insinuation that this was anything but a peaceful, legitimate protest from the 'brave people of England and Ireland'.

2. That a democratically elected central committee be
    formed the next Sunday at the Adelphi theatre.

Before proposing the third resolution, the Chairman halted,
looked up from his notes and addressed the crowd:

"Gentlemen, many a time I have seen large public meetings
pass resolutions with as much earnestness and unanimity as you
have shown this day; and yet, when the time came to test the
sincerity, and prove the determination necessary for carrying
out those resolutions, it was found then that the spirit, indeed, is
willing, but the flesh is weak. Now, then, before I put this resolution from the chair, let me point out to you the responsibility
it will lay upon you" There were cheers of encouragement at
this point, "And so I feel bound to ask you, gentlemen, to speak
out your mind. Should any member of the League be dragged to
the lock-up for not having the licence, will a thousand of you
volunteer to liberate the man?"

"Yes!" screamed the crowd at full voice.

"Will two thousand of you come forward?"

"Yes! Yes!"

"Will four thousand of you volunteer to march up to the
Camp, and open the lock-up to liberate the man?"

"Yes! Yes! Yes!" - the chanting and the clamour was really
deafening.

"Are you ready to die?" he shouted at the top of his voice,
stretching out his right hand, clenched all the while; "Are you
ready to die?"

"Yes! Yes! Yes! Yes!" and the hurrahs rolled across the hill.

This response put the Chairman in such good spirits, that, in
spite of the heat of the sun and the excitement of the day, he
launched into a poem:

> "On to the field, our doom is sealed,
> To conquer or be slaves;

The sun shall see our country free.
Or set upon our graves."

There was great cheering and gunfire and passionate waving of weapons and clenched, determined fists before the noise died down somewhat and the remaining resolutions were read and adopted:

That anyone arrested for not paying the 'obnoxious' license fee would be defended and protected by all.

That Commissioners be removed from adjucating on disputes re: licenses and be replaced by a new impartial body.

That only members of the League benefit from the mutual protection undertaking above.

That military marching with fixed bayonets and any firing of weapons by police or military be prohibited unless the Riot Act has been read.

Before long a spontaneous burning of licenses on two bonfires added to the sense of resolve and excitement. The flames hungrily consumed the hated Licenses while hundreds more Diggers enthusiastically paid over their 5/- joining fee to the Reform League.

Night fell and an uneasy peace settled on the town.

THURSDAY 30TH NOVEMBER

10 a.m.

The Diggers, despite the tension, were returning to their work. But with an incomprehensible disregard for the likelihood that it would inflame passions, the Commissioner decided that now was the time to go license hunting. It was foolish fuel to pour on a smouldering fire.

On the New Road, near the Eagle saloon, Commissioner

Johnson's force of policemen surrounded a number of Diggers and demanded to see their licences. Some had them, some not. Those without ran off amongst the pit holes and some four or five Diggers were taken prisoner and marched off. This did not settle the affair, however, for one of the men broke away and made a dash for the tents. As he weaved amongst a cluster of tents housing men, women and children, with three policemen chasing, a police inspector recklessly ordered his men to fire, which one of the constables did. It was only by sheer luck that there were no deaths, although some were wounded.

The crowd swelled and, fearful of what might happen, Johnson sent word to the Camp Commissioner. Rede soon arrived on the scene at the head of more policemen and military and came face to face with a large crowd of angry Diggers. By this time, the whole Camp force was arrayed on the Flat.

The police and their horses were shuffling and twitching and all government enforcers watched with drawn swords and fixed bayonets, casting anxious eyes at an overwhelming number of angry Diggers. Many of the Diggers were also armed with pistols, muskets and knives. All determined to resist enforcement of the pernicious license tax. Shouts of, "We will NOT pay the license. We WILL have our rights" rolled across the Flat in waves.

Rede raised his voice and attempted to reason with them, "My Lads, I know you are angry but I have no choice. I MUST do my duty. My orders come from the highest authority and I cannot disobey them." Rede went on to remind them that their own deputation of negotiators had told them only yesterday that the Lieutenant-Governor had promised that they would get their rights, and their own Mr. Fawkner had been selected as one of the committee to investigate their grievances. At the mention of Fawkner's name there was a loud cheer from the Diggers followed by cries of, ""We will not have drawn swords or fixed bayonet" and, "Where is the

Governor. Send up Hotham" and "We want justice, and we will have it".

Rede waited for the cries to abate and reiterated that he was determined to collect the licenses, only to receive shouted responses of, " We haven't got 'em; We can't give 'em. We've burnt 'em." Rede shook his head and replied, "My Lads, I must read the Riot Act if this behaviour continues" only for this to prompt shouts of, "Read it, read it, read it, read it!" Rede then began to read aloud from a parchment in his hands although his voice was drowned out by a multitude of angry, defiant voices raised with passion accompanied by the waving of muskets and clenched fists.

The noise and excitement seemed to confuse Rede and his colleague, Johnson, (who looked anxiously on the scene) and they seemed unsure of what to do. But then, as the noise ran its course, Rede stated again, " The licences must be shown. We must apprehend all who have not their licences."

Upon hearing this, a universal cry arose, " To the Camp[6] boys, to the Camp." There then began a general movement of the Diggers towards the Camp when suddenly there was a shout of, " Not to the Camp, boys, not to the Camp; back to our own ground on Bakery Hill."

Some of the Diggers made off to the Eureka, some to Bakery Hill - while the Commissioners and commanding officers held a consultation on the New road, evidently unsure of the intentions of the Diggers and what was to happen next. At length the military and police were drawn up into divisions on Bakery Hill and sharpshooters were stationed behind piles of dirt surrounding the Diggers' holes and Johnson set off again to enforce the licenses.

Johnson had asked what he was supposed to do if, in collecting the licences and arresting those who refused to pay, there was resistance? He received an uncompromising reply from the police commander, " If a man raises his hand to strike, or throw a stone, shoot him on the spot." One unfortunate mounted Digger, without a license, was apprehended about this time, taken prisoner and put under the guard of two troopers, "If he tries to escape, blow his brains out" the officer in charge was heard to say as they made their way back to the Camp.

12 NOON.

Deciding that the situation was getting out of hand, Rede gave the order to withdraw the government forces to the Camp and a tense peace ensued.

Outside the compound, soldiers were deployed to keep guard and inside the police also remained under arms. Meanwhile work continued to reinforce the mess-room veranda with sandbags.

And It began to spatter with rain.

3 P.M.

At Bakery Hill, a large number of Diggers had assembled to sign up to the Reform League. They shuffled along in a ragged line, giving their names. Every single one was armed. Some of them were sailors and they were placed in a division by themselves. A large contingent were Irish. In the same area, platoons of men were being put through their paces by an old soldier.

With the Southern Cross waving high above him, Peter Lalor, the leader of the insurrection, climbed onto a stump, and holding the muzzle of his rifle with his left hand, its butt-end resting on a foot, he gestured with his right, "It is my duty now to swear you in, and to take with you the oath to be faithful to the Southern Cross.

Hear me with attention. The man who, after this solemn oath does not stand by our standard, is a coward in heart. I order all persons who do not intend to take the oath, to leave the meeting at once" There was a distinct lack of movement with these words, then, "Let all divisions under arms 'fall in' in their order round the flag-staff."

The movement was made accordingly. Some five hundred armed diggers advanced with serious, earnest faces and the captains of each division made a military salute to Lalor, who now knelt down, his head uncovered, and with his right hand pointing to the standard exclaimed in a firm measured tone:

"WE SWEAR BY THE SOUTHERN CROSS TO STAND TRULY BY EACH OTHER, AND FIGHT TO DEFEND OUR RIGHTS AND LIBERTIES."

A universal full-throated AMEN was given in response and some five hundred right hands stretched towards the flag.

An observer wrote later, *'The earnestness of so many faces of all kinds of shape and colour; the motley heads of all sorts of size and hair; the shagginess of so many beards of all lengths and thicknesses; the vividness of double the number of eyes electrified by the magnetism of the Southern Cross; was one of those grand sights, such as are recorded only in the history of the Crusaders in Palestine.'*

A sustained volley of revolvers and other pistols now took place, and licenses were thrown onto a blazing fire. The meeting then dissolved while the Southern Cross flew bravely over it all. Those who were in favour of moral rather than physical action had by now left the scene with many of the remaining Diggers being Irish or Scottish with a sprinkling of continental Europeans.

During the evening armed bands of volunteers called on stores to equip the Diggers with arms and ammunition if they were without, promising to pay or return them after the affair was settled. Men and women kept assiduously at work pouring lead to make bullets by the hundred in readiness for battle.

* * *

IN AN ATTEMPT TO AVOID CONFLICT, Lalor and his advisors decided to send a delegation to Commissioner Rede to seek an accommodation. It was a rather cold night, the stars shone clear and bright when two of their number, Messrs Black and Rafello, accompanied by Father Smyth, presented themselves at the bridge, which was guarded by the police. Father Smyth then proceeded on his own, his cloth vouching for him, to ensure the safety of the delegation and request a meeting.

Concerned that the enemy should not gain intelligence about their numbers or dispositions, Commissioner Rede came out and met the delegation exactly one yard downhill from the Camp near an old gum tree opposite the local court building. He stood there confidently, wearing his gold-laced cap, his arm in his jacket like a little Napoleon. Sub-inspector Taylor, with his silver-lace cap, blue frock and jingling sword - a regular 'puss-in-boots' indeed - after introducing the deputation, placed himself at the right of the Commissioner and on his left stood a man with splendid blond whiskers, the police magistrate Charles Henry Hackett.

Black began to state the Diggers' position, demanding release of the prisoners only for Rede to explode, "Demand! What position are you in to demand anything?" Black tried to defuse the response and asked whether bail could be organized and, after a whispered conference, it was agreed that bail would be accepted for two of those arrested, the transaction to occur the following morning under the auspices of Father Smyth.

Black then put the second demand forward – that the Commissioner resign to avoid further bloodshed.

"What do you think, gentlemen, Sir Charles Hotham would say to me, if I were to give such a pledge? Why Sir Charles Hotham would have at once to appoint another Resident Commissioner in my place!" and then, puffing himself up, added, "I have a dooty to perform, I know my dooty, I must 'nolens volens' adhere to it."

Black attempted to negotiate further only for an indignant Rede, his pride wounded, to interrupt, " "It's all nonsense to make me believe that the present agitation is intended solely to abolish the licence. Do you really wish to make me believe that the diggers of Ballaarat won't pay any longer two pounds for three months? The licence is a mere cloak to cover a democratic revolution".

Carboni Raffaello, who had not yet said a word, stepped in, "Mr. Rede, I beg you would allow me to state, that the immediate object of the diggers taking up arms was to resist any further licence-hunting. I speak for the foreign diggers whom I here represent. We object to the Austrian rule under the British flag. If you would pledge yourself not to come out any more for the licence, until you have communicated with his Excellence, I would give you my pledge..." but here he was instantly interrupted by Father Smyth who said with finality, "Give no pledge sir, you have no power to do so."

Hackett and Rede then had another whispered conversation before Hackett offered that Rede could promise to take into consideration the present excited feelings of the diggers and use his best judgment as to a further search for licences on the morrow to which Rede, rather unhelpfully, added, "Yes, yes; but, understand me, gentlemen. I give no pledge."

The usual ceremonies being over, Sub-inspector Taylor escorted the delegation back to the bridge, gave the password, and bade the three men goodnight as they trudged back to give their report while the cold, brilliant moon rose into a black night sky, their breath misting as they walked.

FRIDAY, 1st December

About ten o'clock, news reached the Eureka camp that the redcoats were under arms, and that there would be another licence-hunting which prompted Peter Lalor to give the order to hasten work on preparing the stockade. Heaps of slabs, and all available timber were soon piled higgledy-piggledy around the camp. Lalor then gave directions as to the position each division should take up.

But no blue or redcoat appeared.

It was becoming apparent that, while there were men aplenty, there was a severe lack of arms and ammunition. Lalor urged everyone to do their best to procure what they could but refrained from counselling or even hinting that local stores should be pressed for the supply.

By mid-afternoon 1,500 men were drilling in and around the Eureka stockade (where they had moved to be out of sight of the Camp). Paddy Gettins (an Irish pikemaker) and Sandy McNab (a Scottish blacksmith) were working a forge inside the stockade to make pikes for those without guns.

About 200 armed Diggers arrived from Creswick's Creek and 200 Americans, the Independent California Rangers, armed with revolvers and Mexican knives also arrived under the leadership of James McGill, who had trained at West Point, all to cheers and a welcome worthy of Blucher's arrival on the field of Waterloo.

At a meeting of the senior members of the League, Peter Lalor was elected Commander-in-chief and McGill was appointed second-in-command although McGill soon left on hearing that reinforcements were on their way from Melbourne. Most of the American Rangers, all horsed, weaved their way out of the stockade in good order and headed south, the drumbeat of hooves and the jingle jangle of harness and weapons ringing into the distance as they rode off to intercept the artillery and reinforcements.

With senses tuned to the highest level, virtually no-one went to work on the diggings; instead rumours flew about and preparations for conflict continued including building up the defences at the Eureka. A cold night passed without further disturbance.

SATURDAY, 2nd December

Before the sun rose, alarms rang in the Digger's camp when a large body of troopers sallied forth from the government Camp and began to manoeuvre at Bakery Hill, but nothing further transpired and they soon returned to their Camp with a noticeable easing of anxiety and alarm as they retreated.

Defensive preparations continued at the Eureka with slab barricades being erected amongst the holes and carts readied to create obstacles and provide cover. Horses and bullocks were pressed into service to reinforce the stockade with fresh timbers, but it was a ramshackle affair, nothing more than an enclosure to keep the Diggers together, rather than with an eye to military defence.

In conference with his officers, Lalor outlined his plan, "If government forces come to attack us, we should meet them on the gravel pits, and, if compelled, we should retreat by the heights to the old Canadian Gully, and there we shall make our final stand".

The population at large were clearly supportive of the Diggers although talk was about moral force rather than physical being appropriate because of an understandable fear that if the Diggers were to gain control of the Camp, property might become 'insecure' and confusion reign. Judging by the good state of order amongst the Diggers and the remarkable absence of drunkenness over the last few days however, these fears were probably groundless.

Although the stockade had been built up, it was not viewed as an aggressive statement and between one and two o'clock it was comparatively deserted. Those who remained (some one hundred) were those who either had a long distance to go to reach their tents (and the day was very hot) or had no tent or friend to visit in Ballaarat.

As night fell a sense of excitement mixed with anxiety and expectation made it difficult to sleep and many collapsed onto their beds exhausted with fatigue but comforted that the morrow was the Sabbath and perhaps tensions would ease accordingly.

* * *

AT THE CAMP, the high command had heard back from their spies and were pouring over a map spread across a table. They had received intelligence that the Diggers intended to stop rein-forcements from Melbourne coming to their aid and had despatched the Californian militia and so weakened the forces in the stockade. Now was the time to strike. Arrows and squares had been drawn on the rough cartography and Captain Thomas was explaining his proposal. There was little to question, this was simply a mopping up exercise, and he was given the go-ahead. The meeting broke up and Thomas called his subordi-nates together to issue his orders.

THE EUREKA STOCKADE

*B*allaarat
Sunday 3rd December, 1854

IN THE WEE, small hours of Sunday morning Captain Thomas stepped out into the warm night air. It was dark with light coming from torches and a brazier. He looked up at the stars, noting the Southern Cross standing out clearly in the empty sky, and then down at a body of 276 armed men, quiet, staring ahead, drawn up for inspection.

He adjusted his sword belt, pulled his gold-encrusted cap tighter on his head and walked quickly down the ranks with the officer of the day at his side. He gave a word or two of encouragement and then returned to his mount, being held by a constable in his blue police uniform. He grasped the reins, wheeled his horse and gave the order to march, heading out of the Camp gate with his officers and infantry following.

Everyone had been told to proceed with as little noise as possible but the sounds of an army on the march, even one this small, were hard to subdue. Mr. Hackett, the police magistrate who had attended the aborted negotiations with Black, Rafaello and Father Smyth rode beside Thomas.

The sun was rising as they neared the stockade. They could hear alarms being shouted behind the barricades. A blood red morning sky foreshadowed the carnage to come. Without hesitating, the five battalions were drawn up as planned facing the stockade.

In the stockade, the Diggers numbered perhaps 170 on foot including a large contingent of Irishmen bound together by a common ancestry and a long history of animosity towards the English, who had served their ilk ill for centuries. But most of the them were armed only with pikes. The shepherds' holes inside the lower part of the stockade had been turned into rifle-pits and were now occupied by the remaining California Rangers, some twenty or thirty in all, who had kept watch during the night.

The police and soldiers began to advance.

The 40th and 12th infantry divisions moved forward while the Mounted police advanced on the right and the 40th dragoons on the left. A further division of troopers were kept in reserve to deploy as needed. The cavalry broke into a trot, then a gallop, hooves thundering into the earth, sabres drawn.

Later, Thomas was to relate that the first shots came from the stockade and that they killed one of the troopers from the 12th and one from the 40th. This was disputed by others; none could say for certain who opened fire first.

When the first shots rang out, Captain Ross took up his position at the foot of the flagpole with his men. And Captain Thonen and his division, who were stationed to the south in front of a gully, under cover of the slabs, answered the government fire, causing the dragoons, who were now galloping closer and fully within range, to swerve to avoid the barrage.

Other Diggers took cover and began pouring fire into the advancing infantry who were themselves firing volleys at the defenders. The cries of soldiers and Diggers hit by musket balls filled the air while acrid smoke filled the nostrils and the percussion of muskets and revolvers provided a clamorous backdrop that would have scared the hounds of hell.

To the east of the stockade, the German captain, Vern and his men kept up a sporadic fire as the infantry troops advanced steadily for the holes. Standing near Captain Ross, a brave American officer, who had the command of the rifle-pit men; fought like a tiger; he was shot in his thigh at the very onset of the assault, but, although hopping all the while, he stuck to Captain Ross heroically.

The dragoons from the south, the troopers from the north, were now galloping at full speed towards the stockade, the steel of their sabres flashing in the sun, pointed at the defenders as their mounts hurled them forwards.

Peter Lalor, raised himself on the top of the first logged-up hole within the stockade to order his men to retire amongst the holes and as he was pointing a chance shot hit him, throwing him to the ground.[1] A musket ball had shattered the bone close to his left shoulder and he lay in great pain and bleeding. He was hidden under a pile of slabs by his comrades in case the stockade was overrun, which was looking likely.

The infantry now aimed and, as one, let loose a full discharge of musketry which mowed down all who had their heads above the barricades. Ross was shot in the groin. Another shot struck Thonen in the mouth, and felled him on the spot.

The command of "Charge!" rang out and the redcoats rushed with fixed bayonets to storm the stockade. A Captain Wise, leading the charge, was shot in the leg as he clambered over the barricade. He continued to advance, dragging his useless leg and shouting encouragement to his men. Another shot from behind a wagon hit him in the other leg and he collapsed to the ground where he lay, cheering his men on as he bled to death.

Those who suffered the most were the score of pikemen,

mostly Irish, whose task was to stick the cavalry with their pikes if they rushed the holes. They stood their ground manfully from the time that the whole division had been posted at the top, facing the Melbourne road in double file under the slabs. But pikes were no match for bullets and overwhelming force. They were cut down mercilessly but their bravery gave time for many of their comrades to make their escape.

A wild "hurrah!" burst out. One of the police troopers had now reached the centre of the stockade and he tore down the offending Australian flag, which had been nailed to a pole[2].

With cuts, kicks, and a casting aside of the flimsy barricades it was done. As they advanced, the infantry thrust their bayonets into the bodies of the dead and wounded strewn about on the ground. One woman was mercilessly butchered by a mounted trooper while covering her wounded husband, pleading for his life.

It was all over in about fifteen minutes although the killing went on for most of the day as fugitives were hunted down.

As the soldiers and troopers completed securing the wider area a journalist, alarmed by a bullet passing through his tent, rushed out and was immediately fired on by a trooper and dangerously wounded. Despite protesting, handcuffs were put on him while he lay bleeding[3].

Captain Ross had by now surrendered and was giving up his sword, when a soldier, perhaps unsure of the chivalric gesture or simply with a blood lust, fired a mortal ball into his breast.

The roar of battle had now ceased to be replaced by the occasional shot, the groans of injured men, the sound of boots and rifle butts landing on men who had laid down their arms and the crackle of flames gleefully set by the victors licking around tents and barricades, burning injured men to death, as the troops secured the stockade,

The field was rent by the sobs of poor women crying for absent husbands and here and there, children could be seen, frightened into silence. A little terrier lay on the breast of one of the dead men and howled most pitifully. It was removed, but kept returning and when his master's body was thrown with the other corpses into a cart by a trooper, the little dog jumped in after him and lying again on his dead master's breast, began howling once more.

Some of the defenders managed to escape, another 114 surrendered and were rounded up. Estimates of the Diggers killed on the field of battle[4] ranged from 17 to 34, and as many as 60 in total died, including those who later succumbed to their wounds. Most of them were Irish. Lalor later noted that "the unusual proportion of killed to wounded was because of the butchery of the military and troopers after the surrender". Of the soldiers and police four were killed, including Captain Wise who died of his wounds, and 12 were injured.

Victory complete and absolute, Thomas ordered the troops back to Camp, the dragoons, sword in hand, rifle-pistols cocked, took charge of the prisoners and brought them in chains to the lock-up, pricking them forward with sabres and bayonets. The sergeant of a detachment remarked in a jeering tone, "I think we roused 'em up early enough this morning. Joe's dead now." On the way and at the Camp the Southern Cross was carried about in triumph, waved about in the air, then pitched from one trooper to another, thrown down and trampled underfoot. "We have waked up Joe!" they joked and others replied, "And sent Joe to sleep again!"

In the lock-up, prisoners were crammed in so tight that it was impossible for all to lie down and they took turns to stand or rest. The prisoners' growls and howling reached the ears of Commissioner Rede and about two o'clock in the morning the doors were flung open and all the prisoners were removed between two files of soldiers to the Camp storehouse - a more spacious room, well ventilated and comparatively clean.

· · ·

DECEMBER, 1854

All armed resistance collapsed and Martial Law was imposed. News of the battle spread like wildfire across the colonies and beyond but what the military thought was a victory turned into a public relations disaster, seen as a suppression of a minor insurrection with disproportionate, brutal force. Thousands turned out in Melbourne to condemn the authorities and side with the Diggers' demands.

* * *

MEANWHILE, some 70 miles further north, despite the earlier 'Red Ribbon' remonstrations against the license and the potential for an armed response, the Bendigo fields had remained peaceful and news of the Eureka Stockade came as a shock rather than a call to action. The repression of the Diggers was complete, or so Commissioner Rede thought as he rode roughshod over the diggers to stamp out any potential for another uprising.

Despite the conflict, by year end Robert and his partners had produced enough gold from their Kangaroo Flat pitch to pay their license fees and recover the cost of Bess and the puddler. Even better, Robert had also continued to add to his savings while Mary Ann and the children were coping as best they could in the rough and sometimes dangerous conditions. Just how dangerous was particularly brought home to Mary Ann when she heard the distressing story about a Mrs. Thomas who had died of a centipede bite to her finger, which caused her to issue a stern lecture to the children about staying away from creepy crawlies. She redoubled her efforts to keep the home swept clean at all times.

ECLIPSE

Loddon Junction
1855-8

FOR A FEW WEEKS after the Eureka Stockade, Commissioner Rede exercised his newly re-established authority ruthlessly and there was no sign of further unrest. However, of the approximately 120 diggers arrested only thirteen were brought to trial on 22nd February, 1855 and charged with high treason. After only half an hour's deliberation the jury came back with a verdict of Not Guilty and the thirteen were feted by the citizens of Melbourne who paraded them through the streets, shoulder high, upon their release. Rede was quietly demoted and reassigned in disgrace from the camps to an insignificant position in rural Victoria.

A Commission of Inquiry was set up (which was scathing in its assessment of all aspects of the administration of the goldfields and particularly the Eureka Stockade affair) and produced several recommendations including a restriction on Chinese immigration, the abolition of the hated gold licenses (replaced by an annual miner's right and an export tax based on the value of gold shipped), abolition of

Commissioners (replacing them with Mining Wardens), and cutting police numbers significantly. After 12 months, all but one of the demands of the Ballarat Reform League had been granted and Peter Lalor[1] was elected to the Legislative Assembly.

* * *

AT THE BEGINNING of 1855 Robert decided to try his luck south of Bendigo at Loddon Junction. Albert and Jack had decided to move on and William Begg had proved to be less than reliable and inclined to drinking and gambling so it seemed to make sense to break camp and make a fresh start. He had heard about a new find at Yandoit creek near Loddon Junction, about 30 miles to the south and, after thoughtful discussion, the family abandoned Bendigo, loaded everything up on a cart and headed south.

They made their way towards Castlemaine and camped for the night – they were now becoming very proficient at this - and James, George and William at least were now of an age to be more of a use than a hindrance. The next day, they journeyed through Campbell's creek and crossed the Loddon at Guildford where the Guildford Arms provided a convenient place to stop for dinner. They drove straight on for another 6 miles, passing a refreshment tent on the left hand side of the road and then turned right along an unmistakable, well-worn track, following several prospectors ahead of them on foot.

It was a fine day. Around them rolling pastures of green were bounded by the heights of the Jim Crow hills and the occasional scrub of quartz ranges. At the Jim Crow Creek, 3 miles from the Yandoit, Robert and Mary Ann were struck by the magnificent scenery and stopped to drink it in. On the western bank of the creek, a stony embankment some 15 feet high, there was an extensive plain, several miles long, with an easy-going, spongy turf and dotted here and there were groves of magnificent trees, their branches spreading wide, providing shade and a home for numerous varieties of birds. Continuing through this plain they approached the Yandoit diggings across natural shrubbery in which brightly coloured birds flitted and gambolled.

Their eyes then fell on the object of their journey, King William's gully, which spread out before them more like a broad valley than a constricted gully. Unlike the Bendigo diggings, green turf here had not yet been tramped out and the extensive, spreading boughs of many majestic trees provided shelter for the tents and huts that the diggers had constructed. There were a few hundred tents there already but even from this distance it was noticeable that the old rags and porter bottles which infested more mature diggings were not evident. Indeed, the whole scene presented an image of general cleanliness and good order.

On the right, Robert noted that the Yandoit creek would afford a regular water supply and beyond that there was a fine chain of waterholes. They could see men busily washing and cradling and all over the ground windlasses were continually at work alongside the metallic chorus of pick and spade revealing new holes and the rumble of the cradle.

Although nowhere near as numerous as Bendigo, there were some stores and more were being constructed as they watched, the hammering of nails into wood echoing across the valley.

They made their way towards the tents and found a spot to make camp, hobbling Bess under a tree, who found some fresh grass to chew while Robert sent two of the boys to bring back some water. The rest of the day was spent erecting a tented home and paying a visit to a nearby store to add to their supplies. While there, Robert took the opportunity to talk to the locals about the situation and put it about that he was looking for one or two diggers to partner with him when he began digging the next day. There was no shortage in this regard as about a hundred men were arriving every day.

Robert teamed up with two seasoned diggers from Ballaarat. Griff Hawkins, a spare man with thinning hair and a big bushy beard and David Nicoll, taller and solid as teak with a scraggly black beard. They were both about Robert's age and had arrived together at King William's Gully the same day. They had both participated in the protests but had not been involved in the Stockade itself. Around a campfire of an evening the three of them would talk about what had happened with Peter Lalor and they celebrated when news of the acquittal of the arrested diggers came through. "Mebbe there'll be some changes now" Hawkins offered although he also accepted that things were much better where they were than had been the case 'under that devil, Rede'.

They were both hardened miners who thus far had made enough of a living on the goldfields to survive but had not yet found anything to change their lives. They saw in Robert someone equally skilled and determined to make good.

At the end of their first month, they had struck gold and were squirreling away several ounces most days as the hole went down six, then ten, then twenty feet. They had rigged up a windlass at the top of the hole and, while one of them worked at the bottom, the other would wind down a bucket and haul it up again before carting it off to the creek for washing where the third man would be working the cradle. Robert had roped in James and George who would assist at the cradle for most of the day.

Mary Ann had created order out of the chaos as best she could and William and Benjamin had begun to explore, when they were not doing their chores, finding other children on the diggings to pal up with, while little Elizabeth stayed close to her mother.

The site grew. Blacksmiths, a tent-maker, general stores

flying a union jack, doctors and others soon established themselves. Although there was no public house, sly-grog shops mainly offered bottled porter and ale. Amazingly there had been no bushranger activity and whereas horse stealing was common on the other diggings (the newspapers were full of notices offering rewards) not one had been lost here – yet. There were no gold-buyers at the diggings, so a trip to Jim Crow was necessary to sell and this in turn meant that thousands of ounces of gold tended to stay in private hands at Yandoit. So far, there had been no visit from a Commissioner and while two policemen had turned up one day, they didn't stay and vanished as quickly as they had appeared.

The increase in activity brought bad as well as good men to the site. On the night of 2nd April armed burglars broke into the shop of John Rankin, a Scotchman who had set up a butcher's shop, and in the process of a botched robbery shot him dead. The Mt. Franklin police were called in to investigate and subsequently arrested a John Smith at the head of King William's gully. At Mary Ann's insistence, Robert immediately bought a mastiff to chain at their tent. Robert called him Percy and the name stuck.

And in July, Mary Ann announced that she was pregnant again, much to the surprise of both Robert and herself.

1856/7

The rush had seen perhaps 10,000 arrive at the Yandoit diggings. The green fields had long ago disappeared and the gullies around the creek and its tributaries had been swamped by the frenzy of yet another goldfield. The two main gullies were King William and Nuggetty.

Robert, Hawkins and Nichol moved from hole to hole in search of a big find, sinking their claim some 25 feet down in search of elusive nuggets. Two of their holes had turned up just enough to keep body and soul together but they kept on doggedly because others had made good around them. The mining took them through dry red marly soil to about twenty-five or thirty feet. The only unusual thing about this field was that at about fifteen feet down they always struck foul air which required the use of wind sails to allow them to breath and work effectively. Fortunately the ground was compact and allowed such excavation to be undertaken without fear of a collapse, although that didn't protect one poor man who was killed when a winch broke and a bucket full of earth plummeted down thirty feet, landing on his head and killing him instantly.

The gold lay in thickly scattered patches and each hole typically produced about six to eight ounces per load if it was in the right place although a hole next to theirs had turned out seventeen loads the day before, each averaging eighteen ounces. It was unusual to find large nuggets although, to prove the rule, one nugget weighing some 4 lbs had been found on the Saturday before last, so you never knew what was coming next and it was this hope that kept the thousands toiling from dawn 'til sunset six days a week.

* * *

BY NOW JAMES – who had turned 13 in March - was working full-time with them at the cradle (he was too young to work the winch or to dig out the hole) and George and William too would help at times. Mary Ann had given birth to a son on 4th April and she had insisted on naming him Robert after his father, much to Robert's concealed delight.

The year ended with success at a new hole they had broken in late autumn and as Robert and Mary Ann saw out the old year they celebrated knowing that there was almost enough hidden away to allow them to start thinking about the farm that they had discussed in Bendigo.

* * *

ON THE 26TH MARCH, 1857 at about 6:30 in the morning, a number of the miners and all of the Bright family shielded their eyes as they witnessed the rare event of an almost total eclipse of the sun. They had been warned not to look directly at the sun and used some broken glass to protect their eyes as they witnessed almost 90% of the sun disappear behind the black shadow of the moon and afterwards Robert had to explain to the children how this marvel had occurred and what it meant. He had a rough idea, there had been discussion about the forthcoming event for a week, but he had only a rudimentary grasp of the science and was quick to shuffle questions away for fear of uttering what might later be shown to be nonsense.

Other than the eclipse, 1857 was uneventful, although the quantity of gold they were finding was diminishing, which made Robert start thinking about moving to another location, but they celebrated George's thirteenth birthday on 31st December, 1857 still working the Yandoit field.

1858

With the summer at its height, the heat was a problem for all, not only because of the physical discomfort but also because of the risk of bush fires. On the 9th, 10th and 11th of January the heat was almost unbearable and work had slowed, if not stopped as a result.

On Monday the 11th a sawyer in nearby Daylesford had been forced to leave his sawpit because of approaching bush fires which reached his sawn timber stock and furiously consumed everything, including 3,000 shingles which had been stacked about a quarter of a mile away. A large tract of the countryside had been left charred by the fire and showers of sparks required constant vigilance to avoid a conflagration all about. Some embers had even made it to the Bright's canvas roof and it was only quick thinking from Mary Ann that managed to douse it before it was able to do any serious damage.

In June, Mary Ann told Robert that she was pregnant once more. Robert simply smiled at the news and kissed Mary Ann. "Well done lass. Maybe a sister for Elizabeth this time". Mary Ann laughed and kissed Robert back before putting on a kettle to celebrate with a cup of tea.

Robert and his partners continued to hop from hole to hole, steadily but modestly adding to their haul while around them others would from time to time find something remarkable. In October, a nugget weighing 440 ounces was recovered to much excitement

But the initial optimism and camaraderie of the early days at Yandoit were rapidly fading as the population increased and with it so too did lawlessness. A Mrs. Hines was robbed of £48 one night in her tent, a store was forcibly entered another night (Mr. Wardell's) and £100 stolen, Mrs. Spinks of Conner's gully was robbed of £14 when her tent was broken into - the assailant stealing a petticoat that contained the money, Even the court house was robbed of £11 and another tent at Doctor's gully was robbed of everything while the owners were away working.

And then as 1859 was drawing in upon them.....

While Robert and the older boys were working the claim and Mary Ann was at home mending tears in Robert's shirt (and teaching Elizabeth how to sew), Robert junior and Benjamin had gone out to play.

It was a warm, humid day having rained the day before and it was threatening rain again, but it was dry for now and Mary Ann was unconcerned as the boys ran off to the creek to find Benjamin's friends or perhaps see what was happening at the cradle with James or George or William as they had done many times before. Benjamin was 7 and little Robert 2 years old, going on 3, He wanted to be wherever his older brother was and do whatever he did, much to Benjamin's annoyance. However, his mother had told him to look after his little brother and he was not so rebellious as to disobey her.

They were half way to the creek, running along the paths that criss-crossed their way amongst the holes that were being worked or had been played out. Benjamin was leading when he heard Robert behind him cry out.

He turned in exasperation to see Robert sprawled on the ground, his legs dangling over the edge of an abandoned hole. His little arms were flailing as he tried to find something to grip but there was nothing to grasp and with each struggling effort he slipped further and further.

With his heart in his mouth, Benjamin ran back as fast as he could to catch his brother and, as Robert was about to fall, no more than three yards away, he flung himself forward to catch his hand.

He made it. But the momentum of his running carried him forwards and the weight of Robert pulled him to the lip of the hole too.

One of the miners nearby, a young man by the name of Michael Reilly, looked up to see what was happening and immediately realised the seriousness of the situation. He dropped the bucket he was carrying and sprinted as fast as he could across the uneven ground towards the unfolding tragedy, Large strides eating the ground, breathing hard, heart pumping, jumping over piles of dirt and stones, desperate to get to the boys in time.

LOST

*L*oddon Junction
1858

BENJAMIN HAD FOUND a large stone to grab with his left hand while he held on as tightly as he could to Robert's hand with his right. The wet mud however made it hard to grip tightly and Robert's struggling was making it all the more difficult.

Reilly was now within ten feet of the two boys. But Benjamin couldn't keep his grip on the smooth surface of the stone and with a sudden movement he had lost his grip and began sliding.

He frantically kicked out and reached with his free arm to find something to hold onto and stop their inexorable slipping and sliding. Robert's weight was a millstone but he wouldn't let go. He had been told to look after his young brother and that was all there was to it.

* * *

THE TWO BOYS plunged together over the edge, hand in hand, without a sound, Robert looking into Benjamin's eyes, Benjamin returning the stare.

A sickening thud and a small splash a second or two later arose from the hole as Reilly arrived. He crouched at the muddy edge and looked down some thirty-five feet into a water-filled pit and saw both boys still, unmoving. The small boy was face down in the water. The older boy appeared to have cracked his head, blood was staining the water as he lay half submerged. They were still holding hands.

Reilly called out for help and it wasn't long before a rope ladder had been dropped into the hole and Reilly clambered down. However, on reaching the bottom of the pit, he could see that it was hopeless. Neither boy had moved. The older boy's eyes were open, staring up to the sky but a large gash on his head had killed him instantly. He turned the younger boy over, his muddy face lifeless. He couldn't stop tears welling up. He didn't know who they were but it was such a desperately sad waste. He closed their eyes and muttered a heartfelt prayer.

* * *

REILLY and two other miners as well as a woman, the wife of one of them, stood at the entrance to Mary Ann's tent. The miners each carried a lifeless small body. Tenderly they held the boys in their arms, their grimy faces with lines etched where tears had made their way through the sweat and mud, despite their attempts to staunch the unmanly flow.

The woman stepped into the tent calling out, "Mrs. Bright. Are you there Mrs. Bright?" Mary Ann looked up from her sewing, Elizabeth at her side. She didn't know this woman well although their paths had crossed a few times over the past year. "Can I 'elp you?" she asked.

"I have some awful news for you, Mrs. Bright. I wish I didn't.

Jim wanted to tell you but I told 'im that it were better comin' from a mother".

"What do you mean?" Mary Ann answered with alarm, fearing that something must have happened to Robert or one of the boys at the diggings.

"I can't say it easy, so I'll just say it. Your two youngest boys 'ave 'ad an accident. They're both dead. I'm so, so sorry".

Mary Ann's ruddy face went pale. She heard what had been said but it didn't really register. She was unable to say anything and the woman added, "Shall we bring your boys in?" and, without waiting for a reply, beckoned to the men outside..

On seeing Benjamin and Robert, lifeless, Mary Ann let out a long, heart draining groan and flung herself across the two small bodies now lying as if asleep together on the bed. Elizabeth started crying, not understanding what was happening and the woman went over to her to reassure her that things would be alright. Mary Ann was sobbing, tears cascaded down her face and dropped in a pitiful shower onto the faces of her two sons. She turned to look at the men and beat both hands on her breast, then cried out with such pain that it tore at the heart.

The woman ushered the men out with Elizabeth and went over to Mary Ann. Put her arm around her and buried Mary Ann's face into her breast while saying softly, "You just cry it out, love. Just cry it out".

They had sent someone to find Robert to break the news and it was only a few minutes later that Robert burst into the tent followed by James, George and William. He saw the two boys on the bed and groaned, "Oh, it's true" and went over to the two boys to smooth their hair and touch their lips. Then he turned to Mary Ann and took her from the woman to clasp her tight. The three boys just stood there, unsure of what to do, until James rounded George and William up and took them outside to leave their parents alone.

* * *

THE FUNERAL WAS a low key affair led by a Presbyterian minister who worked on the diggings during the week and held open-air services on Sundays. The two pitifully small coffins were carried by Robert, James, Hawkins and Nichol to a makeshift cemetery that had sprung up on unproductive land near the camp. The two boys were buried together after a brief service and a simple marker was erected.

Mary Ann was numb with grief. She walked to the cemetery, stood at the grave, walked back like a zombie, almost present but not quite. It was distressing for Robert too and he had to exercise great control of his emotions to stay strong for his wife and provide direction to the children.

It was the worst day of Mary Ann's life. The very worst. And she cried herself to sleep that night in a household that was quiet, reflective and still stunned by the loss.

* * *

MARY ANN DIDN'T REALLY SURFACE for a week. She was some six months pregnant and was not coping well with bouts of sickness. The shock had also drained her and she spent hours just lying down on her bed, not saying anything and immersed in her own thoughts. James had matured immensely in this time and had taken charge of the children while his parents worked through their grief. Robert was pensive, devastated at the loss and deeply concerned for Mary Ann.

It was a week later, just before Christmas, that Robert took Mary Ann for a walk, something he had started to do to provide some focus on life beyond the grief even though he was conscious of the need to avoid tiring her. As they were walking he started thinking out loud, "Perhaps it's time for us to move on, Mary Ann. We've saved enough to set us up on a small farm.

The boys are old enough now to help with the work and I've a lot to teach them. And you deserve a proper home after these past years. What do you think?"

Mary Ann looked up at Robert. She had been crying again and the tears had stained her cheeks but this made her stop. "You mean leave 'ere and get our own place?"

"Yes, that's exactly what I mean".

"And give up the diggings?" Mary Ann asked.

"Yes, become a farmer, live on and off the land".

"D'you mean it, Robert?"

"Yes, I mean it. It's becoming more and more dangerous here and the gold is running out. We need to move anyway. Let's make it a complete change, Get away from the memories, start again".

Mary Ann started crying again, but this time it was with joy, "Oh yes, Robert. Yes. Yes" and she wrapped her arms around him and wouldn't let go.

NEW START

❧

*M*cCallum Creek
1859-61

The leaders of the Exploring Expedition have been chosen. Mr. Richard O'Hara Burke, long superintendent of the police of Castlemaine district, is first in command, and his second is Mr. Landers, who recently brought the camels from India. Mr. Wills from the Melbourne Observatory, is appointed astronomer to the expedition; and Dr. Becker accompanies it as naturalist. The expedition will start in the course of next month, making Cooper's Creek their point of departure.[1]

The Argus, 25th July 1860

* * *

THE MAN WAS WALKING at an easy pace across the paddock chewing a stalk of grass that he had just picked. The sun was shining in a blue sky and the cabbage tree hat on his head was doing a good job of shading his balding pate. He had rolled up the sleeves on his red check shirt and he gazed about him languidly as he walked; he was in no hurry. A few cows were grazing within 100 yards or so and the sun was shining in a blue sky. Birds sang and a slight breeze ruffled the leaves of the odd gum tree. All was at peace with the world.

However, a bull standing watch over the small herd was less sanguine and took exception to this interloper. It raised its head, snorted and pawed the ground before it started lumbering forward to see off this challenge. Red check man picked up this movement out of the corner of his eye, turned to get a better view, yelped with alarm and started running at full tilt for the nearest fence. He was an ungainly athlete; his arms pumped wildly at his side, he hopped as much as ran and he stumbled over the rough terrain. His hat flew off his head and fluttered away, ignored by the determined, onrushing beast.

The bull was clearly gaining with every step, its hooves drumming with menace on the hard-packed earth. Red check man gulped in searing breaths as he looked behind him to gauge whether he would make it. And, not without some panic, he looked back to the fence, which seemed to be running from the bull too and was getting further and further away.

The crack of a stock whip broke into the scene and a horseman appeared. The bull veered away and red check man made it to the fence after all, clambering over the rails in ungainly haste and crumpling on the far side in a heap. The stockman rode up to him.

"Are you alright mate?" the stockman asked and red check man slowly regained his footing and nodded in the affirmative, breathing heavily and wiping the sweat off his brow.

"Name's Bright. Yours?" the stockman asked.

"Barrett, John Barrett" he gasped.

"You sure you're alright?"

"I am, thanks to you".

"Why were you on my land?" Robert asked, for it was Robert Bright who had come to the rescue.

"I didn't realise; I was just having a walk. On me way to Back Creek[2]. I'm sorry".

"Well, no harm done I suppose. Let me get your hat" and Robert rode back a few yards, picked up the hat and returned it to its owner.

"Thank you, Mr. Bright. I'll be on me way then". And still breathing heavily, red check man went on his way leaving Robert to continue moving the cattle back to the milking shed.

Robert had been as good as his word and the whole family had headed south towards Back Creek – a rapidly growing town thanks to several finds of gold in the area in the last couple of years. They arrived with Mary Ann heavily pregnant and she gave birth to another son in March 1859. They named him Benjamin again.

On the nearby McCallum Creek he found a small farm to rent with a ready market for its produce in Back Creek. He was tempted to join in the 'Scandinavian' rush, but he had made a promise to Mary Ann and he was going to keep it.

The 'Scandinavian' rush began seriously as they arrived with claims of the ground being "alive with gold". As a result hopeful diggers flocked to the region, windlasses were working every-where, the noise and dust infused everything and a forest of tents mushroomed. By the end of 1859 some 15,000 people were at the rush. The main street in Back Creek was now taking shape – it had been named Scandinavian Crescent in March that year. Hundreds of shops and businesses opened to cater for the needs of the diggers, including Robert's dairy supplying milk and cheese to this swarming population.

Amherst also had its prospectors and a few years earlier had vied with Back Creek as the main centre for the area before the big rush began. The road from Back Creek to Amherst now took on the name of Camp Street and the launch of *The Amherst and Back Creek Advertiser* followed by the *North-West Chronicle* signalled the establishment of a significant settlement.

Every time Mary Ann went into town for supplies, she would see construction - everywhere permanent buildings were being erected to replace the initial temporary tents. On one trip she was mesmerised by the sight of a 200 ounce cake of gold in a gold broker's window in the crescent and in another, 1,500 ounces of gold nuggets. There seemed to be a new bank each time too to care for the golden haul, the National, the Bank of Australasia, the London Bank of Australia, the Victoria.

There were, in all, six streets of stores; the names of Oxford Street with its narrow row of shops, Bond Street and Russell Street in particular triggered Mary Ann's memories of being arrested in London. Ballaarat Street and Sturt Street[3] also took their place. A theatre had even opened in Oxford Street just before they had arrived. At the Robinson & Co. store a Post Office was opened.

In order to break through the basalt cap to reach the gold leads, mining companies introduced blasting techniques, so now as the 1860's broke, the sound of explosions added to the general mayhem – and accidents and deaths too.

As the eventful year of 1860 merged into 1861, the town's wild growth stabilised somewhat and in October, 1861 Back Creek was renamed Talbot. By now about 100 companies were operating mines and their signs, such as the Great Extended Conway Castle, the Talbot Paddock Company, Prince Alfred, Morton Extended and Independent were displayed throughout the town while the Crescent hosted 23 restaurants, a variety of hotels and ale stores, tobacconists, 4 butchers, 5 boot shops or boot makers, 3 tent shops, 6 drapers, several chemists, milliners, saddlers, confectioners and billiard saloons.

Robert had used their savings from six years on the diggings to rent 25 acres of land bordering the McCallum creek and had fenced it and stocked it with some Holstein Friesian milch cows and a bull, some ewes and a tup, a yard full of laying hens and a noisy rooster. He had also set aside an acre to grow root vegetables, turnips, carrots, parsnips, potatoes to feed the family. About 2 acres was still forested. He still had Bess, the horse he had first bought on the diggings, although she was getting a little long in the tooth and they had two dogs that Robert and his sons had trained to keep watch.

It had been going on for two years of hard physical work for all of the family, repairing fences, erecting new ones, gradually improving a run-down slab-built cottage and erecting a shelter for the animals and storage. James, who was now a sturdy 17 year old and the 'numbers man' with a head for business, George, going on 16 and William, going on 13, were very much involved in running the farm and in addition to Elizabeth, who was now 7, Benjamin made up the family.

They were happy. The scars from the tragedy at Loddon Junction had still not healed, but Mary Ann no longer cried herself to sleep and Robert was at peace with himself watching his sons and his small farm grow. Life back in the countryside was a blessed relief from the years on the diggings. He occasionally congratulated himself on what he had achieved, thinking of his time as a farm labourer in Cambridge and how his current situation would have been an impossible dream there. Mary Ann and Elizabeth were thick as thieves and Elizabeth, with a downturned mouth or a forced tear could wind him around her finger to obtain whatever she wanted – within reason.

Although not totally self-sufficient (Mary Ann would still buy things like flour and tea from the shops at Back Creek), they were quite independent and they found a ready market and a good enough income for their farm produce with the rapid increase in population resulting from the lure of the goldfields. The only cloud on the horizon was the health of little Benjamin, who was a sickly baby and who seemed to struggle to take his mother's milk. They had brought in the local doctor, but he had been less than useless and so they had soldiered on using their common sense and the advice of some of the local women, mothers all, who, knew best of course.

However, despite all efforts, Benjamin continued to struggle and one morning at the end of the year Mary Ann went to his crib to find that life had ebbed away overnight. She was distraught and brushed away Robert's attempt to console her, "It's a curse" she sobbed with anger, "Why does God take every Benjamin from us - your brother, my two sons. 'It ain't right. It just ain't right". The boys and Elizabeth kept their distance, unsure of what to do and Robert, with a tilt of his head and eyes guided them outside to leave them alone with their grief once more.

Over the following days Mary Ann kept to herself, not speaking unless she had to, speaking harshly when she did. The funeral was not just a pitiful affair as the small coffin was lowered into the small grave, it was also something that seemed to age both Robert and Mary Ann beyond their years. Just when things seemed to be going right for them this was sent to try them once again.

"When will it ever end, Robert?" she cried after the service had ended and they walked away from the cemetery. "What 'ave we done to deserve this. It ain't right, it just ain't right" and she buried her head into his chest, all cried out, as Robert held her tight, unable to find any words adequate enough for the emotions.

* * *

LATER THAT YEAR, Mary Ann announced to a very surprised Robert that she was pregnant again. The news lifted her considerably and they saw in the new year with hope rather than grief and Robert treating her like a fragile eggshell.

SETTLING IN

*M*cCallum Creek
1861-2

The Government of Sydney are stretching a second telegraphic wire
between Sydney and Adelaide, by way of Deniliquin and the Murray,
and avoiding Melbourne ; while the attempt to repair the Tasmanian
submarine cable has been abandoned.

The Intercolonial Cricket Match has terminated once more in
favour of Victoria. On this occasion the battle-ground was Sydney.
The Argus, 23rd February, 1861

* * *

THE NEW YEAR broke much as every one before it although this
time with a cloud over Mary Ann that hovered every waking
hour and subdued everything. Life was to be endured now, not
enjoyed. However, it was difficult to stay miserable when the
sun shone in a blue sky, the trees and bushes bloomed, the birds
sang and the daily beat of life played out amidst the bucolic
peace of life on a farm. And she had Robert and her boys and

little Elizabeth who, bless her, had done her best to lift Mary Ann's spirits after losing Benjamin and had taken on more of the household chores.

Like any farmer, they were at the mercy of the weather but in the summer of 1860/61 they were blessed. An abundance of rain had fallen and creeks that usually dried up and waterholes that were usually empty were well-filled and the whole country, usually parched and bare by now, was green with grass as vibrant as it had been in winter.

The good weather had, it was hoped, been supportive of the great expedition that was the topic of discussion at all social events. This was the status of the Burke and Wills expedition that had set out from Melbourne with such a great fanfare six months earlier.

Seeking to become the centre of an overland telegraph route connecting Australia with Java and Europe, the Victorian government had offered a reward of £2,000 to encourage an expedition to find a route between South Australia and the north coast of Australia and, despite his lack of bushcraft or prior relevant experience, Robert Burke had been appointed to lead the expedition and William Wills had been appointed surveyor and navigator. The two explorers, together with seventeen men and 26 camels, 23 horses and 6 wagons had left Melbourne on 20th August the previous year watched by some 15,000 spectators. It was said that their equipment weighed about 20 tons including enough food to last two years and extraneous items like a cedar-topped oak camp table with two chairs.

They had travelled along the same road that Robert and Mary Ann had taken to Bendigo several years before and then struck north to Swan Hill and beyond, reaching Menindee on 12th October having taken two months to travel 470 miles, a journey that the regular mail coach did in little more than a week. By then, two of the expedition's five officers had resigned, thirteen members of the expedition had been fired and eight new men had been hired.

But now they had gone missing and such was the concern that search parties had been dispatched.

Relaxing after a day's work, James, stumbling over several words, read out loud an article from the Melbourne Argus of 23rd February, 1861 that Mary Ann had found in Talbot on a shopping trip. It was eight days' old, but was nevertheless of great interest to them all:

The missing party, who failed to overtake the leader with despatches, and at the date of last summary were exposed to great privation in the bush, were recovered by the party sent to their relief. The party consisted of Police-trooper Lyons, Macpherson (a saddler), and Dick, a native. Their narrative is one of considerable interest. They followed the traces of the leader to a point which they estimated at four days' journey to the northward of Cooper's Creek, from which they were compelled to return, by their inability to find food or water. Mr. Burke had travelled with great rapidity, and had made no considerable halt at any of the camps which they had found.

At a certain stage of his journey, Mr. Burke had buried some flour for the use of those who were to follow him, but the shifting sand had so covered the traces of the deposit, that even the native who accompanied the smaller party, and who had been with Mr. Burke when the flour was hidden, was unable to find it. They fell in with a party of natives who promised to provide food for Lyons and his companion, in return for gifts promised them by the native, on his return with succour, for which he was then setting out alone. This promise the party kept for a few days, providing waterhens and other birds, but they then deserted the white men.

Macpherson, however, had observed the natives making use of a kind of meal from a plant then in seed, and induced a boy to show him the plant. Quantities of it were then gathered, and, pounding it into meal, the two men sustained themselves with it until the arrival of the native with help from Mr. Wright's camp, at Menindie, the setting out of which was reported last month. The men had been out in the bush for 47 days, and had started with only seven days' provisions, relying on overtaking Mr. Burke at Cooper's Creek, and finding the flour buried by him on the way.

"What chance they'll ever find those poor men?" Mary Ann said after James put the paper down.

"Little or none, I'd say" Robert replied, "The bush is dangerous even close to civilized parts, but out that far and with the black fellahs ready to attack, my guess is that they're dead by now".

"We don't know that, Dad" James replied.

"I know, but you mark my words, they won't be coming back" Robert replied with a shake of his head.

"Just you make sure that you don't do anyfing as silly" Mary Ann chided looking hard at James, George and William who had all been talking excitedly about exploring just fifteen minutes earlier.

* * *

HEAVY RAINS in June were a mixed blessing. It rained continually, eventually causing McCallum Creek to flood. Part of Robert's land was submerged, but fortunately his vegetable patch was unscathed and the house and chicken yard was on the highest ground so this escaped the rising water. At one point flooding rose to a depth of eight feet at the usual crossing place on the Ballaarat road delaying Cobb's coach reaching Back Creek from Ballaarat until half-past four the next morning when the water had sufficiently receded to make it possible to cross the creek safely (it should have reached its destination about seven o'clock the previous evening).

In the midst of this angry weather, Mary Ann delivered

another son. Although they were concerned that it might be a difficult childbirth given Mary Ann's age, it went quite smoothly. They named him Frederick – although neither of them discussed it, they would not visit misfortune on the child by naming him Benjamin or Robert.

The next month, there was another torrent of rain that began at four in the morning and continued non-stop until eight that evening. Much of the Flat became impassable and come four o'clock the swollen creek covered the new bridge by the All Nations hotel in Back Creek. At nine o'clock the dam at that point was washed away in a torrent of sheer power, hurling broken wood, tents and other debris downstream. Fortunately it did no serious damage and the water had begun to subside by midnight.

In October, violent thunderstorms with rolling peels of thunder and sheet and forked lightning struck, even killing a parrot in a cage at the Geelong and Ballarat hotel in Back Creek and knocking the landlady unconscious for several minutes. There was also the risk of bush fires that could quickly get out of control and no-one was immune from raids by bushrangers, although the Bright's farm was probably too small an enterprise to attract such attention.

Notwithstanding these events, on the whole, the weather was a friend to them. In November, after a wet Spring, the sun shone from clear skies and promised the bounty of plentiful crops and healthy livestock.

* * *

IN AUSTRALIA, civilization continued its inexorable spread and in Melbourne an Australian cultural icon was about to be launched. On the 25th November, *The Argus* reported the initiation of a race for the 'Melbourne Cup':

THURSDAY, NOVEMBER 7, 1861

Notwithstanding the very short interval that has elapsed since the Jockey Club Meeting, the attractions of Flemington Course appeared yesterday to have lost none of their powers of fascination, for the attendance on the part of the general public was much larger than we remember to have seen on the ground on any day for the two years last past, with the single exception of the occasion of the Two Thousand Guineas Stakes being run for.

The weather was especially favourable to the enjoyment of the visitors, and the turf being throughout in excellent order, was in the best form to ensure the horses of the best class the full measure of advantage due to their intrinsic superiority. There was a very fair show of fashionable company upon the Grand Stand. Early in the afternoon his Excellency Sir Henry Barkly arrived, attended by Capt. Bancroft, and the presence of the Governor threw and increased animation into the scene. His Excellency visited the saddling paddock during the half-hour preceding the Cup Race, and noticed, apparently with interest, the general character and condition of the competitors, as they passed up and down and stripped for saddling. The enclosure on the hill, open to the public on this occasion at a charge of one shilling for admission, was patronised to the extent of about 2,000, the Grand Stand added some 600, and the elevated ground outside with the crowds next the rails on the course, furnished about 1,500 visitors to the course; so that the total number present may be estimated at about 4,000 persons.

The most perfect order prevailed throughout the day, and the police had little more to do than enjoy a view of the racing.

On the ground were the usual racecourse amusements, and the ordinary minor speculative games of skill or chance that frequently tempt the unwary and the rash to diminish their stock of ready money by the unwise means they employ to add to it. The refreshment booths drove a thriving trade throughout the day, and the refreshment rooms of the Grand Stand, where Messrs. Spiers and Pond were the caterers, were also largely patronized, and the good things of their providing met with general approval......

Next came the great event of the day, the MELBOURNE CUP, for which seventeen of the twenty two acceptances came to the post, the absentees being Bolero, scratched on Monday, Moscow, scratched on Wednesday, Partisan and Defence withdrawn at one o'clock p. m. yesterday, and Eagle's Plume, who was weighed for and mounted, but, after taking his preliminary canter, was returned to the saddling paddock, and sent straight homewards.

The appearance of the principal favourites was carefully scanned as they afforded opportunities for the observation of the cognoscenti and it appeared to be generally admitted that, whatever might be the difference between their relative merits, they had all been profited to the utmost of their capability by the care and attention bestowed upon them by their respective trainers. The condition of Archer, Mormon, Flatcatcher, Inheritor, and Despatch in particular was superb. The Sydney horses were admirably brought out and the winner, Archer, looked the very perfection of health and power, a fitting competitor for the Victorian champion, who looked pounds a better horse than on the Two Thousand Guineas Day. The rival merits of this formidable pair were eagerly discussed, but the confidence of the Victorians increased as the hour of starting arrived, and, probably from being off their own ground, the Sydney party ceased to support their horse, who was consequently passed in the quotation prices both by Mormon and Despatch, whose friends were very "fond." Very little disposition was shown to invest on the outsiders, and, except a few pounds which were laid out on The Moor, Nutwith, Prince, Antonelli, and Fireaway, we might say that the betting was confined to the four or five leading favourites.

About twenty five minutes to four the flag fell and a good start was effected, Flatcatcher, Medora, and Mormon getting to the front in a few strides. As the horses rounded the turn, coming to the straight running, a terrible accident occurred, through Twilight, Medora, and

Despatch falling, with fatal results to the two last mentioned mares, and inflicting very severe injuries on their riders.

This unhappy contretemps reduced the field to fourteen, and these came along at a tremendous pace past the Stand, the front rank being composed of Mormon, Archer, Fireaway, and Antonelli. At the river side the two Sydney horses were in front, but on nearing the Old Stand Inheritor beat a retreat, and Antonelli became the immediate follower of the Sydney crack. From this point, however, Archer never more closely approached, and the changes took place in the order of precedence amongst his followers; for the New South Wales hero kept away from his horses, and came in comparatively an easy winner by several lengths.

A MARRIAGE

ℳ cCallum Creek
1863-7

By 1860 THE population of Victoria had increased to the point where it exceeded that of its gold rush rival, California. Melbourne was booming and so was the hinterland including Talbot, which had become a substantial centre, so much so that in 1864 it had a Court House, borough offices, seven schools, a street of good shops, two breweries, churches, two soap and candle factories, sixteen hotels, coach services and general carriers, and a number of crushers. Even so, the population had declined substantially from the heady days of the Scandinavian rush and it had settled at a still substantial 3,400 souls.

With the three elder boys maturing into manhood and Elizabeth becoming a pretty young woman, the farm became a settled, relatively prosperous home for the Brights supplying the busy Talbot/Amherst townships and beyond.

Robert had taken advantage of new laws[1] to buy the farm, so now they were land-owners too. James had started to teach

William and George to read and write and the family had become a part of the community, participating in local dances, attending the theatre in Talbot and participating in local farm-related competitions. The boys had even played some cricket although none had a natural bent for the sport. They also attended church each Sunday, all rolling up in their cart with Jenny, the successor to Bess, between the shafts.

However, as they reached the middle of the decade all was not rosy. Over the summer of 1864/5 Victoria had been experiencing drought and it became more difficult to feed and water the animals as a result. Because of the lack of rain, many farmers had not ploughed their fields over the winter and on into Spring. Beef herds had been reduced to skeletons. According to newspaper reports, some had tackled the problem by boring wells or with new techniques – one farmer sewing clover and English grass seeds during the drought (believable or not, it was reported that his grass had been waist high at one point and now looked like an English meadow). Robert, however had taken no such steps but had coped because of the small size of his dairy herd relative to the land, because of his proximity to the creek, and by boring a well. Thankfully, in May 1865, rains provided some relief.

But the next year drought continued to stalk the land and bush fires too were an ever-present threat. The result was forced sales of animals, poor crops and insolvencies. One of Robert's neighbours, James Neave, a brewer, had been bankrupted because the continuing drought had made his water supply unfit for brewing purposes and he had lost business with his beer turning bad and crop failure. The drought had also impacted property prices, so even selling his land produced insufficient funds to pay his creditors. It was a stressful time for him and his family and a warning to Robert.

William also found himself in some trouble. He was a headstrong young man now, 18 years old and with an eye for the opposite sex. He had stayed overnight at the Adelaide Lead, a few miles to the north after meeting a girl there while delivering milk, butter and cheese from the farm. It was while walking out with her on Monday, 22nd October that they were witnesses to a 'vigilante' attack.

Apparently a married miner, Joseph Knowles had seduced a 17 year old girl named Anne Jeffrey who was an apprentice of Knowles's wife, a dressmaker. When Anne became pregnant his wife had left him and Anne moved in with Knowles to the shock and affront of their respectable neighbours.

While William and his paramour were walking by Knowles's house a mob of angry miners gathered outside, then, the anger spilling over, Anne's father beat down the door and dragged his daughter out. At the same time a party of miners seized Knowles and marched him to the nearby Primitive Methodist chapel where the minister conducted a mock trial and he was sentenced to be tarred and feathered.

At the urging of his girlfriend, William had been following along with other residents watching the spectacle with some curiosity.

It then turned ugly. A mixture of warm tar, pitch and resin had already been prepared and the mob proceeded to strip Knowles to his waist and pour the mixture over him, daubing extra portions where any flesh remained uncovered.. A bag of feathers was then produced and the defenceless victim was rolled into the feathers. Amidst shouts, one of the onlooking crones commented with glee, "His own muvver wouldn't know 'im now". She then started shouting for the same treatment to be given to Anne Jeffrey but that was a step too far for the men, although that didn't stop her being roughly handled by the women who pulled her dress over her head to expose her underclothes, shouting abuse all the time, before she too escaped.

Then with abusive shouts, Knowles was told to 'make tracks', which he did without any haste, coolly remarking, "I suppose that's it, now you've taken your revenge". However, worse was to come because while this had been going on, others had set fire to his house and the flames could be seen leaping into the air amidst the fierce crackling and crashing of burning timber. By now the police had arrived and William and his girlfriend, being onlookers, had their names taken along with other participants and other witnesses.

As the burning of the house was not 'strictly legal' (as reported in the *Talbot Leader* later) those identified by the police were subsequently charged with riot and conspiracy.

Back on the farm, William had relayed the events to the family and thought that that was the end of the affair but a few days later a warrant was served on him at the farm, much to the consternation of Robert and Mary Ann. William was questioned extensively by his parents before they accepted that he had just been a bystander (Robert's recollection of being caught in a similar situation at Burwell many years before perhaps helped with his understanding and support for his headstrong son).

William was required to attend court at Maryborough on the following Wednesday, November 7th and Robert went with him to offer whatever support he could. The case dragged on to the following day before a verdict was given. The lawyer, Mr. Samuel, representing William and others accused applied for the discharge of Messrs. Shaw and Sanders and William because they were not involved in any way in the proceedings. But the judge shook his head, "Each of these men were present at the time. Each of them is guilty because they did not raise their voices to protest"

Mr. Samuel then argued that the event was not a serious riot and that an adequate response would be to bind the prisoners over to keep the peace. The judge considered his suggestion for a few seconds then pronounced, "I hereby order the prisoners to be bound over to keep the peace for three months in their own recognisances of £20 each, without sureties". He then added as he looked sternly over his gavel at the three men, "I must remind each of you that by your presence on this occasion you were responsible for a breach of the peace. I trust that this sentence will be a warning to others to prevent a similar lawless occurrence".

With that William was released and Robert and William returned home, wiser perhaps.

But life went on and, of course, James, George and William (now aged between 19 and 24) had well and truly introduced themselves to the local female population.

James had been courting a red-haired, pretty 20-year old Scotch miner's daughter, Mary Andrew. She had come to the gold rush with her family from New Monklands[2] in Scotland, where she had been born. She was working as a house servant in Talbot and James had met her at a dance in Talbot the year before. Her father, David Andrew, was employed on the Talbot goldfields working for one of the hundred or so mining companies that were blasting their way through the rock to follow the gold lead. He and Robert got on well enough, drinking together from time to time at social events and Mary had befriended 14-year old Elizabeth, who looked up to her. Mary Ann, like most mothers, thought that James – the son of a land owner – could do better, but James would have none of it. He was serious about his Scotch lassie, and during the winter of 1867 he asked Mary's father for her hand in marriage which was eagerly accepted.

This put the 'cat amongst the pigeons'. James had been the literate member of the family and Robert had come to rely upon him to help manage the farm. So Robert was faced with a decision. They were talking one evening. The boys were out, Elizabeth and Frederick abed:

"Mary Ann, with James's marriage I wonder whether we

should think about selling up" Robert began hesitantly. Mary Ann stopped her sewing and looked up.

"That's a big decision, Robert. Why?"

"Well, it's not just James. The drought, you know, things haven't been easy and who knows when it will break? And if it doesn't we could find ourselves in the same position as Jimmy Neave and others"

"It's early days yet, Robert. We've managed this far"

"Yes, I know, but without James it's going to be much harder and we can't expect the boy to stay on when he has his own family to take care of"

They looked at each other. Mary Ann could see lines of worry in Robert's face and suddenly she realised that he was no longer the strong, irrepressible force he had once been. They were both getting on and yes, maybe it was time to ease back if they could.

"So what would you do?" she asked.

"I'm not sure yet. We should be able to sell up and have some money to get by, even after helping James set himself up. Perhaps I could find a job in Talbot or.." and here he tailed off.

"You should speak to James and get his ideas, Robert. Before you do anyfing rash".

"Yes, I will"

"Cup of tea?" Mary Ann offered and the conversation switched to easier subjects.

* * *

OVER THE NEXT several weeks Robert and James and Mary Ann discussed options and it was finally decided that they would indeed sell the farm – not because of James's marriage but because they all feared that things could get very much worse with the drought continuing apace. They also decided to set up a carter's business. With the population growth and the need to move goods between Melbourne, Maryborough, Castlemaine and the Bendigo goldfields they were sure they would have plenty of business and it would be much less risky and less work whether Robert and the boys all worked together or Robert carried on the trade on his own.

So Robert Bright & Sons, Carters came into being and before Spring had passed the farm and all livestock had been sold and the family had moved into a small property by Mt. Greenock a few miles away.

* * *

THE MORNING OF 12TH DECEMBER, 1867 was warm and clear. The day would be hot and dry and St. Andrews, the Presbyterian church in the centre of Talbot waited patiently, shaded and cool inside, ready to host the wedding of James and Mary – David Andrew and his family being regular churchgoers at the Church of Scotland.

St. Andrew's Church, 15 Heales Street, Talbot

A little after noon, Robert and Mary Ann had taken their places in the second pew with William, Elizabeth and a fidgety 5 year old Frederick – all in their Sunday best. James, with George as best man sat in the front pew, every now and then looking anxiously back to the entrance. On the other side of the aisle, the Andrew family talked quietly as they waited for the service to start.

With a small commotion as a door opened behind the altar, Reverend John Nicol appeared and took his place at the head of the aisle and then, with the striking up of the wedding march[3] on a piano, David Andrew entered with his daughter, veiled, in a simple pale green dress, carrying a small bouquet of flowers. They walked up to Reverend Nicol slowly, matching their steps to the music, and James and George took their place.

The service was brief and straightforward. Everyone remembered their lines and Mary Ann watched on with a tear welling in her eye as she remembered her own wedding and saw her young son now a man. The service ended with James kissing his bride before being led away to sign the register. Henry Cross, a church acolyte, signed the certificate rather than have Robert mark his cross alongside David Andrew's signature.

GRANDPARENTS

 ❧

Kangaroo Flat
1868-71

CLOSE OF TRANSPORTATION

We have now arrived at what may be called an Epoch in Western
Australia, which, we may tell in Melbourne and publish in Adelaide
— the last ship-load of crime and criminals has arrived. In future it is
presumed that all who come augment our population shall be virtuous.
Inquirer and Commercial News , Jan. 22, 1868

* * *

THEY ONLY STAYED at Mt. Greenock for a short while. James had
helped his father establish his carrier business with George and
William working alongside him and then he had left home and
moved several miles to the west with his bride, to Mt. Lonarch,
to set up home on a small farm that he had rented and stocked
with his psrent's financial help.

The Mt. Greenock house had been a temporary solution while they sorted themselves out and before long Robert found a more appropriate property to rent at Kangaroo Flat[1], to the south of and within easy reach of Talbot with room to stable a horse and a cart and the associated equipment to run the new business. They settled into their new life as carters, finding good opportunity running goods to and from Talbot to Melbourne and Bendigo, Robert usually at the reins and George or William riding 'shotgun' – literally, as this was the heyday of bushrangers like Ben Hall[2] who had not long before terrorised New South Wales.

In 1869, Elizabeth – now a pretty and accomplished 16 year old – met a young man who was introduced by James's wife as a friend of their family. He was 26 years old, a Scotchman from Paisley, a wood cutter by trade, the son of a carpenter, and his name was Thomas Seargeant. Despite the difference in their ages they made a good match.

Over the following year the intensity of their relationship increased until one day Thomas pulled Robert aside. He shuffled his feet and with hesitation began, "Mr. Bright, I ken Elizabeth may be a young woman, but there's many younger married ere now, err, I mean, I'd be honoured if I had your blessing to marry your dochter". The last was rushed out and he looked up at Robert when he had finished half expecting to be knocked back. But Robert considered things for a few seconds and instead said, "And Elizabeth? How does she feel about this?" The door burst open and Elizabeth flew in with Mary Ann following behind, "It's what I want, father" she said quickly standing beside Thomas and holding his hand.

Robert looked over at Mary Ann, "It seems like I'm the only one who isn't in on the secret".

Mary Ann laughed. Elizabeth had been discussing this for a month with her mother and Mary Ann had taken a liking to this strong, confident young man. "With James's wife and Thomas 'ere it looks like the Scotch are beatin' down our door" she said with a smile.

* * *

ALMOST A YEAR LATER, on Tuesday, 30th August, 1870, the Brights were once again witness to the marriage of one of their children. The service was held at St. Michael's church[3] in Talbot and the 17 year old Elizabeth had never looked more beautiful in a white dress especially made up by Mary Ann for the occasion.

The wooden church was soon to be pulled down and a new bluestone building erected - indeed the foundation stone of the new church had already been laid two weeks before. So this could be the last time that the Reverend Mahalm would conduct a marriage service in this building which added a certain poignancy to the wedding.

After the service, Thomas and Elizabeth, with their parents, adjourned to the parsonage next door to sign the papers, Thomas placing his signature on the document with a flowing hand and Elizabeth putting her cross beneath to mark the event. Thomas kissed his young bride again and beamed a wide smile, then kissed his mother and Mary Ann for good measure, thoroughly pleased with himself. Elizabeth was a little overwhelmed if the truth be known but she was surrounded by people who loved her and she thought, who could ask for more?

Following the service, a bagpiper marched ahead of the bridal couple, leading everyone to the *Goodman's Phoenix* hotel that had been built just the year before next to the Bank of Australasia. This was where the families had arranged a wedding reception for both families and friends. It's two ballrooms were put to good use late into the night with ale and whisky flowing freely and a ceilidh atmosphere infusing the event with music, dancing and a sense of something particularly well done.

With all the merriment around them, Robert and Mary Ann sat at a table, toasted each other, and reflected on the great distance that they had travelled – not just physically but socially too.

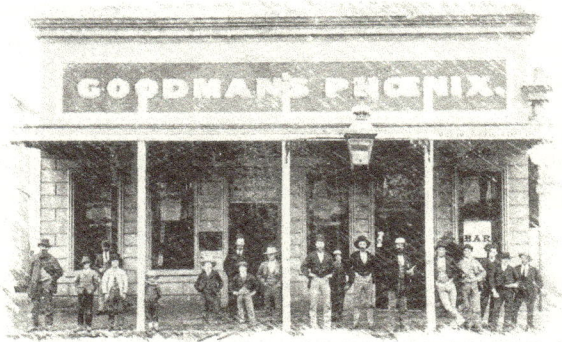

Goodman's Phoenix Hotel, Scandinavian Crescent, Talbot

THE NEXT YEAR Robert and Mary Ann became grandparents, James and Mary delivering a son whom they named Robert, much to the satisfaction of Robert himself who saw this as the completion of a long circle and a 'bright' hope for the future. A pun that he took great pleasure in using on more than one occasion.

AND WILLIAM GOT into trouble again.

Unlike James and George, William had always been more adventurous, less conservative. With this free-wheeling spirit he had also found it easy to make friends. He was also a good-looking, well-built young man and found it easy with his ready smile to talk to and win girlfriends notwithstanding the Victorian mores that permeated even this far into the colonies from England.

On reaching his 21st year in 1869, he had decided that he should stand on his own two feet and rather than stay with the family at Kangaroo Flat, he found a job as a farm labourer three hours to the south on the Jones farm near Mt. Beckworth – not too far from Clunes.

He had occasional amorous flings with the local girls and in the winter of 1871 he had taken up with the farmer's young daughter, Mary Jane. She was 16 going on 17 and was as pretty as a picture with blonde hair, a pale Welsh complexion and a slim, petite, blossoming body. She was equally as adventurous as William and they made a good match. They would walk out together, go to church together, laugh, play, dance and scramble in the hay together.

And so it was almost inevitable that in the November of 1871 Mary Jane broke the news to William that she was pregnant with his child.

At first William didn't know how to respond, "Are you sure?" he asked and Mary Jane replied testily, "Of course I'm sure. My parents will be furious".

William waited a few seconds and then took Mary Jane's hands in his and said, "Will you marry me, Mary Jane Jones?"

She looked at him intently and threw his first question back at him, "Are you sure?"

William frowned and replied, "It's the right thing to do and besides, I'll be envied by everyone to have such a beautiful bride".

Mary Jane hugged him and they kissed.

"The problem now is escaping a skelping from your Dad" William said as they sat down side by side on a nearby wall.

Despite herself and the worry, Mary Jane laughed at this aside and William joined in. He was sure that things would turn out fine. They always did.

They spent the next hour talking about how to break the news, where they would live, what they would do and, with the sun beginning to slip below the horizon, William walked Mary Jane back home. She would break the news to her mother first and the day after tomorrow they would meet again to plan the next steps.

In the end, despite an outburst from her father and a tongue-lashing for William and Mary Jane, who could do nothing but take it as they stood sheepishly in front of him (with Mary Jane's mother wringing her hands in the background), it was agreed that they would marry as quickly and quietly as they could after the banns were read at the Jones's local church in Clunes. It was agreed they would move into a small cottage on the farm until things could be worked out.

William made his way back to his parent's home at Kangaroo Flat and broke the news to them. Needless to say, it was not welcome and Robert came down quite hard on William, lecturing him about the need to act more responsibly and take hold of his life. Mary Ann was more supportive. William had always been the extrovert of the family and his recklessness mirrored her own spirit to some extent. After a dispiriting evening, the tone at breakfast the next morning was more conciliatory and William explained that they would be staying at the Mt. Beckworth farm for the near term before they decided whether that was something they wanted for the long haul.

Robert and Mary Jane's father, John Jones met soon after. They were of a similar character and both regretted the situation that they found themselves in but also both agreed that the best thing was to arrange a speedy marriage - and a quiet one to avoid wagging tongues as much as possible.

* * *

AND SO IT was that on 27 February, 1872 William and Mary Jane were married at Saint Paul's Church in Clunes at 6 o'clock in the evening without any grand ceremony by the Reverend Herring. Both William and his new bride signed the marriage certificate with a cross. Robert, Mary Ann, James and George attended the service (Elizabeth was looking after Frederick) as did the Jones's close family and afterwards, they adjourned to the farm, where Mary Jane's mother had laid on a simple meal.

St. Paul's Church, Clunes

Toasts were made to the married couple with best wishes for the future, despite the unspoken shame brought on the two families. The Bright family didn't stay long for it would take a couple of hours to get back home and night had fallen. With the 'party' at an end, William and his new bride retired to their cottage for the evening, not celebrating but resolved to make everything work.

About four months later, on the 10th July, Mary Jane gave birth to a daughter to whom they gave the name Eliza Ellen.

And, at the end of that year, Elizabeth celebrated her first-born, another daughter, who was named Mary Ann.

. . .

COME celebrations on New Year's Eve 1872, Robert and Mary Ann were now grandparents three times over with a young Robert, Mary Ann and Eliza joining the ranks of this pioneering Australian family.

GAINS AND LOSSES

Kangaroo Flat
1873-75

Fortunately, in this colony, still prosperous, there are not many poor who should be so, or who cannot help it. The industrious colonists of this new and beautiful land are nearly all through the favour of God, in a position to combine in the celebration of Christmas social enjoyments with its religious observances, and this is how the great festival of the Church should be celebrated. There is a season for sackcloth and ashes, for penitence and tears, but this is one for rejoicing with all man's heart and soul.

Excerpt from The Advocate,, 24th December, 1875

* * *

ON THE 3RD DECEMBER, 1873 Robert celebrated his 60th birthday. A few weeks earlier he had become a grandfather to Thomas (Seargeant) when Elizabeth delivered her second child and a new Mary Ann Bright[1] when William's wife brought her second child into the world.

Because Robert's birthday fell on a Wednesday, the family had arranged a surprise party for the following Saturday evening, the 6th December at Kangaroo Flat. It was a grand family gathering, 14 people altogether, including 5 grandchildren and Elizabeth's husband Thomas as well as William's wife Mary Jane.

They arranged to arrive at the house about noon and Mary Ann saw to it that Robert had to run errands in town that morning with George; he rarely worked on a Saturday these days.

It was a hot, dry day with the sun beating down from a clear blue sky and when they returned Robert and George were both talking about the delights of a glass of ale. By now the other members of the family had hidden themselves in the house, having also hidden the horse and cart in which Thomas, Elizabeth, William, Mary Jane and their children had arrived. George pulled up outside the house, the horse shuffling as the cart rocked back and forth and Robert climbed off the cart with his shopping under his arm. George too had clambered down and was making to lead the horse into the stabling as Robert made for the entrance to the house.

As Robert entered, Mary Ann was sitting in the parlour on her own. She was worried that one of the children would cry or make a noise but, by some magic, that didn't happen.

"Hello Robert, did you get everything?"

"Yes, it's all here" and he laid some provisions on the table. The bedroom door then burst open and everyone tumbled out with cries of "Surprise!" and "Happy birthday!" and peals of laughter as Elizabeth hugged him and gave him a kiss and then a round of hearty handshakes and claps on the back followed amongst a rough tumbling of people offering their congratulations.

Robert was totally surprised but the grin on his face said everything that needed to be said. Drinks were poured and the room descended into animated conversation with jokes and teasing comments and the warmth and happiness of a family that had been forged in the furnace of mutual trials and tribulations.

If truth be told, Robert was not in the best of shape. He had developed a cough of late and the excitement and press of people brought about several hacking explosions as he tried to gather his breath. Mary Ann held him close and handed him a cloth, "Don't crowd 'im, give 'im some air, it'll be all right" and, while everybody looked on solicitously, Robert recovered his composure, "It's nothing. Don't worry about me. Don't fuss. It's just wonderful to see you all. Such a family, makes me proud"

"And annuver one on its way" Mary Ann added, hugging Elizabeth, who was now four months pregnant and who blushed at being singled out.

They settled down and the conversation transcended into jokes, laughter and reminiscences. At one point, Mary Ann offered, "I wish our Benjamins and Robert 'ad been 'ere to see this" and Robert added, "And our families back in England" which sobered the levity somewhat but, with glasses refreshed, the mood lightened once more.

The men moved outside to put up an extended table and benches and build a fire on which they were going to cook the lamb and beefsteaks that Robert had brought home with him. The women meanwhile busied themselves with readying some potatoes, carrots and cabbage and bringing out the plates and knives for the meal. Frederick, now a boisterous 11 year old, escaped the house and the young children to insert himself into the company of the men, albeit drinking water rather than ale.

* * *

In May of the following year, 1874, Elizabeth went into labour again. Thomas called in Dr. Dawling and sent a message to Mary Ann to let her know. With Robert driving the cart, they arrived when Elizabeth had been in labour for six hours.

Thomas and Robert excused themselves and left it to the doctor and women to oversee the birth. It was not easy. They could hear the cries from the birthing room and, when Mary Ann came out for some water, she appeared to be concerned although she didn't say much. Mary Ann returned to her daughter's side leaving the two men outside to wait on events.

Eventually, the doctor came out of the room and announced that Thomas had a new daughter, much to his relief. Elizabeth and Thomas had agreed that, if it were a girl, she would be named Margaret and Robert shook Thomas's hand and they both raised a glass to the newborn. When Robert and Thomas were allowed in to see the new mother they found a small baby in her arms, sleeping. Elizabeth was exhausted. Her face was flushed and she laid back, holding her baby, eyes shut, breathing shallowly. Thomas went to her side, kissed her moist brow and muttered something Robert couldn't hear. Elizabeth opened her eyes, smiled wanly, then shut them again. They were soon ushered out of the room so that the mother could rest.

The doctor came back the following morning. Elizabeth was in some pain complaining about a stomach ache. She was running a high temperature and the doctor told them that he suspected that Elizabeth had contracted childbed fever. He told Mary Ann to apply a cooling compress to bring down her fever, gave Elizabeth some medicine and said he would be back in the next few hours.

Later in the day he did return but, if anything, Elizabeth was in worse shape and he was clearly concerned. He told Mary Ann to stay with her, keep her as comfortable as she could; try to bring her temperature down with cold compresses and feed her a simple broth to try to build up her strength.

Through the night, Elizabeth struggled to sleep, she now complained of worsening stomach pains and chills. Her brow was hot to the touch even so. When Elizabeth tried to feed little Margaret, the baby obviously had some difficulty, so both mother and child presented a troubling sight.

Two days after giving birth, on 5th May, with Mary Ann sitting by her side holding her hand and Thomas on the other side of the bed stroking her hair, Elizabeth looked at her mother and then at her husband and whispered, "Take care of Mary Ann, and my dear Thomas and little Margaret" and then she closed her eyes and after several laboured breaths, breathed her last.

The Doctor confirmed that Elizabeth had died of puerperal peritonitis and turned his attention to trying to save little Margaret who was clearly not doing well.

* * *

HE FAILED. Five days after entering this troubled world, Margaret succumbed and joined her mother. The doctor wrote: 'Too low vitality from birth and loss of its mother' on the death certificate. A simple statement that could not even begin to measure the depth of sadness that settled on the household.

* * *

MOTHER AND CHILD were buried together in the Amherst cemetery on the 7th May, 1874 with both families mourning the loss of a beautiful, gentle child and one who had not even had a chance to live her life. Mary Ann faced up to the loss stoically. She was becoming immune to loss, if that were even possible, and retreated into a shell that others were not allowed to penetrate. Robert, too, was hit hard by this. Vitality seemed to go from him and he left the business more and more to George, instead sitting at home with Mary Ann, talking, when they did talk, in low tones and with a resigned acceptance of their misfortunes.

* * *

THE FOLLOWING months saw Robert sink deeper into himself. His cough had worsened in a wet, cold winter and at the end of September, Mary Ann had called in the doctor once more with Robert's failing health. The doctor diagnosed bronchitis and told Mary Ann to keep Robert warm, feed him a meat broth and gave her some expectorant to help bring up the phlegm sitting on his lungs.

"Now, you just stay in bed Robert Bright" she chided when he tried to get up after waking late one morning in October. "We need to build up your strength and keep you warm and rested, so no chores today". She pushed him back into his pillows but this triggered a spasm of chesty, hoarse coughs and the ejection of ugly, green phlegm into the ever-present hand-kerchief. She wiped his sweated brow with a flannel and stroked his hair as he sank back; the coughing had wearied him and he accepted that he was going nowhere that day.

William and James both came to visit. They visited every month or so anyway, but their father's plight worried them. He was no longer the strong, commanding figure he had once been. While he still had his faculties, he was nevertheless much weak-ened and they sensed that this was no ordinary illness. They each sat and talked, Robert trying to joke with them and they with him and all of them pretended that this was just a passing matter of no account but when they left and spoke with their mother outside the bedroom, their concern and hers was very evident.

* * *

ON THE MORNING OF THURSDAY, 28th October, 1875 after a troubled night with Robert's wet coughs and struggle to draw breath that tore at Mary Ann's heart, she was sitting by his bedside, bathing his forehead.

"D'you remember when we first met?" he asked her.

"Yes, course I do" she replied with a smile.

"I knew then I wanted to marry you" he said.

"Go on, Robert Bright "

"Really, I did. You were such a perky little thing and so pretty. My only worry was you wouldn't like me"

"Robert, you 'ave been everyfing a girl could ask for. You make me very 'appy. Even when we was scraping and scratchin' on those bloody goldfields"

Robert smiled and tried to laugh, but as he did a spasm of coughing broke out, leaving him exhausted once more.

"Now you just settle back and get some sleep. Doctor's gonna be 'ere later and we'll soon 'ave you back on yer feet". She kissed him on the forehead, tucked him in and crept out of the room to put on the kettle for a cup of tea.

A half hour later she heard him cough violently and went back in to help him with Frederick following. Robert looked at both of them as they entered the room, smiled weakly and then shut his eyes to collapse back on the bed. He let out a long breath. And as Mary Ann took his hand he squeezed it.

And he breathed his last.

* * *

THE DOCTOR ARRIVED an hour later and was let in by a disorientated Frederick to find Mary Ann crying softly, still holding Robert's hand, with her head next to his and her other hand stroking his hair hesitantly as if somehow she could bring him back to her by this simple act of love.

* * *

THREE DAYS LATER, on the 31st October, Mary Ann, James and his five-year old son Robert, George, William and Frederick stood at the side of a freshly dug grave in Amherst cemetery, where Elizabeth and Margaret had been laid to rest some two years earlier. The other children were kept away with James's and William's wives acting as babysitters and, in any event, a very pregnant Mary Jane was not considered fit for the journey. It was felt that Elizabeth's children were also too young to attend.

It was warm, but not hot, with clouds scudding across the sky. As the coffin was lowered by William, James, George and Elizabeth's husband, Thomas it started to spit with rain. No-one even looked up to the sky and the Minister began his service, "Ashes to ashes, dust to dust..." The raindrops pattered down, soft, as if hesitant to disrupt this momentous event, mixing with the tears in Mary Ann's eyes.

James came over to stand next to his mother and put his arm around her protectively. He wiped away tears of his own. William and George looked on and thought of the happy times they had spent with this man, their father. A man who had broken free of a system weighted against him, who had made a good life for them all, who had suffered under the venal sentence of transportation to the other side of the world and yet who had risen above the stigma and the adversities to build a life for himself, their mother and them. A man who had founded a family in this new land. Yes, he had a lot to be proud about and they were certainly proud of him. A true pioneer.

And they were very worried about their mother. She had been dealt a heavy blow and was suffering. They tried to ease things for her but it was difficult knowing how because until now she had been the strong one, the person who held the family together, who made it all work. But now, her grief was tangible and she seemed to have shrunk into herself, almost unaware of everything going on around her.

They had talked amongst themselves about what should happen now and although they agreed that George would continue his father's business, they hadn't figured out much else. Would she be better off living in Talbot rather than out in the country? They hadn't broached the subject yet and, in any event, George could stand in for their father while she remained at Kangaroo Flat and Frederick, although only 13, was certainly old enough to pull his weight. What they did know was that they would look after her, whatever it took.

* * *

AND SO THE eventful year of 1875 drew to a close, the brothers and their mother perhaps closer than they had been since they were children and all wondering what the years ahead would bring.

COMING OF AGE

*K*angaroo Flat
1877-80

SOON AFTER ROBERT'S FUNERAL, Mary Jane had given birth to twin girls who were named Elizabeth in memory of William's sister and Margaret after her little baby. Mary Ann took great pleasure in being a grandmother once more and over the next two years began to spend quite a lot of time with William and Mary Jane and their four girls.

She got on well with Mary Jane, a free-spirited lass after her own heart, and the children were a constant source of entertainment and every now and again worry, but always engaging.

William continued to work at the Jones farm and James was busy building up his farming activities at Mt. Lonarch. George and Frederick were kept hard at work with the carterage business. They had left the 'Robert Bright & Sons' name painted on the cart and even though the mining boom was slowing down in Talbot, they were respected for getting the job done at a reasonable price so were never short of work, although it could keep them away from home overnight quite often with journeys to Melbourne and Bendigo.

Frederick was growing into an athletic youngster and had taken up cricket in his spare time, playing for a local team in Talbot. It was therefore with great excitement that he journeyed to Melbourne with George on 18th March in the year of 1877 to deliver produce to a warehouse. The excitement came about because George had promised to go with him to see the touring England cricket 11 play an Australian 11 at the Melbourne ground. Admittedly the great W.G. Grace was not playing for England, which took a little of the shine off the occasion, but the chance for Australia to pit its finest against the mother country was a treat to relish. England were very much the favourites, ready to teach the colonials the finer points of the art.

In the first innings, played on the 17th, Australia had scored 245 thanks to a masterly display by Charles Bannerman who had retired hurt with 165 runs to his credit. England had then been bowled out for 196 with Midwinter taking five wickets. In Australia's second innings, without Bannerman fully fit (he had a split finger) they struggled and found England's bowlers too hot to handle, ending up with 104, Shaw taking Bannerman's wicket for 4 runs and dismissing four others cheaply. It looked like England would canter home.

Charles Bannerman

On the 19th, a beautiful Monday, perfect for cricket, they arrived at the ground soon after play had started and paid their 2/- entry fee, taking up a position near the grandstand. Australia had started the day with 83 runs on the board and nine wickets gone, so the expectation was that England would soon take the last wicket and go on to knock off the required runs to win. However the two Australians, Kendall and Hodges, would have none of it and dealt effectively with Shaw and Ulyett, the bowlers who had caused so much trouble the day before, Kendall hitting Ulyett for four runs not long after to bring up 100 for Australia. England then brought Lillywhite on to bowl. Although Kendall held his end, Hodges was soon bowled and Australia finished with 104, leaving England 145 to win.

The crowd was smaller than the day before when 10,000 had been watching, hoping for Bannerman to repeat his triumph of the first day, but still about 2,000 were in the ground now anticipating that when England took the field they would make quick work of the task. Frederick had been engrossed with everything and had been cheering every Australian run enthusiastically. He was, however, worried as the two English openers emerged from the pavilion just before one o'clock to face the Australians already in their positions.

Kendall had been handed the new ball and to the delight of Frederick and most others in the ground he made quick work of both batsmen, Hill going for a duck and Greenwood for 5. Perhaps there was a chance? Charlwood, however dispelled some of the optimism, hitting Kendall to the chains for 4. The score clicked to 20. Then, immediately after this, Jupp was beaten by Midwinter and, despite making a stand, Charlwood was bowled by Kendall. The score now stood at 30 and the ground began to buzz with excited anticipation.

The match continued cautiously with singles being scored

and the Australian bowlers containing their opponents. Another wicket fell. At tea, the score stood at 59 with six wickets still to fall. Frederick was beside himself with glee, praising his heroes and personally assuming some of the possible glory that beckoned.

The play resumed with Ulyett bringing up 60, but he was soon after clean bowled by Kendall. The score now stood at 62 with five wickets gone, five to go. Frederick opined that, "We have to take Selby's wicket. He's their danger man" and indeed he was making steady progress and looked comfortable at the crease. George nodded his agreement; he really hadn't enough knowledge of the game to venture an opinion but it was thrilling to see Frederick so animated and Australia holding its own.

Selby started to come out of his shell and made a succession of good strokes bringing 90 up on the scoreboard. England now needed 55 to win and Selby looked like he might do it on his own. Hodges then replaced Midwinter and forced Selby to mistime a shot, sending the ball high into the sky into the safe hands of Horan standing near the boundary. Armitage and Lillywhite, who followed were no match for Australia's bowlers and were dismissed. It was now Emmett and Southerton guarding the last wicket with 100 up and 45 needed to win.

The tension in the ground was palpable. A miracle seemed about to happen and none wanted to break the spell. Kendall trundled down to the wicket, his left arm like a windmill, releasing the ball to Emmett. He played, mishit the ball and it cannoned onto his wicket. England all out for 108 and Australia had won the match.

The crowd exploded with delight. Frederick jumped up and hugged George then hugged a stranger next to him. He was in seventh heaven. Several of the Australians, including Charles Bannerman and Tom Kendall were called out from the pavilion to receive the delighted applause and cheers of the crowd and it was a thrilled Frederick who left the ground with George at the end of the celebrations. On the journey home he couldn't stop talking about the game and he bathed in the reflected glory of Australia beating England.

Somehow it seemed to prove something.

* * *

CYCLES

On Monday evening last the town of Benalla was thrown into excitement by the report that a constable had been shot by the notorious Kelly.

On enquiring on Tuesday morning at the police station, we learned that a mounted constable named Fitzpatrick had been sent out to execute a warrant for the arrest of one of the Kellys. When he arrived at the house, he saw the party wanted, and at once informed him that he was to accompany him back. The prisoner asked to be allowed to have something to eat before starting, which request was granted, the constable keeping guard over the prisoner while he was eating, when suddenly a door opened, and Ned Kelly, for whom the constables have been seeking for the last eight or nine months, came forward with a loaded revolver and fired point blank at the constable, and missed him.

At the same time, the mother of this respectable crowd came forward with a shovel and struck the constable over the head, and only for the great strength of the new helmet worn by the constable the blow would have finished him. We have seen the helmet, and feel quite convinced that the blow was not a playful one, the whole side of it being completely smashed in. Fitzpatrick put his hand down for his

361

*A*t dinner one Sunday, months after the great victory over England, with William and his family visiting, Mary Ann asked William and George if they had heard anything about a bushranger named Ned Kelly and his gang, "I 'eard from Mrs. Bantry that not two days ride from 'ere the country is in a real 'ows yer father about this Ned Kelly bandit" she began.

William jumped in, "Yes, near a place called Benalla or Greta I think. There was a shooting of a trap and the leader of the gang, an Irishman called Ned Kelly, has gone on the run."

"Well, you be careful on the road, George. With bushrangers out and about you never know what might 'appen" Mary Ann cautioned.

"He's two days ride to the west of here, Mother, he's not going to trouble us. Besides, from what I hear it's not as simple as it sounds".

"What d'you mean? George" William asked.

George, settled into his chair and began, "Well, as I was told, he's from a poor Irish family with four girls at home. The trap that was shot had been given the flick by one of them and he was trying to get his own back by arresting one of her brothers when this Ned Kelly came back home and there was a scuffle and the gun went off".

"Where did you hear that?" William asked, his curiosity piqued.

"When I was in town a couple of days ago, having a drink with some mates" he replied.

"I don't care what the trufe is, George, if there's a man'unt there'll be guns and if there's guns there'll be trouble and I don't want this family caught up in it." Mary Ann said with determination.

"Well, as I said, Mum" George replied, "This is all happening two day's ride from here and if he's being hunted, the last thing he'll want to do is show his face this close to Melbourne and Talbot. We'll be all right on the road and I've got Dad's musket if there is trouble".

Mary Ann shook her head but said no more and conversation turned to the weather and the state of the roads until there was a commotion outside and Mary Jane stood up from the table to settle what sounded like a dispute amongst the children. Mary Ann laughed at Mary Jane's resigned expression and joined her as they went outside.

* * *

SIX MONTHS later Mary Ann's world came crashing down yet again. George had been chopping wood outside when she heard Frederick shouting with alarm, "Mother, come quickly, there's something wrong with George!" The door burst open and Frederick ran to her, "Quickly, he's collapsed. What to do?"

Outside she could see that George was lying among split logs and splintered wood chips next to his axe which was lodged in the earth where he must have dropped it. He was holding his chest and struggling to breath. As Mary Ann hurried to his side he gave one convulsive heave and fell back. She knelt down – not without a little difficulty – and felt his brow. George had closed his eyes and his arm had by now released its hold on his chest and had dropped to his side, lifeless.

It was all over in seconds and Mary Ann just held him, shocked, almost unable to comprehend what had just happened.

* * *

GEORGE'S DEATH was a blow that none of the family had expected and it consequently had a correspondingly harder impact than it might have done. They were not prepared and it resulted in a scrambling about as James and William busied themselves with looking after George's affairs, and Mary Ann's. It was 1879 and Mary Ann was now 65 years old. Still very much aware of what was going on around her, but naturally not as active, complaining from time to time about the aches and pains of age.

* * *

JAMES AND MARY also celebrated the birth of a new addition to the family that same year, a bonny daughter named Marion and William and Mary Jane, not to be outdone, also produced a son, named William junior.

Amidst the celebrations of a growing Bright family and the shock of George's loss, discussion turned to Mary Ann's welfare. James and William quickly agreed that William and his family should move in with his mother and Frederick should take over the carterage business.

But they also wondered whether Mary Ann wouldn't be better of living in Talbot where help and medical attention would be more readily available and it would be easier for James and his family to visit. Frederick was getting on for 16 and it wouldn't hurt him to be closer to job opportunities in town as well if the carterage work fell away.

The town that had once boasted a population of 15,000 had less than a fifth of this now with the gradual demise of large parts of the mining industry as the leads ran dry and there was a surplus of acceptable accommodation available at cheap rents. So it was decided that – provided they could get Mary Ann to agree – they would find premises in Talbot and move the business and the household into town.

* * *

So IT WAS that Mary Ann, William and his family and Frederick saw in the new year of 1880 in the town of Talbot. It was a great difference from the countryside, but it allowed Mary Ann to walk to Scandinavian Crescent and have tea with friends and family, browse the shops and watch the world hustle by. She particularly enjoyed shopping with her granddaughter, Mary Ann (William's daughter) and they both had fun telling people that they were both named Mary Ann Bright, to the confusion of many a shopkeeper. It was even more fun when Elizabeth's daughter, Mary Ann came along too although she, of course, was not a Bright but three Mary Anns together was a worthy statement!

When not with the family she would sit contentedly in a rocking chair on the veranda of her new home watching the people, the carts, the horses hurry by and her mind would drift with recollections of times and people past.

The months passed pleasantly, grandchildren came to play, she captivated their minds with stories of life in London and on the goldfields, James, William and Frederick spoiled her rotten. And she felt the press of age on her shoulders.

With the advent of Autumn she caught a bad cold that then sank onto her chest so she spent the next several weeks battling to get rid of it with the doctor attending regularly.

* * *

ON THE 11TH JULY, 1880 - a sunny day, she stepped out of the house and settled herself in her rocking chair on the veranda, well wrapped up because, although it wasn't 'London' cold, it wasn't that warm either, but she relished the fresh air and enjoyed watching the world pass by. The sun smiled on her.

She smiled too as she thought on times past, relived good and desperate times with Robert, walking back from church after they were married, the day he came home with a gold nugget the size of a small plum and the excitement it caused. She thought of her family in England, the clacking of the loom and her father and brother concentrating on their task as the light faded. She wished that she could speak to her mother, to show her how things had worked out after all.

She reflected on the children she had lost and shed a tear for each of them. So hard. So hard to bear. Then she thought with pride about James, William and Frederick and all her grandchildren. Three good boys who would make a good life for themselves, she was sure and their offspring too. She wondered about Emma and Liz – what had become of them? Strange, she hadn't thought about them for years. She hoped things had gone well for them both. And as she thought about them, she remembered vividly walking down Oxford Street with that damn Dutch clock under her cloak. Her heart beating with the thrill and the cockiness of having pulled it off. She almost laughed out loud as she recalled that.

And then she thought of Robert again. The day he proposed. Walking back from St. John's in Launceston after meeting Reverend Browne, Robert's smile. In her hands she held a bible with the dried wild flowers from the bouquet that Robert had given her still lying between the pages. She touched them as if to make contact with Robert somehow. She missed him so much.

* * *

WILLIAM CAME HOME to find her in her chair asleep, the bible in her lap. The sun had not yet retired for the day and it cast a beautiful honey-rich glow across the drifting clouds. He tried to wake her.

But she had gone. She was with Robert now.

William cried out loud with anguish and beat his fist uselessly on a post. He pulled his mother to him and tears fell from his cheeks onto her greying hair.

He realised an age had now passed and that the family would have to carry on in her stead. To live up to everything that she had represented: strength, courage, fortitude, determination, love. He shook his head as he asked himself, 'How would they manage without her?'.

* * *

MARY ANN WAS BURIED TOGETHER with her beloved Robert in the Amherst cemetery. Trees arched over the field of graves, providing shade and shelter, rainfall had greened the grass and hedges. It was quiet, peaceful – a gentle breeze rustling dead, brown leaves that clung tenaciously onto their branches and the music of birdsong the only sounds.

The children erected a fine tombstone with a wrought iron railing to mark that here lay two people of distinction who deserved respect and attention; people of note. These two souls were part of the foundation of this great new country of Australia. They had made a difference and now they were at rest.

Tears stained the headstone as they each said their goodbyes. And as they walked away, an onlooker might have concluded that it was the end of a story.

But it was also the beginning of many, many more.

Amherst Pioneer Cemetery, 2019

AFTERWORD

Author's notes.

The names recorded for posterity in the history books are those of the politicians, industrialists, aristocrats, military leaders; generally those who chose their parents well. But the lives of unheralded millions of people that swirled in and out of history are at least just as important, perhaps more so given that they were the mass of humanity that shaped our world.

There are readily available records about people like Governor Arthur and the heroes of the Eureka Stockade so there is no point repeating them here, but I have provided below a little more colour about some of the real people, less well known, whose lives were intertwined with Robert's and Mary Ann's stories in Book I and Book II:

Edmund Bryant was born in 1803 in Somerset, England, the youngest of four brothers. He was clearly an adventurous soul who appears to have had more ambition than capability, which was put to the test after his brother Francis died. He and his brother James emigrated to VDL in 1824 on the *Aguillar* with a letter of recommendation from Lt. Governor Sorrell after soliciting a land grant from the Earl of Bathurst. They took up land near Jericho, about 70 kilometres north of Hobart. He returned to England in 1824 and married Jane Mogg in 1825 bringing her back to VDL in October 1825 with his brother Francis, wife and children. He also brought pure-bred sheep and cattle and a 2 year-old thoroughbred stallion, Viscount[1], as well as goods for sale. The brothers had a store in Hobart and a butchery, imported sheep and cattle and ran stock on various properties. Edmund leased Trafalgar and was in occupation by October 1831. As early as 1836 he shipped 1,000 sheep to Port Phillip and was a signatory to a letter from Port Phillip settlers to Governor Sir Richard Bourke requesting land grants. In 1839 his lease on 'Trafalgar' expired and he purchased nearby 'Kingston' from John Batman. 1845 was not a good year for him. He was having trouble meeting his debts and in March 1845, while living at 'Kingston', near Ben Lomond, 8 or 9 bushrangers led by Daniel Priest (transported for life on the *Lord Lyndoch* in 1838) and John Smith (also serving a life term off the *Marion Watson in 1842*) seized Edmund and his family and stole several goods. Three months later, on 7[th]June, an insolvency hearing took place in Launceston followed by another hearing on 22nd June applying for his discharge from insolvency. Two months later, in August, Edmund was visited by two more bushrangers at his 'Shepherd's hut' at Kingston (Wilson and Leaman who were once at Norfolk Island and had escaped from Bridgewater penitentiary). It would seem that this was the last straw and within two months he had moved his family to Port Phillip district, arriving in Melbourne on the 31st October, 1845 - around the same time that Robert and Mary Ann would have been considering emigration themselves. He acquired 'Cairn Curran' in 1848 and died there less than a year later, on 21st April 1849, aged only 46.

Benjamin Bright (Robert's brother) was Robert's twin brother, presumably named after the Brights' second son (who died before his first birthday in 1808). Cambridge Family

History Society records show that Robert and Benjamin were both baptised at St. Giles, Cambridge on 5th December, 1813 - the sons of James and Elizabeth from Castle End, Cambridge. He married Rebecca Chapman in 1837 at St Giles, joined the army in Ireland around 1839, served as a private with the 43rd (Monmouthshire) regiment and fought in South Africa in 1851/3 receiving the South Africa medal and was then posted to Madras, India in 1854 where his regiment assisted in putting down the Indian mutiny. He died of acute dysentry in Bangalore on 8th June, 1855, probably caused by eating contaminated food or water - the same time that Robert was working the Bendigo goldfields, both unaware of what had happened to each other.

Benjamin Bright (fourth child) was born 8th July, 1851 in today's northern suburbs of Melbourne in the Merri Creek area according to church records and was baptised at St. Peter's, Eastern Hill, which is the oldest Anglican church standing on its original site in the inner Melbourne city area. The building was first used for services in 1847. As another son named Benjamin was born in March 1860, I have assumed that this Benjamin died as a child before then although I have no records to say how or when exactly.

Benjamin Bright (seventh child) was born on 5th March, 1859 and died 10 months later in 1860 at McCallum Creek .

Elizabeth Bright/nee Gee (Robert's mother) was born 10th March, 1776 at Longstanton, Cambridgeshire. She married Robert's father, James Bright, on 20th January, 1793. She died in 1835, still in Cambridge, aged 59 - three years after Robert was transported.

Elizabeth Bright (Robert's sister) probably named after her mother (Elizabeth nee Gee), she was born in 1795 at Longstanton, Cambridgeshire. She died in 1826, aged 31, at St. Giles, Cambridge.

Elizabeth Bright (fifth child) was born in Bendigo in 1853.

She married Thomas Seargent in 1870 aged 17 and was only 21 years old when she died, a few days after giving birth to Margaret, in Talbot on 5th May, 1874. Margaret also died two days later. They are both buried in the Amherst, Victoria cemetery.

Frederick Bright (eighth or ninth child – see John Bright) was born in McCallum Creek, Near Talbot on 11/6/1862. He was alive when Mary Ann passed away but I cannot find other data.

George Bright (Robert's brother) was born in 1811 and was probably named after the Brights' first son who died not yet five years old in 1808. There are no other records that I have been able to trace to find what became of him.

George Bright (second child) was born 31st December, 1844 in Launceston. He was alive on 25th October, 1875 when his father passed away but had died by 11th July 1880 according to notes on Mary Ann's death certificate.

James Bright (Robert's father) was born on Christmas Day, 1773 in Whittlesford, Cambridgeshire. He married Elizabeth Gee on 20th January, 1793 at St. Botolph, Cambridge. He died in October, 1849 – fourteen years after his wife - probably unaware that Robert had married and that he had three grandsons by then, one named after him and others to take his name down the generations.

James Bright (first child)

James Bright

Records show his birth as being in Launceston on 16th March 1842 *and* 1843. 1843 ties to the age shown on his marriage certificate.

He would have been named after Robert's father. He married Mary Andrew on 12th December, 1867 and his profession is shown as Carrier, his wife a servant from Scotland and his father-in-law a miner.

He learned to write, became a farmer at Mount Lonarch,

Victoria about 40km to the west of Talbot, and saw the 20th century arrive, living through the First World War and dying on 23rd May, 1929 at the grand age of 85.

The Mt. Lonarch estate stayed in the Bright family for 90 years. He is buried at the Amphitheatre cemetery in Glenlogie, Victoria.

James Bright's signature & residence at Kangaroo Flat, Talbot on 28/10/1875 from Father's death certificate

John or Robert or Benjamin Bright (eighth child?) Records on birth and death certificates of other family members show that a child named Robert had been alive but was dead by 1859, however the name is totally absent on subsequent family records. Likewise another Robert was dead by 1875 but he doesn't appear on previous or later records and another Benjamin was dead by 1880 but isn't recorded as being alive on previous family records. I haven't been able to trace any birth or death certificates for these names. This doesn't mean that they didn't exist but it could also all be clerical errors or memory lapses or misremembered data from those who recorded the information when the certificates were prepared. I have not written this person or persons, if they existed, into the story.

Robert Bright (sixth child) was born 4th April, 1856 at Loddon Junction. I cannot find a death certificate but in March 1859 (on the second Benjamin's birth certificate) he is noted as deceased.

Willian Bright (third child)

William was born in Launceston in 1848. He was probably named after Mary Ann's father. He married a 4-month pregnant, 17 year old Mary Jane Jones on 27th February, 1872 at St.

374

Paul's church, Clunes – his occupation was shown as Labourer and he was resident at Beckworth (about 12km west of Clunes) at the time.

James witnessed the marriage certificate but William and his wife signed with a cross. He later learned to at least sign his name (see above). His wife, Mary Jane Jones, gave birth to a daughter, Eliza Ellen, on 10th July the same year. They had many more children including Mary Ann Bright whose photograph appears at the beginning of this book. He became a farmer and died in Tamworth, NSW on 14th September, 1925 at the age of 77.

William Bright

William Bright's signature & residence (son, Talbot) on 12/7/1880 from mother's death certificate

Francis Colgrave was a ploughman by trade and was 25 years old when he disembarked at Hobart Town off the *Circassian* on 16th February, *1833*. He had been sentenced to 14 years transportation at Huntingdon assizes on 7th March, 1832 for stealing a chest of tea and clothing. He had been incarcerated before for housebreaking and his brother, Samuel had also been transported for life earlier following four offences of theft and assault. Francis earned his Ticket of Leave on 9th March 1839 and received a conditional pardon on 28th October 1841, marrying his wife Isabella Watkins on 7th October, 1842. By 1858 he was the owner of a house in Evandale and continued farming on 12 acres of land through 1890. He died at his home on 27th October, 1890 aged 85. His wife died a few days later. They had several children and his son, Francis, owned 90 acres at Blessington in 1881.

William Cousens (Cousins) was apparently 17 years old when he arrived in Hobart on the Georgiana in 1834, which would make his birth year 1816 or 1817. The Cambridge gaol report noted his 'bad character' but there is no other evidence to support this assessment. He was orderly on the voyage and his Certificate of Freedom was granted on 23rd July, 1839 at the expiry of his 7-year sentence – the same day as Robert. There is, unusually, no note of any misconduct on his record. On arrival he was assigned to a Mr. J. Hooper and in 1835 was assigned to a Mr. A. Fisher. He seems to have disappeared thereafter into history. There is a record of the death of William Cousins in Launceston in 1875. He was a labourer by trade and the cause of death was a compound fracture of the arm. It is possible they are one and the same.

Sarah Crocker/nee Goulding (Mary Ann's mother), Sarah Ann Golding or Goulding, was born in 1776 on the 21st July in Westminster, London. She married John Crocker at St. Leonard's church in Shoreditch on 29th March 1796 and gave birth to a son, John in 1798, a daughter, Sarah in 1800 and another son, William in 1805. In 1808 her husband died aged only 32. But the next year she married again, this time to William Crocker, quite probably her husband's brother. At the age of 37 she gave birth to Mary Ann on 3rd May, 1814 and then another son, Peter eighteen months later. As narrated in this story, her second husband died, aged 48, in 1825. Mary Ann left England in 1834 never to see her mother or siblings again. Her mother continued to live and work in Bethnal Green and Shoreditch, dying a pauper aged 83 in July 1859.

William Crocker (Mary Ann's father) was born in 1775 in Shoreditch. He married Sarah Goulding on 21 May, 1809 and died in June 1825 (or possibly 1826) in Shoreditch aged 50 or 51.

Mary Creed was as an Irishwoman born in 1806, a house servant, from County Cork. She was sentenced to 14 years for stealing. On arrival in Hobart on the *Edward* in 1834 she was removed to the prison hospital. On May 1, 1835 she was punished with solitary confinement for being drunk and disorderly. A couple of months later 'having recovered from the complaint for which she was invalided' she was gaoled for 3 months at the Hobart female factory, in the second-class section (i.e. for a relatively minor offence). On being released she was returned in March, 1836 for being drunk. In April, May and July of that year she was in further trouble then, on 17th October, she died, still in the Hobart House of Correction, aged 30.

Sarah Davis was a house servant by occupation, from Spitalfields and 16 years old when she arrived on the Edward in Hobart. She had been given 14 years for stealing clothing from her employer. Although the story has Mary Ann and Sarah sharing a cell in March and April 1836 at Launceston's House of Correction, I don't know this for a fact, but it's certainly a possibility because Sarah was sentenced to 6 months in the Crime Class at the Factory on 16th January that year. She had just completed seven days in solitary confinement on bread and water for using abusive language two days before Mary Ann joined her in the cell on 4th March. She was more than a match for Mary Ann! Her rebellious and wayward actions saw her constantly in and out of the Factory: drunk and disorderly, absent without leave, absconding, using abusive and obscene language, refusing to attend Chapel, being unable to account for property etc. In 1838 she was given nine months hard labour for *'misconduct in having had money in her possession without satisfactorily being able to account for the manner in which she became possessed of it'*. In July that year her term was extended by three years and in December it was extended a further twelve months for absconding. On the 20th January 1844, she was ordered to serve a probationary period before obtaining her Ticket of

Leave which was granted on 14th December that year and, staying out of trouble, she was recommended for a conditional pardon on 16th March, 1847 – the condition being that she not return to the United Kingdom until her term had been served. She finally received this at the age of 31 on April 9th, 1849 per the convict record book (but advertised in the Cornwall Chronicle of 13th January that year) – fifteen years after arriving in Van Diemen's Land but three years earlier than her extended sentence demanded. She must have convinced someone in authority that she was a reformed character. After that....?

Elizabeth Diamond (real name Primmet) was born in Shoreditch, London on 13th March 1818. She was 17 years old when she arrived in Hobart on the *Edward*. Like Mary Ann, she was not immediately assigned but records show that she was soon working for a Mr. Ferguson (probably in or near Launceston). She was given 14 days solitary confinement on bread & water October 11th, 1834 for being out after hours and another 21 days solitary confinement on bread and water for being absent without leave two months later. She married a free settler, Charles Best, on 14th October, 1835 (perhaps explaining her absences). There are no other records of her falling foul of the system. By July 1848 she had moved to Kensington, South Australia and records show she was in Castlemaine, Victoria in 1857 (five hours to the south of Bendigo, where Robert and Mary Ann were staying at that time). In all, she gave birth to twelve children, including a Mary Ann in 1857. She moved back to Tasmania (the name had been changed from Van Diemen's land on 1st January, 1856) – probably by 1886. Her husband died at Deloraine, Tasmania in 1892 and she, herself passed away at Westbury, to the west of Launceston on 12th September, 1905 – 25 years after Mary Ann - at the grand old age of 87.

Margaret Drury was born about 1812 in Corbally, Ireland which would have made her 23 when she was transported. She was convicted of stealing from her aunt and her uncle and was sentenced to 7 years, transported on the *Neva* from Cork, heading for Sydney with 150 other female Irish convicts, 34 children, 9 free women (with their 21 children) and 26 crew. The *Neva* didn't make it. It was shipwrecked approaching the Bass Straits northwest of King Island on 12th May, 1835. Most drowned, including all the children, but a few survivors (including the ship's commander, the first mate and 7 of the crew) were drifting for about 8 hours on rafts made from parts of the wreck. In all, 15 survivors, including 6 convicts made it to shore. Margaret was one of the convict women who survived and she was eventually sent to the Launceston Female Factory. There is no record that I have found of how long she was there, but we do know that she was charged with being drunk on 25th November, 1835 at the Factory. A week after this, one of the crew survivors, Peter Robinson, applied for permission to marry her and that took place at St. John's church, Launceston on 12th January, 1836. Marriage was clearly not straightforward. She was now assigned to her husband but on 21st March, 1836 she was imprisoned for 21 days on bread and water for harbouring a convict on assignment. It was her husband who laid the charge! I have woven Margaret into Mary Ann's story as they would most probably have met when Mary Ann was also serving one month in March of 1836 and 3 months a year later when Margaret was again in the Crime Class for 6 months (from 25th February 1837), for being drunk and indecently exposing her person – again her husband laying the charges. She was back at the Factory in July, 1839 for 6 months for having absconded and during this time served an unusually long 30 days in solitary on bread and water for disobeying orders. She earned her certificate of freedom in 1840, two years before her sentence expired, and settled with her husband in George Town before moving to Victoria, possibly lured by the gold rush or as a result of the Geelong, Portland Bay and Port Fairy Emigration scheme set up in 1845 to encourage settlement in Port Phillip by tradesmen and labourers. Possibly the same scheme used by Robert and Mary Ann to pay for their emigration to Victoria as narrated in the story.

Mary Gillard was a farm girl from Tiverton in Devon, England transported for 7 years for housebreaking. She was nineteen years old when she arrived in Hobart off the *Edward*. She had a fiery spirit which was clearly not doused by her experiences on the voyage when she was almost swept overboard. She was in the Launceston House of Correction in 1835, 1836 and 1837. Charges included disobedience and having possession of tobacco, for which she received one month's hard labour. This clearly had little effect for she was back in the Crime Class again in 1837 for refusing to attend chapel and refusing her dinner. The next year,1838, was an eventful one where she kicked against the traces. In February, she went AWOL and received 14 days solitary confinement. In June, she went AWOL again and received 3 months imprisonment of which 7 days were spent in solitary on bread and water. In September, she was given 7 days solitary on bread and water for fighting in the nursery ward and in November she was given 6 months in the Crime Class for going AWOL once more. In 1839 she received 12 months hard labour at the Launceston House of Correction for going AWOL yet again; in 1840 she was given 10 days solitary on bread and water for 'neglect of duty' and then in 1843 she gave birth to an illegitimate child. The next two years were quiet but in 1846 she served 9 months hard labour. However, on the 18th July, 1848 she was recommended for a Conditional Pardon and, despite being absent from her place of residence and receiving 14 days hard labour in 1849, the Pardon was approved at the end of January, 1850. Her sentence must have been extended because it should have been served by 1841. She sounds like quite a character. I have no further information, but I hope that things worked out for her. She seems to have had an unquenchable spirit.

Dr. James Hall was born in 1784 in the same district as Mary Ann, in Shoreditch. He had an eventful life including serving on HMIS *Selafail* – the flagship of the Russian squadron operating in the Adriatic (1805-7) and serving on HMS *Jackson* after the abdication of Napoleon in 1814[2]. For James Hall, the *Georgiana* in 1832 was the fourth voyage as a Surgeon Superintendent to Australia (previously he had sailed with the *Agamemnon* in 1820, the *Mary-Ann* in 1822 and the *Brothers* in 1824). After his arrival at Sydney in 1822, he took a leading part in a bitter political fight alleging that Ann Rumsby, a young convict from the *Mary Ann*, had accused her master, Dr. Henry Grattan Douglas, of impropriety. She denied Hall's story and was convicted of perjury. This was quashed by Governor Sir Thomas Brisbane and Brisbane's supporters portrayed Hall as litigious and meddlesome; he was even accused of challenging the colonial secretary to a duel - which Hall denied – and of sending 'false and slanderous reports' to England regarding prostitution of women prisoners at Emu Plains. Then, on the *Brothers* voyage in 1824, he ran afoul of some of the crew and of the women convicts because of his efforts to stamp out prostitution. On arriving at Hobart he laid charges of piracy and attempted murder. He claimed to have been assaulted by some of the women and alleged that the chief mate had been the instigator. His case was considered to be one only of aggravated assault and conspiracy, not mutiny or attempted murder, and nothing further transpired, indeed Hall's lack of tact was seen as the main reason for the trouble. Another report was then sent to England about Hall's 'very improper conduct' observing that he was 'undeserving (of) any further advancement in his profession'. On his return to England he obtained an appointment in the *Andromache*, from which he was invalided in November 1835. In 1836, with a permanent liver complaint, he retired on a pension and he died on 30 March 1869 at Gladstone House, Southsea, England.

Mary Higgins was a housemaid, born in 1805, married to Thomas Higgins, living in Surrey. She was transported for life for stealing a watch and pledging a gown, presumably taken from her mistress. She arrived in Hobart on the *Hydery* on 11th August, 1832 from Plymouth. Despite a lot of sickness on this ship, she appears to have managed the voyage without serious physical issues and the Surgeon awarded her a 'Good' rating. Four months after arriving she was found drunk in a 'disorderly house' and caught stealing a pair of stockings worth 1/6 from her master, Mr. Linckman, to whom she had been assigned. She was confined in a cell at the Cascades for six days and committed to the Crime Class for three months. The records show she was still there in March 1834 and I have placed her in Mary Ann's ward in this story although I have no direct record to confirm this. She was again in trouble in November 1838 – out after hours - and was sentenced to six months hard labour in December 1845, however this was commuted on the authority of the Lt. Governor; reason unknown. Compared to many of her peers it would seem that she was reasonably free of trouble.

John Hurley (or Harley) appears to have been a hard man. A Londoner, born in 1806, he was a waterman by trade. He arrived in Van Diemen's Land in March 1831 on the *Red Rover* having been sentenced to seven years for housebreaking, like Robert Bright. He was assigned on arrival to a Mr. Bastian, was soon thereafter punished with fifty lashes for abusive language, absconded and was recaptured in Hobart in September 1832 and was sentenced to six months hard labour. In 1833 he was serving six months again and while in gaol spent six days on the Wheel, a particularly hard physical punishment. He was then put on the Notman road gang, notorious for its iron discipline (see Robert Nutman, below). In 1834 he was given a twelve month hard labour sentence for conveying a letter from a convict on the Grass Tree Hill road gang to persons in Hobart to obtain supplies. That was later extended by two months for burning his bed. Two weeks after permission to marry Mary Ann was refused in 1836, he was sentenced to two months on the Reiby's Ford road gang for fighting with fellow servants – possibly teased and frustrated at his marriage plans being thwarted. In the first half of 1837 he was in more trouble and the records show that he was banished from the district. There are several notes of him being drunk throughout his time as a convict and it is tempting to surmise that Mary Ann escaped what might well have been an abusive marriage. I have found nothing definitive after he received his Certificate of Freedom in 1837, although there are records of a John Hurley marrying a Mary Ann Hodder in 1848 and departing for Port Phillip/Melbourne in 1848 from Launceston. The same man? Possibly.

Mary Hutchinson (nee Oakes) was born in 1810 at Parramatta, New South Wales, one of fourteen children. Her parents were missionaries and her childhood was spent near the Parramatta Female factory where her father was superintendent (1814-22). Not yet 16 years of age, she married John Hutchinson, a Wesleyan minister and missionary and they went to Tonga but were eventually forced to return to New South Wales. They then went to Hobart where, in 1832, John Hutchinson was appointed superintendent and she was appointed matron of the Cascades Female House of Correction with specific responsibility for health and behaviour. The infant mortality rate at Cascades was a scandal because of the conditions and five of her twelve children also died while she was at the Factory. Her husband's recurring illnesses left her in control of an institution which by 1850 housed over 1,000 women. An inspector commented on her disciplined management in 1851: *'The cleanliness of the prison was almost dazzling, and the order and discipline appeared faultless'. 'Dead silence' everywhere was observed'.* When ill health forced her husband to retire in 1851, her continued employment *'as a subordinate in the Establishment of* *which she had been virtually the Superintendent'* was considered inappropriate; but as a woman she was not thought suitable to be Superintendent. She was, however, appointed matron-in-charge of the smaller Launceston 'factory' where she remained until 1854 when she retired on a pension of £60 p.a. She died in Hobart in 1880 aged 69.

Ann Murray came from London, sentenced in the same court as Mary Ann to transportation for seven years at the age of 19 for stealing but instead served 3 years 8 ½ months in Newgate. Released for 10 months, she was back in trouble for stealing clothing and was this time transported, aged 24, on the *New Grove* on 4th September, 1834 – four months after Mary Ann on the *Edward*. On arrival she was assigned to a Mr. Abbott in Hobart, but was absent drunk and returned to Cascades. The rebellious Ann obviously enjoyed a drink. At her trial she explained, 'I was very much in liquor' to justify her actions. She was back and forth from assignment to Cascades five times in 1835. 1836 saw more of the same. In 1837 she had moved inland but it was the same story through 1839, being assigned to a succession of masters including Mr. Langmaid in 1838 (as had Mary Ann). Her final censure was in 1840 – 'disorderly conduct and making use of obscene language in the hearing of the females of her master's family' while assigned to Mr. Hardwick of Norfolk Plains. She had been in and out of the Crime Class (7 ½ months in all), had been in solitary confinement on bread and water for a total of 24 days and, for this final transgression, served 3 months with hard labour at the Factory. In 1839 she had a child, Eleanor, and was eventually married to the father, Edward Peat, in 1842 - he had applied three times for permission before succeeding (1840, '41 and '42). In all she served 17 different masters and had 22 periods of punishment. She died in Launceston in 1873, eight years after Edward Peat, a grandmother, at the age of 62.

(Her story is more fully told in 'Convict Lives, Female Convicts Research Centre, ISBN 978-0-9871443-4-8)

Robert Notman was a Scotsman known as 'Old Bobby Nutman' and his cruelty to prisoners placed in his charge was renowned throughout the colony. He was reputed to have whipped men nearly to death and that old convicts feared him greatly. However, he was also known to adopt a much more compassionate manner to political prisoners. "He told us that murderers, thieves and robbers who had been placed under him heretofore, could not be governed without being flogged.." (from Samuel Snow, who was banished to VDL for participating in the Patriot War in Upper Canada in 1838). Notman eventually returned home to Scotland.

Dr. Joseph Steret was serving as Assistant Surgeon on the *Conqueror in 1820.* In 1824 he was on the *Bellerophon* and in 1825 he was assigned to the *Ranger* from the *Jasper.* His notes on the voyage of the *Edward* reflect well on his skills and his compassion.

Emma Wells was born in Southwark, London on 9th January 1817 and was 18 years old when she arrived in Hobart on the *Edward.* On board she had earned a 'Very Good' rating from Dr. Steret. She was assigned to Reverend John Mackersey, the Presbyterian Minister of Kerklands, living at the Kerklands Manse near Campbell Town south of Launceston. She married William Watson on 10th August, 1835, a freed convict from Stirling, Scotland who had arrived on the *Morley* twelve years earlier (in 1823). She was heavily pregnant at her wedding and gave birth to a son, also William, three days later. On 30th November 1836 she was imprisoned for 15 days for 'improper conduct towards her husband' but suffered no other *recorded* penalties or marital discord. She gained a Conditional Pardon on 7th February 1840 and her Certificate of Freedom in 1842. She lived in Launceston until 1846 when the family moved to Melbourne, arriving on the *Henry* from Launceston on the 4th August, 1846 with four children. In all she gave birth to eleven children, including one daughter named Mary Ann. Her son, Edward passed away on 24th November 1860 in Yerling, Victoria and less than a month later Emma died in childbirth, aged 43, on 13th December 1860 at Brushy Creek, Mooroolbark, Victoria. She is buried with her husband William at Boroondara Cemetery, Kew, Victoria.

APPENDIX 1

The contribution that convicts made to the economy is evident from the increasingly anxious local clamour in support of the maintenance of transportation :

* * *

Launceston, March 5th, 1839

[DRAFT]

To Her Majesty the Queen – Lords – or Commons (as the case may be.)

THE HUMBLE PETITION of the Colonists inhabiting the Northern Division of the Island of Van Diemen's Land – respectively set forth the following: –

- That Petitioners have heard with concern that the Select Committee of the Commons House of Parliament, appointed to enquire into the System of Transportation, have concluded their Report with certain Resolutions, of which the First is as follows: – "That Transportation to New South Wales and Van Diemen's Land should be discontinued "as soon as practicable."

- That Petitioners humbly beg to express it as their conscientious opinion that the Resolutions of the Committee are, as respects this Colony (for of New South Wales they cannot speak of their own knowledge), founded on evidence at once partial, incomplete, and in many instances wholly unfounded in fact.

- That Petitioners do not pretend to say which is the best system of Secondary Punishment for the Mother Country to adopt; but Petitioners would humbly suggest, that upon a question upon which so many intelligent men have differed in opinion, the most grave and mature deliberation should be given to any proposals for change in the existing System.

- That whatever the *comparative* effects of the Transportation System might appear to be, upon sufficient trial of other modes of Secondary Punishment, it is confidently believed that its positive results are widely different from those which the Select Committee have deduced from the incomplete, yet exaggerated evidence received by them.

- That in particular, as respects the character of the Free Population of this Colony, the effect which a large labouring convict population has had upon *their* social condition, has been entirely misrepresented. As a body, the free settlers of Van Diemen's Land, of the present day, need not fear comparison with any other equal number of the Queens subjects in any part of Her Majesties dominions, whether as to HUMANITY, as to good morals, or as to their attention to the ordinances of religion. Indeed it is believed, that the very presence of a convict class, as to whom it is merely a rhetorical exaggeration to say that they stand in the relation of master to *slave*, – operates rather as a provocative to highly exemplary conduct than otherwise. The Free Settlers do not amount to more than –– ministers, whom they voluntarily support; *besides* ––– clergyman of the Church of England; ––– ministers of the Church of Scotland; ––– priests of the Roman Catholic persuasion; and various catechists and lecturers, supported by Government.

They have --- Branch Bible Societies, Saving Banks in the chief towns, and various other Societies of a benevolent and useful character. – Their whole aspect in fact is that of a moral, intelligent, active, and industrious community of Britons; and of the truth of this they challenge investigation.

- That it were an absurdity to assert that vice does *not* exist, and exist to a very great and deplorable extent, among the Convict Classes; but it would be an equal absurdity to *expect* any such state of things in the Colony. But seeing the nature of this portion of the population, (which Petitioners believe has too seldom been kept in mind; whereby much has been referred to *the System* which ought to have been referred to the original or inherent depravity of the Convicts) - Petitioners cannot but consider that a much greater extent of vice and crime might have been expected, than what is really to be found among the Convict classes.

- That, indeed, while it is admitted that vice abounds, there are a vast number of instances, and the proportions of them is believed to be increasing daily, in which Convicts, or men who have been such, have become sober and well–conducted, and not a few of them religious members of society.

– That *Transportation*, coupled with assignment, has now had the experience of nearly half a century; and from that experience, the following results may be affirmed of it, as, either having taken place, or (*under the correction of ascertained evils*) being attainable for the future:

Transportation removes the criminal, in the great mass of instances *forever*, from the seat of his crime.

Assignment eases the State of the cost of maintenance and superintendence of criminals, to a very great extent.

The Convict, as he becomes free, finds himself in a society in which, though known as having been a prisoner, his past condition is not felt as an insupportable reproach to him; while he can obtain good wages for his labour; every Convict, by the time he has arrived at his freedom, having attained an expertness in one or more of the various trades and callings useful in a young country, – featuring the system of Transportation, that enables it to vie, at least as far as this point is in question, with the best devised Penitentiary Systems of America.

The Transportation System is susceptible of every degree of necessary severity; while its adjunct, Assignment, (which Petitioners emphatically deny to be in the mass of cases a condition of hardship, but affirm it to be, on the contrary, one of great physical comfort,) – need not be resorted to, until, as indeed late regulations have directed, a probationary term of punishment should previously be gone through by the Convict, in the service of the Government.

The want of adequate religious instruction has been the greatest fault of the Transportation System in past years; yet perhaps no system offers a better opportunity for forwarding such instruction in an effective manner. With the increase in wealth, religious observances have rapidly increased among the Free Settlers, and are daily spreading their healthy influence downwards, at little or no cost to the Mother Country.

Another evil of the past – *the disparity of sexes*. This evil has been greatly diminished by the late immigrations of females from Britain; and if this excellent plan were continued, there would soon be little room left for objection on this head. The freed Convict would then see before him the increased probability of domestic repose and comfort – the strongest of incentives to the reformed culprit to persevere in his renunciation of vicious courses.

- That, as Petitioners submit – if *there* be the actual or attainable advantages, which Transportation and Assignment hold out, the expediency of entirely changing the existing system for novel speculations in penal discipline, at no doubt with immense cost to the Parent Country, must be considered as doubtful in the extreme!

- That the Petitioners believe that they are benefited by the existing System. They do not desire to conceal this belief. They emigrated under the existing system; have embarked large capitals, and (by the aid of them and their industry) have acquired extensive property under it – it may be truly said under the faith of its continuance; they have laboured industriously, and enjoyed in past times much hardship, and risked much danger under it; but the result is one of which, if they wished, they could not conceal – unprecedented prosperity, as manifested in a large import and export trade, and the advantages resulting from which the Mother Country is a joint participate; in a highly improved territory; and large and flourishing towns and villages. They naturally do not desire to see their property shaken to its very foundation, by a change in the system of Secondary Punishment, – operating powerfully as that change would, on the supply of labour in the Colony; – more particularly as, from the limited extent of Crown lands available for sale, this Colony, unlike the neighbouring Provinces, has not the means of carrying on an extensive immigration of labourers: – But Petitioners rest their prayer, less on the injury to them and their families which any great and sudden change would entail, than on the danger which they think they can see resulting therefrom to the interests of the Mother Country.

Under all these circumstances, it is the humble prayer of Petitioners that Her Majesty the Queen, (Lords, or Commons, as the case may be,) will not introduce any measure having for its object to abolish the System of Transportation, coupled with Assignment, as the national system of Secondary Punishment: – Or that, before introducing such measure, a Commission of Enquiry be first sent out to Van Diemen's Land, to ascertain, upon undoubted evidence, on the spot, the exact moral and social condition of all classes in the Colony.

APPENDIX 2

Petition proposed by Dr Jones at Bendigo meeting, 2nd July, 1853

Humble Petition of the Undersigned Gold Diggers and other residents on the Gold Fields of the Colony

Sheweth

That your petitioners are the Loyal and Devoted Subjects of Her Most Gracious Majesty Queen Victoria the Sovereign Ruler of this Colony one of the dependencies of the British Crown

That in the present impoverished conditions of the Gold Fields the impost of Thirty Shillings a Month is more than Your Petitioners can pay as the fruit of labor at the Mines scarcely affords to a large proportion of the Gold Miners the common necessaries of life

That in consequence of the few Officials appointed to issues Licences the Diggers Storekeepers and other residents lose much time at each Monthly issues in procuring their Licenses

That the laborious occupation of Gold digging and the

privation attendant on a residence on the Gold fields entail much sickness and its consequent expenses on Your Petitioners

That in consequence of the Squatter Land Monopoly a large proportion of Successful Diggers who desire to invest their earnings in a portion of land are debarred from so doing

That newly arrived Diggers must lose much time and money before they become acquainted with the process of Gold Mining

That in consequence of Armed Men (many of whom are notoriously bad in characters) being employed to enforce the impost of Thirty Shillings a Month there is much ill feeling engendered amongst the Diggers against the Government

That in consequence of the non-possession by some of the Miners of a Gold Diggers License some of the Commissioners appointed to administer the Law of the Gold Fields have on various occasions Chained non-possessors to Trees and Condemned them to hard labor on the Public Roads of the Colony - Your Petitioners maintain this to be contrary to the spirit of the British Law which does not recognise the principle of the Subject being a Criminal because he is indebted to the State

That the impost of Thirty Shillings a Month is unjust because the successful and unsuccessful Digger are assessed in the same ratio

For these reasons and others which could be enumerated Your Petitioners pray Your Excellency to Grant the following Petition:

First.   To direct that the Licence Fee be reduced to Ten Shillings a Month

Secondly   To direct that Monthly or Quarterly Licenses be issued at the option of the Applicants

Thirdly   To direct that new arrivals or invalids be allowed on registering their names at the Commissioner's Office fifteen clear days residence on the Gold Fields before the License be enforced

Fourthly   To afford greater facility to Diggers and others resident on the Gold Fields who wish to engage in Agricultural Pursuits for investing their earnings in small allotments of land

Fifthly   To direct that the Penalty of Five Pounds for non-possession of License be reduced to One Pound

Sixthly   To direct that (as the Diggers and other residents on the Gold Fields of the Colony have uniformly developed a love of law and order) the sending of an Armed Force to enforce the License Tax be discontinued.

Your Petitioners would respectfully submit to Your Excellency's consideration in favour of the reduction of the License Fee that many Diggers and other residents on the Gold-fields who are debarred from taking a License under the present System would if the Tax were reduced to Ten Shillings a Month cheerfully comply with the Law so that the License Fund instead of being diminished would be increased

Your Petitioners would also remind your Excellency that a Petition is the only mode by which they can submit their wants to your Excellency's consideration as although they contribute more to the Exchequer that half the Revenue of the Colony they are the largest class of Her Majesty's Subjects in the Colony unrepresented

And your Petitioners as in duty bound will ever pray etc.

APPENDIX 3

Petition presented to the Governor of Victoria re: the Mining License fee :

To His Excellency Charles Joseph La Trobe
1st August 1853

Humble Petition of the Undersigned Gold Diggers and other residents on the Goldfields of the Colony

Sheweth

That your petitioners are the Loyal and Devoted Subjects of Her Most Gracious Majesty Queen Victoria the Sovereign Ruler of this Colony one of the dependencies of the British Crown

That in the present impoverished conditions of the Goldfields the impost of Thirty Shillings a Month is more than Your Petitioners can pay as the fruit of labor at the Mines scarcely affords to a large proportion of the Gold Miners the common necessaries of life

That in consequence of the few Officials appointed to issues Licences the Diggers Storekeepers and other residents lose much time at each Monthly issues in procuring their Licenses

That the laborious occupation of Gold digging and the privation attendant on a residence on the Goldfields entail much sickness and its consequent expenses on Your Petitioners

That in consequence of the Squatter Land Monopoly a large proportion of Successful Diggers who desire to invest their earnings in a portion of land are debarred from so doing

That newly arrived Diggers must lose much time and money before they become acquainted with the process of Gold Mining

That in consequence of Armed Men (many of whom are notoriously bad in characters) being employed to enforce the impost of Thirty Shillings a Month there is much ill feeling engendered amongst the Diggers against the Government

That in consequence of the non-possession by some of the Miners of a Gold Diggers License some of the Commissioners appointed to administer the Law of the Goldfields have on various occasions Chained non-possessors to Trees and Condemned them to hard labor on the Public Roads of the Colony - A proceeding Your Petitioners maintain to be contrary to the spirit of the British Law which does not recognise the principle of the Subject being a Criminal because he is indebted to the State

That the impost of Thirty Shillings a Month is unjust because the successful and unsuccessful Digger are assessed in the same ratio

For these reasons and others which could be enumerated Your Petitioners pray Your Excellency to Grant the following Petition

First. To direct that the Licence Fee be reduced to Ten Shillings a Month

Secondly. To direct that Monthly or Quarterly Licenses be issued at the option of the Applicants

Thirdly. To direct that new arrivals or invalids be allowed on registering their names at the Commissioner's Office fifteen clear days residence on the Goldfields before the License be enforced

Fourthly. To afford greater facility to Diggers and others resident on the Goldfields who wish to engage in Agricultural Pursuits for investing their earnings in small allotments of land

Fifthly. To direct that the Penalty of Five Pounds for non-possession of License be reduced to One Pound

Sixthly. To direct that (as the Diggers and other residents on the Goldfields of the Colony have uniformly developed a love of law and order) the sending of an Armed Force to enforce the License Tax be discontinued.

Your Petitioners would respectfully submit to Your Excellency's consideration in favour of the reduction of the License Fee that many Diggers and other residents on the Gold-fields who are debarred from taking a License under the present System would if the Tax were reduced to Ten Shillings a Month cheerfully comply with the Law so that the License Fund instead of being diminished would be increased.

Your Petitioners would also remind your Excellency that a Petition is the only mode by which they can submit their wants to your Excellency's consideration as although they contribute more to the Exchequer that half the Revenue of the Colony they are the largest class of Her Majesty's Subjects in the Colony unrepresented.

And your Petitioners as in duty bound will ever pray etc.

NOTES

1. ASSIGNMENT

1. On being assigned, the crime for which they had been transported would be confidentially communicated to the new master or mistress who was obliged, under penalty of a fine, to keep the information to themselves unless the convict gave permission otherwise.
2. Picking Oakum: the process of picking apart tarred ropes to be shred into fibres. The work was unpleasant and monotonous and before long created sores on tar-blackened fingers.

2. VIGILANTES

1. The Longford Hall cricket club was started on the 10th September the following year, 1836. (Longford is also the burial site of Charles Arthur, the aide de camp and nephew of the Governor who appeared earlier in this story at the Cascades Female Factory with his father. He played for Tasmania in the first-ever first class cricket match in Australia 15 years later, in 1851, against Victoria).
2. Fuller Pilch was an Englishman, considered the greatest batsman of his day (until W.G. Grace) and was the pioneer of forward defensive play; striking the ball in front of the wicket with a stroke that was known as 'Pilch's Poke'

3. RESTART

1. Truganini (1812-1876) was considered by many to have been the last full-blooded Aboriginal Tasmanian although she was outlived by Fanny Cochrane Smith (1834-1905). She was buried in front of the chapel at the Cascades female factory in May, 1876 but was eventually exhumed and cremated, her ashes being scattered over her homeland in the estuary of the Derwent and Huon rivers to the south of Hobart, as she had requested.
2. The assurances given were patently made in bad faith - there is no suggestion that Robinson or Arthur intended anything else but to exile them to Flinders Island. The settlement became more like a prison than a haven as conditions deteriorated and many of the residents died of disease and homesickness, never to return to their homeland.
3. Dinner meant the mid-day meal at this time.

4. COUNTDOWN

1. Snitch – slang for 'to inform on'
2. A ticketer – convict slang for a man or woman with a Ticket of Leave

5. AWOL

1. Cockney rhyming slang – North and South = mouth
2. Slang – Pocket it = put up with it.
3. Licensing laws in Launceston required landlords to eject any convicts on the premises after 8pm during the week and to refuse entry on Sundays at any time – unless they were travelling with a regular pass or with the authority of his or her master. Probably laws honoured more in the breach than the compliance.
4. Doggett's Coat and Badge: The oldest rowing race in the world (since 1715) took place (and still takes place) on the River Thames in London between up to six apprentice watermen rowing against the tide in their wherries over more than 4 ½ miles (although nowadays they row with the tide). The prize was a red coat (Doggett's coat) and a silver badge. Each competitor receives a miniature of Doggett's Badge that they can wear in their lapels. It was a good advertisement for trade at the time. Winning the Doggett's Coat and Badge is still a sought-after honour to this day.
5. This is a waterman's song from the time: 'The London Wherryman". Stratford St. Mary is a pretty, historic village in Suffolk – to the north-east of London in *John Constable* country – with a magnificent flint church . Farringdon is in London, not far from Mary Ann's birthplace.

6. CRIME CLASS

1. Panopticon – architectural form of a prison designed by Jeremy Bentham in in the late 18th century.
2. The 'Ten Bells' was a pub located at 12 Red Lion Street. It was pulled down in 1851 and rebuilt a few meters away at the corner of Commercial and Fournier Streets. It later became associated with Annie Chapman and Mary Kelly, two of Jack the Ripper's victims. Annie Chapman may have drunk at the pub shortly before she was murdered and the pavement outside of the pub was possibly where Mary Kelly picked up her clients.

9. TANTALUS

1. Brown nose - a sycophantic person. i.e. they have their head so far up somebody's backside that they have a brown nose.
2. Nose ender – slang for a straight blow full on the nose.

10. TICKET

1. Although the founder of Melbourne is debated, John Batman certainly has a strong claim. In 1835, as a leading member of the Port Phillip Association he explored much of Port Phillip finding the current site of central Melbourne and noting in his diary, "this will be the place for a village". The city was named Melbourne two months earlier than this conversation took place, in March 1837, for William Lamb, 2nd Viscount of Melbourne, the Prime Minister of the United Kingdom.
2. John Glover was a well-respected English landscape artist and member of the Royal Academy who emigrated to Van Diemen's Land in 1831, arriving on his 64th birthday. In 1832 he acquired the neighbouring land grant to Batman's Kingston estate and made his home there. His relationship with John Batman was known to be very difficult.
3. The *Neva*, shipwrecked on the night of 12th May, 1835 – see Afterword: Margaret Drury

11. PATTERNS

1. Franklin accompanied Mathew Flinders on his voyage to Australia (1801–03), and served in the Battles of Trafalgar in 1805 and New Orleans in 1815 before undertaking exploratory voyages in the Arctic. He served as governor from 1836 to 1843 and is recognised for his efforts to promote the development of cultural pursuits in the colony. He is best known for his search for the Northwest Passage in 1845. Their fate was unknown until 1859, when a final search mission found skeletons and a written account of the expedition through April 25, 1848.
2. Floor'd (slang) - so drunk as to be unable to stand.

12. FATE

1. A small pail with a handle on the side
2. A style of calligraphy used to enhance documents. The letters were made with a broad-edge pen and sometimes carefully retouched with a fine pen. The forms, especially the capitals, could be simple or elaborate.

13. FREEDOM'S CALL

1. Reibey's Ford, 6 miles south-west of Launceston, was the site of a frequently flooded ford. Convicts were constructing part of the road and bridge from Launceston to Devonport. Today called Hadspen, the town has preserved several buildings which date from the early 1800s as well as the modern bridge across the river. The Red Feather inn, built in the 1840s, an adjacent convict era gaol and four cottages form a cluster of heritage buildings in the middle of town.
2. The Hibernia is still there. It was named by Josiah Pilcher after the ship that transported him, and for Ireland. Its current name is the 'Irish'.
3. Lushy cove – convict slang for a drunk man
4. The official name of the day to commemorate the plot led by Guido Fawkes to blow up parliament on 5th November, 1605 and replace a protestant king with a catholic. In the late 1800s the name had evolved in popular parlance, becoming known as Guy Fawkes Night or Bonfire night as it is to this day in England although no longer commemorated in Australia.

14. LIAISONS

1. See Appendix re: Petition
2. Built by John Fawkner in 1824, this is possibly the oldest brick building still standing in Launceston today. At the time it had 23 rooms and a bar. It was here, four years earlier, in 1835, that John Batman and his friends laid plans to cross the Bass Straits and establish a settlement in what would become Melbourne. Today it is known as the Batman Fawkner Inn.
3. Two-up: this involves betting on how two coins will fall. It may have evolved from pitch and toss, a game of tossing a single coin into the air and betting on the result that was played by poor English and Irish at this time and earlier. It was widely played especially during the gold rush in the 1840s and later, and has become a traditional Australian betting game.
4. Cockatoo: the slang name for a person designated to look-out for possible police raids.

15. THE PATRIOT KING

1. Built 7 years earlier in 1832, the *Patriot King* was a well-known inn in the town. John Williat, the landlord, lost his license the next year (1840) when one of the Licensing Board 'objected strongly' to a renewal saying he had been insulted by Williat and alleging that he was in the habit of 'tampering with the constabulary', that he violated the laws with impunity and that it was impossible to obtain a conviction against him on account of his intimacy with the constabulary of the district. Amongst others, Edmund

Bryant spoke up for him but the Board voted 12 to 8 to remove his license. Williat, however, regained his license the next year. The inn was later renamed and stands today as the *Blenheim Inn*.

16. FABRIC

1. Glen Dhu derives from the Gaelic 'Glen dubh', meaning dark valley.
2. Rusty guts – slang for a rough, blunt, old fellow
3. At this time, police officers did not use whistles to summon support, but a wooden rattle, much like rattles that used to be seen at football matches.

17. ROSETTA

1. Rosetta's name was subsequently changed to Leichardt. It is situated south-east of Launceston between present day Kings Meadows and St. Leonard's.
2. Early evening on the 11th of June, 1840 a seventeen year-old, Edward Oxford, fired two pistols at Prince Albert and Queen Victoria as their carriage passed onlookers – he maintained that there were no bullets and none were found. The jury eventually acquitted him on grounds of insanity which infuriated Victoria but there was nothing she could do. He was finally released in 1867, given a new alias, John Freeman, and shipped to Melbourne where he married a local widow, became a regular churchgoer and wrote newspaper articles highlighting the state of the city slums.

22. NEW BEGINNINGS

1. See Appendix 1

23. TURMOIL

1. Eardley-Wilmott protested against "the most extraordinary conspiracy" and the "grossest falsehoods that ever oppressed an English gentleman" to no avail and he died in February in 1847 in Hobart, just before his 64th birthday. It was said, of a broken heart. At his death, public sentiment changed and the citizens of Hobart subscribed to a Gothic mausoleum for him which was erected in 1850. It still stands in St David's Park. La Trobe's subsequent report confirmed that Stanley's Probation system was a complete disaster and in 1846 transportation to Van Diemen's Land was suspended for two years.

24. GO NORTH!

1. In fact gold had been discovered at Nine Mile Springs by a convict in 1840 but the government had hushed it up for fear of convicts rebelling to seek out their fortunes. In the 1880s it became known as the Lefroy goldfields.
2. St Peter's is the oldest Anglican church standing on its original site in inner city Melbourne. The foundation stone was laid on 18 June 1846, and the building was used for services from 1847. During the subsequent gold rush years, four hundred baptisms and the same number of weddings took place each year.

25. SNOW

1. Today known as the Croxton Park hotel located in modern-day Thornbury and previously as the Red House, it burnt down in 1867 but was rebuilt as near as possible to the same design soon after.
2. Attributed to Scotland's poet, Robert Burns who published the song some sixty years before and described it as an old song that he took down from an old man.

26. GOLD?

1. Quolls, as these animals are called today, are carnivorous marsupials. They are primarily nocturnal and spend most of the day in a den

27. GEORGE WILSON

1. The Bush Inn was previously named the Traveller's Rest. Built in 1840, it was the first public building in the district and the village sprung up around it. The village name was changed to Gisborne the year before, in 1851, after Henry Fyshe Gisborne, a former Commissioner of Crown Lands.
2. Five Mile Creek was later renamed Woodend.
3. Francis McNeiss McNeil McCallum (Captain Melville) was a notorious bushranger. He was convicted in Perth, Scotland of house breaking and transported to Van Diemen's Land 14 years earlier in 1838 (aged 15). Throughout 1852, he led a gang of bushrangers, targeting the Black Forest road, and gained a reputation for both boldness and the chivalry that he showed to many, especially women. Later that year, on Christmas Eve, he (under the alias of Thomas Smith) and fellow bushranger William Robert Roberts were arrested in Geelong. He committed suicide in prison in 1857.
4. Today called the 'Royal George'.

5. From the late 1780's to the 1850's the flintlock musket was the original weapon of choice in colonial Australia. At around this time, however, weapons had developed and now had rifling - spiral grooves inside the barrel that caused the musket ball to spin as it travelled the length of the barrel, giving the ball distance and accuracy. The Enfield musket, a percussion cap weapon firing a paper cartridge loaded down the barrel, was used by British troops and colonial police forces as well as the serious and casual bushranger if they could find or afford this weapon, in preference to the earlier flintlocks.

6. *nackle-ass*, a term of contempt meaning poor, mean, inferior, paltry.

7. *Scamp* – slang for a highwayman.

28. THE DIGGINGS

1. The Inn was established in 1846 and the discovery of gold in Bendigo Creek was reportedly announced here a year earlier in 1851. Being the only inn between Elphinstone and the Bendigo goldfields, it became a popular rest stop for those seeking drink, food and accommodation on the track from Melbourne to the goldfields. At the height of the rush in 1852, it was reputed to have made an annual profit of £40,000 and about this time developed a reputation for drunkenness, murder and mayhem. It was soon to be burned down and a new brick and stone building was erected later in 1852. It was abandoned in 1934. In 1971 the surviving structures were bulldozed.

2. Present day Bullock Street

3. A cabbage tree hat was similar to a boater – made from finely woven natural straw with a high tapering domed crown and wide flat brim. It would have a layered hat band of coarser plaiting with zig-zag border edges. It was the first distinctively Australian hat.

4. A slab hut was made from slabs of split or sawn timber, often roofed with bark and/or earthen sods.

5. Matchboxes then were cylindrical containers with a cap, larger than modern rectangular boxes, with matches stacked vertically.

6. Yakka - Australian slang: strenuous physical work

7. Damper: a bread made of flour, water and salt, cooked over an open fire

8. Trap: slang for a policeman

9. Quid – slang for £1

10. Lag: a convict sentenced to transportation

11. Ridge: gold

12. Scarper: run away from trouble

13. It was illegal to *sell* liquor, but not to have it on the premises.

30. RED RIBBONS

1. This involved mixing six pannicans of flour with half a tablespoon of carbonate of soda, the same amount of tartaric acid and a spoonful of salt. Water was then added & the resulting dough kneaded into a loaf. When ready to bake, the loaf was tumbled in a warmed oven. Fire was then applied beneath the loaf and in 90 minutes or so all would be ready.
2. Plum Duff: a steamed pudding with currants or raisins cooked in a cloth-covered pannikin. This was a staple on the goldfields.
3. the evening smoke-o was a regular occurrence and was also known as "blowing a cloud". These informal gatherings took place with the diggers seated on logs beside the tent with a camp fire burning and tobacco, tea and alcohol being consumed. It was a matter of pride as to how long the log because this showed how popular your soirée.
4. Dr. David Jones was President of the Anti-Gold License Association which had been formed a month earlier following the initial meetings with Captain Edward Brown and George Thomson.
5. The aim of the Chartists was to gain political rights and influence for the working classes.
6. See appendix 2

32. THE PRIVATE ESCORT CAPER

1. Now called Heathcote

35. NEW YEAR'S EVE

1. The gullies were named after the events that gave rise to the finds, e.g. Golden gully from the richness of the gold on the surface, Tipperary from the Irish discoverers, Spring Gully because of the small spring at its head, New Chum for the new arrivals opening it, Long Gully because of its length, California because that's where the prospectors came from, Eagle-hawk from these birds nesting close by the first hole. Devonshire from the miners' origin and Peg Leg apparently from the find by three men with wooden legs!
2. The mazurka hails from Poland. It was and is an energetic folk dance for a circle of couples, characterized by stamping feet and clicking heels with sweeping movements across the floor. It had gained popularity and respectability in social circles in England in the 1830s and was the rage in the colonies at this time, much like the Twist stormed dance floors in the 1960s. Mazurkas composed for piano by Chopin reflect his interest in the music from his native land as well as the dance's popularity at this time.

3. Gold was discovered in the Crusoe gully west of Kangaroo Flat in mid-1853 and this started a rush to the district. The Bendigo district's largest gold nugget (377 ounces) was found near Crusoe Gully in 1861.

36. PUDDLING

1. On 22nd October, 1854 a meeting of 10,000 Diggers at Bakery Hill had resolved to protest the conviction of Gregorius (the priest's servant) and called for the Commissioner to be sacked. On 11th November, 1853 another meeting of 10,000 at Bakery Hill resolved to form the Ballaarat Reform League (emulating the Bendigo Red Ribbon League).
2. Sir Charles Hotham had replaced La Trobe as Governor in June after he had backed down on a license fee increase. He was a naval officer, used to strict discipline, and when the Reform League delegation had presented the Diggers' demands on 25th November, he had stated that a properly worded memorial would receive consideration. Rede, however, had been given secret orders by Hotham to increase enforcement 'hunts' despite this apparent willingness to consider the Diggers' demands.

37. PRELUDE

1. The quote is from Robert Burns's poem. It recalls King Robert the Bruce's speech before the Battle of Bannockburn when the Scots comprehensively defeated a much larger invading English army, considered at the time to be the most powerful army in Europe.
2. This was the first mention of the existence of what has become known as the Eureka flag.
3. 'Joe' probably referred to Governor Joseph La Trobe, who was universally disliked or possibly a short-changing storekeeper, Joe McTaggart, who was known to tip off police about unlicensed diggers and sky grog vendors. The cry was first used to warn that police were nearby on a license hunt and it migrated into a taunt and 'war cry' – so much so that by mid -1852 it was legally classified as an obscenity with its use drawing a £5 fine or a one-month prison sentence.
4. Bacchus Marsh was a stopping place for coaches traveling from Melbourne to the Ballaarat goldfield
5. A Canadian Digger from Toronto and a member of the Reform League, Henry Ross is accepted as the man who designed the flag. Three local women, Anastasia Withers, Anne Duke and Anastasia Hayes are said to have sewn it.
6. The Camp holding government forces, which was in sight of Bakery Hill, but not from the Eureka lead.

38. THE EUREKA STOCKADE

1. While the soldiers removed their prisoners after the battle, Lalor remained hidden, bleeding from the wound in his arm. When the last of them had gone, Lalor was helped from his hiding place, put upon a white horse, and rode away through the bush. His arm was later amputated.
2. Trooper John King kept the flag and it was held by his family for forty years until it was lent to the Ballaarat Fine Art Gallery in 1895. Bits of the flag were subsequently cut off and given to visiting dignitaries so approximately 30% of the original flag is missing. It was found after World War II in a drawer at the gallery and its provenance conclusively established in 1996. The remnant of the original Eureka Flag remains today, preserved for public display at the Museum of Australian Democracy at Eureka. In 2001, legal ownership of the flag was transferred to the Ballaarat Fine Art Gallery.
3. Mr. Haslam, the correspondent and agent of the Melbourne Morning Herald, lay there for two hours bleeding from a chest wound until his friends sent for a blacksmith, who forced off the handcuffs with a hammer and cold chisel and took him to a surgeon.
4. Captain Thomas estimated 30 diggers died on the spot and many more died subsequently. The official register of deaths show 27 names associated with the battle at Eureka, mostly Irish but also English, Scots, Canadians, Prussian, Hanoverian, Italian and Australian-born. The stockade was destroyed - its exact site is not known for certain today, although it is commemorated in the town.

39. ECLIPSE

1. Lalor had a distinguished career, later being elected as Speaker of the Legislative Assembly of Victoria.

41. NEW START

1. The Burke and Wills expedition was organised by the Royal Society of Victoria in Australia in 1860–61. It consisted of 19 men led by Robert O'Hara Burke and William John Wills, with the objective of crossing Australia from Melbourne in the south, to the Gulf of Carpentaria in the north, a distance of around 2,000 miles. At that time most of the inland of Australia had not been explored by non-Indigenous people and was largely unknown to the European settlers. The expedition left Melbourne in winter. Bad weather, poor roads and broken-down wagons meant they made slow progress at first. After dividing the party at Menindee on the Darling River, Burke made good progress, reaching Cooper Creek at the beginning of summer. The expedition established a depot camp at the

Creek and Burke, Wills and two other men pushed on to the north coast (although swampland stopped them from reaching the northern coastline). The return journey was plagued by delays and monsoon rains, and when they reached the depot at Cooper Creek, they found it had been abandoned just hours earlier. Burke and Wills died on or about 30 June 1861. Several relief expeditions were sent out, all contributing new geographical findings. Altogether, seven men lost their lives, and only one man, the Irish soldier, John King, crossed the continent with the expedition and returned alive to Melbourne. (Wikipedia)
2. Back Creek – renamed Talbot the next year, 1861.
3. Sturt Street is now called Chapman Street.

43. A MARRIAGE

1. A Land Act was instituted in 1860 designed to 'unlock the lands' from the squatters who controlled most of it. It gave all men the right to 'select' small parcels of land from areas surveyed by the government (including some squatters' runs). New South Wales and Victoria both passed Land Acts in 1861. Cheap land now became available to small farmers.
2. Airdrie, to the east of Glasgow.
3. Mendelssohn's *Wedding March* was written in 1842. It became popular at weddings throughout the Empire after the Queen's daughter (also called Victoria) had selected it for her own marriage nine years earlier in 1858.

44. GRANDPARENTS

1. Kangaroo Flat – today Caralulup
2. From 1863 to 1865, over 100 robberies were attributed to Ben Hall and his various associates, including the holding up of several villages, dozens of mail coaches and prized racehorses. He was ambushed by police and killed in 1865.
3. Talbot. — On Tuesday, (16th August, 1870) the foundation-stone of a new church, to be called the Church of St. Michael, was laid with the usual divine service by the Archdeacon. The attendance at the ceremony was large, considering the state of the roads, and a very considerable sum was placed upon the foundation-stone at the conclusion of the ceremony. In the evening there was a tea-meeting, when several addresses were delivered by the incumbent, Rev. R. Mahalm, the neighbouring clergy, &c; and a collection, as is usual, made. The proceeds of the donations towards the building of the church amounted to about £40. The inhabitants of Talbot deserve much credit for their efforts in the cause of church-building ; within the last ten years they have erected a wooden church, then enlarged it, then built a substantial parsonage, and are now engaged in erecting a substantial and commodious church of bluestone.

From the *The Church of England Messenger*, Melbourne 8 Sep 1870

45. GAINS AND LOSSES

1. A photograph of this child, after she had married, is on the cover of this book.

AFTERWORD

1. Despite Governor Arthur's disapproval, horse races had taken place at Fourteen Tree Plain, Jericho as far back as 3rd April, 1826. A Turf Club was formed at this time with a limit of 50 members. This was the foundation of the Tasmanian Turf Club and was the first in VDL to use the title, "Tasmanian".
2. Hall, James (1784-1869), Australian Dictionary of Biography, National Centre of Biography, Australian National University

ABOUT THE AUTHOR

David Cairns (who is also the Baron of Finavon), has travelled extensively, living in many countries on four continents during a successful career as an entrepreneur and in top management with several public and private technology companies. He holds an MBA from Cranfield and is a Fellow of two accounting bodies and the Scottish Society of Antiquaries.

He is keenly interested in history - and what it teaches us in today's world. He is a public speaker and has also published several articles. *Redemption* is the second and concluding book in *The Helot's Tale* series.

X

ALSO BY DAVID CAIRNS OF FINAVON

The Helots' Tale - Downfall, Book I of the series

A true story. In a Dickensian society the government has introduced the policy of transportation to Van Diemen's Land and New South Wales.

Scratching to survive in the slums of London and the impoverished fields of rural England at the beginning of the 19th century, Mary Ann Goulding and Robert Bright find themselves caught up in the harsh justice system of the time and are transported to Van Diemen's Land, all but slaves in the New World. We travel through the despair of Newgate prison, a death sentence, public hangings, riots, the resurrectionists and a hellish journey for months on the open sea to serve their sentences on an island prison. Brought low, they begin the fightback.

Bushranger Gold

The true story of the McIvor Gold Escort robbery and researched speculation about the leader of the gang who may have been Frank Gardner, perhaps the most notorious and best known of the bushrangers after Ned Kelly.

In 1853, the Australian colonies were rocked by the audacious robbery of a fortune in gold being escorted from the goldfields to Melbourne. It was 'The Great Train Robbery' of the day.

Soon, 400 men were searching the bush to track the gang down. But to no avail. The leader of the gang, Joe Grey was never seen again - or was he? Some of the bushrangers intended to escape on the *Madagascar*, a ship that sailed from Melbourne - and was never seen again.

The Case of the Emigrant Niece

A murder mystery unravelled by two amateur detectives set in

Scotland and Australia in the mid 19th century. Coming soon.